Praise for *His Name is Eric*

A deeply moving and inspiring journey that captures the essence of the love and resilience of this couple. Phillipa's storytelling is heartfelt and powerful, and she captures beautifully their life before the diagnosis and the challenges of trying to make sense of her beloved's cancer journey. A must-read for anyone facing life-changing medical challenges.

— **DR. GEORGE PRATT,**
Clinical Psychologist, Speaker, Author of Instant
Emotional Healing: Acupressure for the Emotions

What an extraordinary and inspirational work! It was incredible that Phillipa Leseberg recalled and documented the experience with her husband to help others avoid a similar, tragic ordeal. She has given us the opportunity to see why it is so important for us to take steps to inform ourselves of all options BEFORE we encounter this situation in our own lives. Reading this book will motivate us to be better prepared for the choices we will need to make and to allow us to steer clear of the worst aspects and, hopefully, the all-too-common outcome of conventional treatment.

— **DR. JOHN F. RUHLAND, ND**

His Name is Eric is simply a stunning piece of writing that I couldn't put down. It is a book that has the potential to change lives. It's an important read for people with a recent diagnosis of cancer because it introduces the reader to the possibility of life-affirming cancer treatments—treatments that are based on the whole person and building the immune system. It raises many questions about how cancer is treated and viewed in the U.S. A cancer diagnosis profoundly impacts so many, and Phillipa and

Eric provide voices to articulate the array of issues a family must face on the journey. *His Name is Eric* is an act of love.

— MARY ARTINO,
Author of Lessons on Loss Not Taught: The Art of Hospice: How Dying Can Hold Insight, Grace, and Beauty

In *His Name is Eric*, Phillipa Leseberg welcomes the reader into a sacred love story with intimate prose and tender care. From the first pages, you know Phillipa and Eric to be two people committed to showing up fully for each other and their lives. When cancer crashes into their world and brings with it immense pain and suffering, that presence only deepens. As Leseberg details each beautiful and heartbreaking moment, *His Name is Eric* becomes an invitation for each of us to witness and treasure all of the everything of our own lives and deaths, as well as to understand healing as something that can never be confined to a hospital room.

— JEN VIOLI,
Author of Putting Makeup on Dead People

Phillipa and Eric's journey through cancer, as beautifully chronicled in this heartfelt book, is a testament to the resilience of the human spirit and connection at a soul level. Reading it resonated deeply with me, as I too have faced my own battles with cancer. Their story unfolds a profound love that shines through the darkest times, reminding us all of the courage that exists in each and every one of us. Gratitude is at the essence of their relationship, showcasing how love can uplift and inspire us in our most challenging moments. This book is more than just a narrative; it's a celebration of life, love, and the indomitable spirit of the human heart. I believe everyone should experience this beautiful love story—it truly touches the soul.

— KARLA OLSON,
Author of The Almost Empty Nester, and Stage 1.5 (two-time) Breast Cancer Survivor

Phillipa has created a masterpiece! It's a truly compelling and engaging read, and I couldn't put it down. I'll be processing it for some time. Her description of the alternative treatments in Mexico was fascinating. It was a perfect read.

— PAULA TOMLINSON,
Director of Software Engineering, Satellites and Rocket Engines, and Stage III Breast Cancer Survivor

Here is a truly remarkable book. Phillipa Leseberg takes us on the roller coaster ride she and Eric, her husband, experience in dealing with his sudden cancer. It is not a sad story, but certainly a moving one, and sometimes with a soundtrack. It's a great love story. After months of hopeful visits to cancer clinics, operations, injections, and chemo, her husband eventually accepted that they just weren't working. Searching for alternatives, Phillipa finds an alternative institute in Mexico that offers treatments for chronic and degenerative diseases. Natural and alternative healing therapies have a profound effect on Eric's well-being. Eventually, she simply asks the traditional medical community to do better. Phillipa's voice is captivating as she vividly paints places and situations in vibrant clarity, putting us there with her. We feel her joy, her sadness, her outrage. Her words wrap around us like the intimacy she portrays throughout her life with Eric. She presents the power of a conscious relationship in marriage. This book will be a pleasure for many readers, and it might bring a few tears. I hope it can get into the hands of anyone coping with cancer or cancer patients. There's a healing in these pages.

— JOHN OSBORNE,
Ph.D., Professor and Film Producer

Phillipa Leseberg's *His Name is Eric* is a raw, authentic, and powerful dive into the emotional rollercoaster of loving someone through cancer. This memoir doesn't just tell a story—it pulls you into the trenches of love, pain, and unshakeable resilience. Phillipa's reflections capture the delicate dance between fighting for life and savoring every fleeting moment. As she and Eric navigate their path, you're not just witnessing a love story, but also a bold exploration of alternative cancer treatments. It's a call to action, urging readers to take charge of their health, ask the hard questions, and challenge the norms of conventional medicine. It's a must-read for anyone facing illness, caregiving, or researching alternative health treatments and seeking a heartfelt reminder of love's strength in the darkest times.

— CRISTINA HORVATH,
Brand and Creative Designer/Artist

HIS NAME IS ERIC

*A Love Story & Exploration
of Alternative Healing
Paths for Cancer*

Phillipa Leseberg

Published by Hummingbird Haven Press

eBook: 979-8-9917433-0-3
Paperback: 979-8-9917433-1-0

To the one and only Eric, my Bebe, who lives on in our hearts and through my stories. This book is my gift to Eric.

To my beautiful Bella girl, I'm so happy to be your mama this go-round.

To those of you who have ever had the courage to question the words from a doctor.

To all who have experienced or lost someone they love to the cancerous curse.

Contents

Author's Note

In writing this book, I relied extensively on detailed journals, text messages, social media posts, and memory. While I tried to represent the events as truthfully as possible, memory can be subjective—and to tie parts of the story together, exact dates may be slightly off. I used the real names of some friends and important people on our journey, with their permission, and changed other names out of respect for their privacy. I did not use the names of the U.S. medical facilities, and I gave the doctors nicknames to protect their livelihood and relationships with colleagues and patients. Finally, I'm not a licensed medical expert, so the information here shouldn't be taken as professional medical advice. Always consult your healthcare provider with any health-related questions or issues.

PART ONE

Preface

I t was early on a gorgeous day in May of 2009, in the middle of the dead-calm Pacific Ocean. The sun was already beating down with no clouds to deflect its rays. The sparkling water off the coast of Kona, Hawai'i, was a vivid turquoise, and in stark contrast, the lava rock was as black as a moonless night.

There were no other boats in any direction—just ours.

Swimming in the bow wave under our dangling bare feet was a small pod of Hawai'ian Spinner Dolphins. We watched them just under the surface of the water, their bodies sleek and smooth, in three distinct shades of gray. They were moving fast, with an out-of-this-world effortlessness.

One of the dolphins rolled over on its side and looked up. It was keeping pace at several miles per hour and casually peering up at us. My heart was pounding. It never got old, these moments with the dolphins.

I glanced sideways at Eric, and my breath caught as I watched a tear slide from beneath his sunglasses. He felt the magic of the moment too.

We sat side by side on the bow of the small boat, our legs fused together, sticking with perspiration from the hot sun.

I took a deep breath, breathing in the deliciousness of us. I was amazed at life's synchronicities that placed me in this present moment. I felt intense gratitude to be here on this boat, next to this man, surrounded by Hawai'ian spinner dolphins.

By the time Eric and I met in person, I had already been swimming with the wild and free dolphins for over nine years, and these ocean angels were a significant part of my daily life. It was, however, his first time to swim with the dolphins and his first trip to Hawai'i to meet me.

Thus began our love story.

It's a story about meeting my beloved online, from across an ocean, and of our precious time together.

It should have been a story of Kiwi girl meets California boy, girl marries boy, moves away from her dolphin friends, and flies off to live happily ever after in a state called Washington.

Alas, the happily ever after was cut short.

It *is* a love story, but it's also the story of our journey navigating the treacherous path of a serious health prognosis and the most unwelcome confirmation that Western medicine simply does not have all the answers.

It's about lessons learned, the ups and the downs, the hope and despair, the shock and horror of traditional treatments, and ultimately fleeing the country to seek alternative offerings.

Could there have been a different outcome?

Read on and decide for yourself. My beloved and I might hope you learn a thing or two, and who knows...our story could help you save a life one day.

— 1 —

California Boy Meets Kiwi Girl Online

I recall the exact moment I met Eric online.

It was April 20, 2009, and I had been living on the Big Island of Hawai'i for many years, swimming almost daily with the spinner dolphins. Eric was living in the city of Kirkland, on the shores of Lake Washington.

I had no radius guidelines set on my Match.com online dating profile, so it could be viewed around the world. I didn't mind where my potential match was located. I just knew he was out there… somewhere.

Eric, on the other hand, allegedly had so many women reaching out to him online, that he restricted his dating pool to a radius of five miles from his home. One day while updating his online profile, he had forgotten to recheck the radius box.

And so, on that fateful day, he unwittingly clicked "save," and his profile showed up worldwide.

Over seven thousand miles away, my seven-year-old daughter, Bella, and I were visiting friends and family in New Zealand. We were sharing a bed at a friend's apartment in Wellington, and my girl had fallen asleep during her bedtime story.

Not quite ready for sleep, I slipped quietly out of bed, sat down at the desk in the bedroom, and opened my laptop. Match.com had sent me an email with twelve new profiles, and I clicked on it to take a peek.

One man stood out to me. I liked his photo and his energy.

In the first shot, he was seated with his hand under his chin and his elbow on the table. He had a light in his blue eyes and was grinning through the camera and out at me. I had a visceral reaction and hurriedly clicked through the rest of his photos. Thank God he had some decent ones of himself, as guys often upload a few terrible selfies—maybe highlighting their nostrils, or capturing a picture of themselves in the mirror of a men's public toilet. Eric, on the other hand, showed that he had at least one friend who was willing to take shots of him and that he cared enough to upload multiple photos.

My reaction intensified when I read his profile. It was impressive. First, he could string a sentence together with better-than-basic grammar, something a number of men dating online seemed to struggle with; second, and the *pièce de résistance*, he had spent time doing deep inner work on himself. He listed the training, coaching, and workshops he had experienced over several years. Additionally, he and his business co-founders had worked directly with Tony Robbins and had a spiritual guru on staff who coached them collectively and individually.

I didn't even read to the end of his profile before I clicked "wink."

After checking through E-Harmony and Match.com profiles for three years and interviewing dozens of online candidates, I was ready. After seven lonely years, I knew my guy would show up. I just didn't know when.

So, on that momentous day in April of 2009, sitting in my friend's guest bedroom, at the desk beside the bed where Bella was fast asleep, I felt hopeful.

The next day I saw an email pop up. It was from him! He had broken all the unwritten rules in the online dating world, including the one about only winking back if someone winks at you, to avoid showing interest too early.

My heart leapt as I read through the long email. Here was someone who was as intense as I was. He had been excited to read about me and had paid attention. He knew I had substance and wasn't frightened away by my intentionally "scary" profile. My goal had been to discourage the men satisfied with only superficial relationships, leaving space for someone who was looking to initiate a deeper and more authentic connection.

I later heard that after reading my profile, Eric blurted out to his friend, "Come and check out this profile! If this lady in Hawai'i is real, I'm going to marry her!"

I appreciated that he was a solid communicator. He knew his mind and heart and could clearly articulate what he was thinking and feeling. He had a voice, and it was his own. It took me two hours to pen an equally meaningful email, and I pressed send.

That was the beginning of it all, the start of our great love story.

I didn't know it at the time, but our story would last only eight years. It was certainly eight years I would have over again.

If only I could.

— 2 —

Two People Melting for Each Other

As soon as I returned to Hawai'i, we fell into a routine of speaking on the phone for an hour or two most evenings, and up to four hours on occasion. Once Bella fell asleep each night, I called Eric for our daily conversation. The two-to-three-hour time difference worked in our favor, as he was a night owl and I was a morning person. One time, we talked all night, and the sun was coming up in Washington as we hung up the phone and went to sleep in our respective beds.

We talked about everything; no topic was taboo. We kept talking until we said goodbye, or one of us (usually me) fell asleep.

We discussed our previous relationships and marriages— Eric had been married three times and I had had two previous husbands. We hypothesized about what had worked and what we had learned from our experiences.

We talked about our girls, both Eric and I had one daughter.

Eric's daughter, Alison, was living close by in Washington and she had four children of her own.

He shared stories of growing up in California with his mom and her boyfriends or her short-lived husbands. He talked about hiding from the rage of alcoholic stepdads and leather belts.

He detailed paper routes and lawn mowing and the beginnings of a fierce financial independence.

He told me of surfing adventures on wild waves and thrilling stories of screaming down steep hills with uncontrollable laughter on handmade go-karts he and his buddies fashioned out of pieces of wood and repurposed wheels and bits of rope.

Playing the saxophone in the school band, stealing kisses, missing the prom, and experiencing full-on teen love and lust.

Then there was the terror of hitting another vehicle while driving his mom's car before he had his license.

I shared with Eric that I was born in a tiny place called Gore, New Zealand. I was brought up in Christchurch, growing into my tall body and gaining confidence at eight years old with the help of an awesome teacher at school and another in the ballet studio.

I disclosed that being born into a family with seven kids was both the best and the worst thing. I liked being in the midst of this huge mess of people, yet I often felt like a stranger, unseen and unheard.

I told him about my big move and teen years in Paekakariki in the North Island. The swim training in warm indoor pools and the competitions in freezing cold bays at surf club carnivals along the Kapiti Coast, representing in our club colors, black and yellow bumblebee stripes. My years of afterschool sports practices and hours of competing on shiny basketball gymnasium floors and on outdoor asphalt netball courts.

I shared the story of my sweet boyfriend of two years at age thirteen and how we only kissed and held hands all that time.

Moving cities and schools and making new friends... starting over.

Leaving my Hamilton home at seventeen to get a degree at the University of Auckland, concurrently training to be a high school teacher.

We talked for hours on end, leaving no stone unturned. We figured out that our big life values aligned, like taking responsibility for our own stuff and not blaming the other for what came up when one of our buttons was pushed. We covered sex and libido and well...everything else.

We weren't necessarily falling in love in those first few weeks, or even in lust, as we hadn't yet met in person, but our hearts were beginning to melt for each other. I had always imagined my guy would say something like, "Don't move, don't go anywhere, and make sure you get yourself off the online dating sites! I'm coming to you!"

And that's exactly what happened. Three weeks after connecting online, Eric was on a plane to Hawai'i. Although my birthday was May 8th, he wanted to celebrate it belatedly when he arrived. On May 13th I got my birthday wish, and we were beyond excited to be meeting in person for the very first time.

— 3 —

Meeting in Person and Spending Time Together at the Mauna Lani Resort

I remember what I wore to the airport to meet him. It was a designer pale green A-line skirt that ended just below the knee, with hand-sewn pearls and sparkles, and a white sleeveless tank top with sequins around the neckline.

My outfit was seriously over the top to pick someone up from the airport, but I wanted to look my best. I was nervous and found myself thinking of all the reasons why it couldn't possibly work. I hadn't been in a relationship for seven years, ever since my separation and subsequent divorce from Bella's dad.

Standing at the airport, I felt like I was in a page from one of the romance novels I devoured as a teen, waiting for my prince to ride up on his fancy steed in all his impossibly tall, blonde gorgeousness.

I found myself holding my breath and consciously forced myself to breathe. Time slowed, the people around me blurred out of sight, when I saw him come through the opaque glass doors into the baggage area. I never shared this with Eric, but in those first few seconds, I noticed that he was heavier than his internet photos, his T-shirt was frayed around the neck, and he needed a haircut. Oh boy!

After hundreds of hours of conversation on the phone, I was excited and panicked at the same time. We awkwardly leaned in to kiss and hug each other.

We stood nervously holding hands, awaiting his luggage at the outdoor carousel. It finally appeared, and we walked across the road to my car and set off for the drive north to my friend's home at the Mauna Lani Resort.

Kim was one of my closest friends and business partner in one of my businesses. She and her husband Rocky had gifted their resort home to us for a week, so we could have the opportunity to get to know each other in person and in private. Thankfully, I had a terrific nanny living with us at my Waimea home who was happy to take care of Bella for the week.

As I was driving, I turned to Eric in a panic and asked, "What if it doesn't work?"

He calmly considered my question for a moment, noted my stress, and responded kindly, "Hey, it's okay. Let's just relax and try to have a good time. If it's terrible, I'll go and check myself into a hotel."

That helped relieve my tension, and we chatted with our usual patter for the thirty-minute drive to the resort.

After we arrived at the luxurious home, replete with pool, two-tier water feature, four bedrooms, gourmet kitchen, and peekaboo view of the Pacific Ocean, I showed him around. I was still a bit jumpy, and at one point, while we were standing by the sliding doors to the pool, he stopped me and reached for my hand. He pulled me close and gave me the best full-body hug I had ever experienced. It felt like we walked into the essence of each other, like all the pieces of the puzzle of love and destiny over all time and across dimensions—past, present, and future—clicked and locked into place.

I knew that being here, in this man's arms, was exactly where I was supposed to be. He had the feeling too, and together we relished every moment of getting to know each other.

There was this piece of furniture, a loveseat that had two sides and no back, and we sat facing one another, staring into each other for hours. We just talked and touched and fell more into that wondrous void where love lives.

Without being consciously aware, Eric happened upon my languages of love…physical touch and romance.

He had spent a good deal of time figuring out birthday surprises for me and purchased several gifts and romantic birthday cards before leaving Seattle. On the plane, he listened to hours of songs and wrote in each one of the cards, as part of my birthday surprise.

Sitting on our favorite piece of furniture, he put his headphones on me, gave me each card and present one by one, and pressed play on the song that accompanied it. I read the card, listened to the song, and unwrapped the gifts, savoring each one.

He knew green was my favorite color, and he gifted me a glass heart with swirls of green and yellow, beautifully created in the glass-sculpting capital of Seattle. There was an emerald and diamond necklace, accompanied by the jeweler's certificate. He knew I was a big tea drinker, and he gave me a mug with an outline of Seattle city.

There was more, and I was blown away by the organization, planning, and care behind the romantic gestures. I had never experienced anything even close to this before.

It didn't take long for us to work our way up to making love, and then we never really stopped. We made love numerous times per day and of course, we knew it wasn't a realistic constancy to keep up for long, but for the first few weeks, it was awesome.

It was looking like I may have found my guy, and I was beyond delighted at the potential of us.

— 4 —

The Dolphin Dance

Eric was supposed to be in Hawai'i for one week, and he stayed for three. He was a business owner with a couple of other ex-Microsoft co-founders, and they agreed to work around his extended vacation schedule. After a week at the resort, we moved up to my home in Waimea for the remainder of his time on the island.

I owned a sweet four-bedroom cottage-style home in the Luala'i development on Parker Ranch, one of the largest working cattle ranches in the country, complete with horses, cows, and real cowboys called paniolos.

Bella had already met Eric at the resort, and as soon as she saw him in our home, she started calling him Daddy. She grabbed his hand and pulled him outside to jump on the trampoline. I loved watching them play, and I took many photos and videos of them jumping and laughing together.

After our initial week, I needed to get back to my wild dolphin swim business, "OneLoveOneSpirit." Eric fit in with my schedule beautifully, and over the next few weeks, joined me on my dolphin swim trips. He was a natural athlete and very comfortable in the water. He listened to me sharing dolphin swim etiquette and started helping me with my clients on our swims. If my heart hadn't already been melting for him, it would have been with that. I was ecstatic that he was a great swimmer, snorkeler, and could free-dive, as a bonus.

We developed something special in the water. On the trips when my guests were replete with their dolphin swim experience and happily ensconced on the boat, eating lunch and lazing in the sun, Eric and I would jump back in the water to do our version of a dolphin dance. We would swim towards each other, hold hands, and roll over one another, initiating a gentle spinning motion…moving through the water as a rotating spiral, connected at the heart.

I heard from several clients that they were quite taken with the way we moved as one through the water. They knew they were witnessing something special.

— 5 —

The Year of Long-Distance Dating and Dolphins

We stayed connected every day and developed a special process early on. We nicknamed it GOCs, for Gifts of Confidence, yet it could just as easily have been called daily gratitudes, or words of affirmation. Eric had given life to the concept with a long-running mastermind group from one of his intense self-development programs. Each GOC would begin with, "I love and appreciate that you . . ." They could be light, funny, sexy, or deep and profoundly meaningful.

We both loved and trusted the process, and although we didn't know it at the time, it would become an ongoing daily habit that would see us through the best and worst of life's experiences.

Eric became a regular visitor to the Big Island over the next year. He came as often and for as long as he could, one to three weeks at a time. He attended Bella's performances at school, her hula and dance recitals, parent-teacher evenings, her birthday, Thanksgiving, and Christmas.

He set up an office for himself within my home office, and we either worked alongside each other, or he joined me on my dolphin swims.

I loved that we connected so well in the ocean and had more opportunities to do the dolphin dance together. I appreciated that he could effortlessly laugh and converse with my clients, and because he was a great storyteller and good listener, they enjoyed him too. I noticed that our clients were fascinated with our relationship, and many asked us how we met and what our stories were.

We had dozens of magical dolphin swim experiences together.

On one occasion, our boat left the Honokohau Harbor and Marina in Kailua-Kona and followed the coast south toward downtown Kona. The clients were excited to meet the dolphins, and I breathed a sigh of relief when we spotted them early. We slowly approached the pod of around seventy dolphins and sat silently observing their behavior. On this day, they were quietly milling about the bay, and I was hopeful for what I called a "top-ten day."

Eric and I slipped into the water and waited for our clients to do the same. We encouraged them not to splash too loudly as it can startle the dolphins, and we liked to be as respectful as possible when entering their space. It was the sort of day I lovingly referred to as "dolphin soup." They were extremely interactive, and we had dolphins to our left, right, and below us, coming up to breathe all around. This was wild dolphin and human interaction at its best.

One by one, the clients jumped back on the boat to warm up, take a break, and eat some delicious local pineapple and papaya. Once the guests were happily relaxed on the boat, Eric and I took a few moments to have fun in the water, without clients.

He enjoyed watching me hold my breath, jackknife at my hips, and dive down to play with the dolphins. I could free dive to seventy-five feet, but it was more fun to go up and down to around twenty-five feet.

I connected with several dolphins as they were coming to the surface to breathe. I took a deep breath, followed the pod down, and a single dolphin came back up to the surface with me. I loved that feeling, suspended in time and space with parallel bodies spiraling to the surface, joined at the heart. It's pure magic.

I saw Eric having his own sweet interaction with dolphins moving alongside him on both sides, like sentinels.

Shortly after, several spotted dolphins joined the pod. I dove down deep and looked up and over at Eric. He was underwater and heading towards a spotted dolphin. Then I saw something I had never seen before. The dolphin literally stopped only feet from Eric, stood vertically in the water, opened its mouth wide, and screeched at him!

I was stunned and swam right over to see how he was coping. He was a little shaken, but doing okay.

A few nights later, the dolphin came to him in a dream and told him that it was a shout-out for him to wake up. It was time to live his life fully, to stop doing what wasn't serving him, and to pursue what made him happy. He interpreted that to mean leaving the company he co-founded yet no longer enjoyed and moving to the Big Island to be with Bella and me.

He had visions of purchasing our own dolphin swim boat, becoming my business partner and captain, and started researching how to make that a reality.

— 6 —

Phillipa Visits Eric in Washington

I visited Eric in Seattle for a week during that year of dating, 2009, as I wanted to get a sense of where he lived and how he interacted with his local environment and friends.

I met a dozen of his friends, went with him to work, and then out to dinner with three different couples in his close circle. Fortunately for me and my heart, he was who he said he was, and he was held in high regard by his friends and colleagues.

We spent a magical week together on his home turf. I was enthralled by the beauty of Washington, and I loved the greenery and abundance of trees everywhere.

Eric enjoyed escorting me around Seattle, particularly the Eastside where he lived. He showed me the University of Washington, the "U-Dub" campus. He pointed out where his classes had been and shared exciting stories of his years there many decades prior. He was proud of both the campus and his achievements. He had been in the Navy, and at the time, he was the only full-time, active, on-duty member of the armed forces at the university. It had been a tough commute and a massive course workload, yet he'd graduated with double degrees in business and computer science.

Knowing how much I loved cetaceans, Eric arranged for us to drive to Anacortes to see orca whales. Although I love all types of cetaceans, I hadn't yet seen an orca. It was a fabulous trip, driving up north of Washington State in Eric's bright red Ford F150 truck, a vehicle he was crazy about. Eric was all man, but just like a boy when it came to fun and fast toys. Red toys were for speed, and yellow toys were for fun.

I was delighted to see a half dozen resident orcas. We also saw minke whales coming to the surface vertically, feeding with their mouths open, like humpbacks, something the captain and crew had never seen before. Eric and I looked at each other with that knowing look. We loved hearing captains exclaim they were seeing something new or unusual and considered ourselves good luck charms when it came to cetacean experiences.

The trip to see Eric started to seed an idea I had about Bella and me moving to Washington. I was ready for a change, and although I loved living in Hawai'i and being with the dolphins, I knew things would be tough financially with the ongoing recession. Both of my businesses were operating at a loss, and it would likely be challenging for Eric to get a high-tech job on the island. So, after his initial disappointment, he agreed it would be the less stressful option for us to start our next life chapter on the mainland. We figured we could always return to Hawai'i once we were better established.

Of course, we had no inkling that we would never make it back to live in Hawai'i together.

— 7 —

The Luckiest Girl in the World

After deciding that Bella and I would move, we were excited about the prospect of being together as a family. Yet, we weren't quite ready to hop on a plane. Bella needed to finish out her school year, and I had to rent out the house and get my business affairs in order.

Although Eric had been sorely tempted to walk away from his work situation with the company he co-owned in Washington ever since we met, he had been doing the responsible thing—persevering, even in a terrible work environment, to keep the money flowing in. He was helping with the finances for my business and personal life and had been for almost a year. But eventually, work became untenable.

One of his business partners, the president of the company, was preparing to give him a golden handshake (as he had done previously with two of the original co-founders) and, fortunately for Eric, this was the best possible option. He signed a five-year non-disclosure agreement and accepted the package to leave. The day he left the company, he was on a plane to Hawai'i.

A week later, on April 20, 2010, exactly one year after we met online, (and yes, he had planned it that way), we had a big development in our relationship.

Early in the day, he walked into my kitchen and hugged me as I was making a green smoothie. He said, "I've made reservations at the Four Seasons Hotel for dinner tonight. Let's celebrate our one-year anniversary of meeting online."

As we were getting ready, I figured something was up. He was wearing a seersucker sport coat and a blue and yellow Hawai'ian shirt. First, I'd never seen Eric wearing any sort of sport coat during the year we'd been dating. Second, almost no one wears sport coats in Hawai'i. It's Hawai'ian shirts only, a sort of one-look-fits-all.

He asked Bella to take a photo of us, and her eyes were as big as saucers as she carefully picked up Eric's fancy Nikon camera. *Click click click.*

We jumped into the yellow convertible Eric had already shipped over when we had assumed he would be joining us in Hawai'i. Yellow, his favorite color, the color of sunshine and fun toys. Eric in his sport coat and me in a shimmery, ocean-blue pleated dress. And off we went.

We arrived an hour before our dinner reservation, and Eric suggested we go for a walk on the beach path. We took a shortcut by the pool and stopped to enjoy the majesty of the setting with everything in its place: lounge chairs, umbrellas, and stacks of towels, perfectly rolled.

"Go and stand over there," he said, pointing. I giggled and sashayed over to the pool.

"OK, I'm ready!" I shouted back.

Pose. Click.

"I'll take one of you now," I said as I grabbed his camera. "Your turn."

Awkward pose. Click.

He reached for my hand, and we walked along the winding beach path towards the water, with so many shades of blue, each more exquisite than the other.

"This…*this* is heaven on Earth," I whispered in his ear as we walked slowly, hand-in-hand, the waves gently splashing along the sandy shore, both lost in thought.

He slowed, turned towards the water, and came closer, enveloping me from behind. He leaned in, kissed my neck, and said quietly, "I love you and I am in love with you, Bebe. I'm so grateful we connected one year ago today. I love and appreciate you…so…much." He squeezed me and we started moving again.

Eric guided me to sit on an olive-green-covered pagoda. He stood in front of me, reached out for both of my hands, and started sinking down on one knee.

Oh my God.

Oh my God.

Oh my God.

He's going to propose! I should have known! He was acting so weird and nervous. Ha ha! That explains the seersucker sport coat. He needed somewhere to hide the ring. Oh my God.

He's really going to propose!

I wish I could remember the exact words of the proposal, but he spoke of love, loneliness, a long search, and the miracle of miracles…the serendipity that connected and brought us together.

"Yes! Yes, I will marry you! Yes, of course, I'll marry you!" I shouted out with absolutely no hesitation.

There were several resort guests close by, and hearing my squeals of joy, they offered to take a few pictures of us. Bubbling with excitement, Eric took many more of me and my sparkly engagement ring.

At dinner, we leaned in to kiss. We fed each other tasty morsels and sipped on champagne in celebration of our engagement.

It was as if we were the only people in the restaurant, and I felt like I was the luckiest girl in the world.

— 8 —

The Build-Up to the Big Day

Since we were already planning to travel to New Zealand in July of 2010 for my family reunion, I came up with the idea to include our wedding in the weekend fun. I ran the idea past my family, and they gave it a green light.

I swung into action planning the wedding with only a few months' lead time. Fortunately, July was the middle of winter in New Zealand, the slow season for weddings, and I was able to schedule a stunning location at a heavily discounted price. I booked the flowers, ordered a cake, hired a wedding celebrant, and found a photographer. I ordered a flower girl silk dress in a deep eggplant for Bella and booked hair appointments for the day of the wedding.

I asked Eric one night, "You know how you promised to learn ballroom dancing in your first email to me? Well, how do you feel about learning a dance for our wedding?"

He responded with a resounding yes.

With Eric's agreement to learn to dance, Warren, my dance teacher, kindly offered to choreograph a night-club two-step dance, including grapevines, leg lifts, half dips, a full dip, and stationary and traveling spins.

I picked up the bulk of the routine first, and Eric learned his part over a two-week visit from Washington. He was nervous but took on the challenge. I drew pictures to help him visualize the steps, the count, the direction, and the lyrics of the song at the main highlights in the choreography, so we could land them with impact. For someone who had only danced on roller skates as a teenager, he was doing amazingly well.

Not long after Eric left to go back to Washington, Bella and I were cooking dinner one evening. I asked, "How would you feel if we moved to Washington to be with Eric?"

I couldn't have been more relieved with her response as she started jumping up and down with excitement, "Yay! Yay! I want to move to Seattle!"

We spent the next weeks and months deciding what to bring and what to store at my Waimea home, which I planned to rent out. I booked our flights and allowed the excitement to build as everything started to fall into place for our next chapter.

I took my dolphin swim team out to dinner and told them I was moving out of state, and I asked them if they would like to keep working with the clients and me from afar. The plan was that I would take the phone calls, charter the boats, schedule the crew, and take care of business, all from Seattle. They were totally on board, and it gave me the time I needed to figure out the future of the business, as I wasn't quite ready to give up my dolphin swim enterprise.

And so, at the end of June 2010, Bella and I moved from Hawai'i to Washington to be with my new love and her dad-to-be.

As Eric had just lost a significant amount of money in a real estate deal that went south, we chose to rent initially. We found a great lakefront condo with a boat slip, right next to the Seahawks football training facility on Lake Washington. We practiced the dance routine every chance we could, and we grew more and more confident.

We went shopping in Seattle to pick up a tux, tie, and shirt for Eric and had great fun choosing a wedding dress for me. I have photos of us in the fitting rooms making funny faces…me wearing dresses in all shapes and sizes, and Eric or Bella holding the zipper together at the back when the dress was too large in one place or too small in another.

After a full day of shopping, and having tried on at least a couple dozen dresses, we were feeling tired and about to give up. However, the retail assistant brought in one last option, and as soon as Eric zipped me up, I knew this was the one. Bella threw open the curtain and I was able to stand back and look at my reflection in the mirror. We all grinned and agreed this was it.

I wasn't initially thinking of wearing white, this being my third wedding. I also wasn't planning on having a long and flowing train. However, when blessed to find a dress that was white, had a long train, *and* fit like a glove, I was sold.

We literally had time to move into our new condo and enjoy a few boat rides on the lake and swims in the pool before we stuffed our wedding outfits and winter clothes into suitcases and flew off to New Zealand for a wedding.

Our wedding.

— 9 —

When Two Become One

I grew up in New Zealand, where the winters are typically cold, wet, and overcast. So, while I was excited to celebrate our big day with my family, I was worried that the weather wouldn't be very good. I woke up on the day of our wedding and rushed to the window to look outside. It was a gorgeous day. This was beyond miraculous for a mid-winter event!

Bella and I enjoyed getting pampered at the hair salon. I had my hair pulled up in a series of large, tight curls, with flowers pushed in strategically, and my girl looked adorable in her ringlets.

We arrived at the venue in the countryside and looked around the grounds. It had the feel of an English manor. The main house, a villa, had been renovated to perfection. It had all the charm of the Victorian era, yet they had managed to install the modern conveniences without looking out of place. There was a barn, a gorgeous pond with a fountain, an outdoor pagoda, and a separate space where large events took place.

There was a room upstairs for the bride and bridesmaids to get ready, and since it was just Bella and I, we had it to ourselves. It was spacious, filled with light, and windows lining two walls. It had comfy chairs covered in beautiful brocade fabric, a chaise lounge, and mirrors of all sizes.

I put a little makeup on my excited eight-year-old daughter, who looked adorable in pearls and a deep-purple silk taffeta dress. I finished my makeup and Bella painstakingly buttoned the back of my wedding dress. I leaned down so she could clasp my sparkly diamante necklace, and I slipped on my matching bracelet. I put in my diamond earrings and finished with clear stick-on nails with French tips.

I was ready.

I looked in the mirror and I liked what I saw—a glowing woman about to wed her big love. The search that had begun long before we met was now over.

On that day, I was marrying my forever guy.

I reached over to the box of flowers and lifted out Bella's bouquet, with rich eggplant-color blooms, roses, and Hawai'ian proteas, and passed it to her.

I asked her if she was ready for the big day. She nodded enthusiastically and reached up to hug me. I picked up the matching bridal bouquet, took my girl's hand, and we walked out of the room.

I peeked around the top of the staircase and saw Eric patiently waiting at the bottom of the stairs. I took a deep breath and started my walk down. He looked up, our eyes locked, and our great joy was captured for eternity by our three photographers.

Click click click

Click click click

Click click click

They followed us around the grounds to get photos before the guests arrived. Eric and I leaned into each other by the huge pond. *Snap.* With Eric's hand gently placed on my back, he guided me up the hill toward trees that were unseasonably golden. *Snap.* We kissed by the trellis on the side of the house. *Snap.* We whispered sweet words into each other's ears. *Snap.* Bella joined us as we walked along the freshly mowed grass and evergreen hedge. *Snap.*

Amazingly, the sky was the brightest of blues and the weather was so unseasonably warm, that we chose to get married outdoors in the pagoda. The venue had draped some white tulle around the sides of the octagonal-shaped raised pagoda and placed a small table and a chair towards the back to sign the registry during the ceremony. The forty or so guest chairs were split in two on either side of the natural aisle in the front of the pagoda. Off to the side was a beautiful large pond with a fountain spraying water upwards in a gentle arc.

Since it was a last-minute wedding, only my immediate family was in attendance with their spouses and kiddos and a few of my close friends from New Zealand. Sadly, my friends from Hawai'i and Eric's close friends and family from the U.S. and Germany had not been able to book flights and/or take time off work to join us.

My youngest brother Aaron was a DJ in his spare time, and he set up a sound system at the venue to play music throughout the day and into the evening. Bella and I held hands, standing under a tree at the beginning of the natural aisle between the Victorian home and a retaining wall lined with trees, waiting for the entrance music to start. Then, when the Savage Garden song "Truly, Madly,

Deeply," started playing, I gave her a hug, bent down to kiss her on the top of her head, and gently guided her in the right direction.

I stood there, breathing in the moment, watching my little girl walk toward her new daddy. Eric was all smiles as Bella proceeded past our guests to take her place on the pagoda.

Snap snap snap

I felt intense excitement and yet calm, deep in my knowing that I was marrying my final life partner.

As soon as Bella was in place, I took a deep breath, reminded myself to slow down and stay in my body, and started the walk towards my big love, my Bebe, my Eric. This was my third wedding, my third walk down the aisle, and I knew how quickly the day could race by. I knew to be conscious, stay present, and enjoy every moment.

Snap snap snap

As I walked, I listened to the lyrics,

"And when the stars are shining brightly in the velvet sky
I'll make a wish, send it to heaven then make you want to cry,
The tears of joy for all the pleasure and the certainty
That we're surrounded by the comfort and protection
Of the highest powers."

I arrived at the pagoda and took my place across from Eric. He reached out for both of my hands. We looked into each other's eyes, and I fought back tears as the music faded after the chorus,

I wanna stand with you on a mountain
I wanna bathe with you in the sea
I wanna lay like this forever,
Until the sky falls down on me.

Eric and I had written our vows together, and he reached into his pocket for his notes to go first. I heard his voice catch slightly,

26

and he paused to collect his emotions. I looked down momentarily and took a breath to prevent myself from losing it too.

"Today I choose you to be my partner in life and to become a family of three. Our miracle lies in the path we have chosen together. I enter into this marriage with you, knowing that the true magic for us is to consciously build upon our foundation of deep intimacy, love, and trust. To me, this means I am accountable, I am constantly learning and curious, I choose to look for ways to love you more, I choose to keep the relationship fresh and ever-evolving, and I choose to express my love to you through my actions, thoughts, and behaviors. When you hear the words, 'I love you,' I am saying I adore you, I admire you, I cherish you, I honor you, and I hold you in the highest integrity."

He looked up and into my eyes, staring into me, seeing me. With vision blurry from happy tears, I reached out and accepted the typed notes from Eric, took a breath, and followed, speaking the same words. I was emotional, but made it through, barely, and we both turned to the celebrant as she announced joyously, "I now pronounce you man and wife. You may now kiss the bride."

Eric placed his hands on either side of my face, and we leaned into each other for our first kiss as Mr. and Mrs. Leseberg. We pulled away after a long moment, and I looked back at Bella and reached out for her. Our smiles were from ear to ear and our hearts stretched big as we clasped hands, Eric, me, and Bella. I squeezed her hand and let go, and as we turned towards the guests, Bella reached down to pick up the end of my long train. Laughing and crying together, we stepped down from the pagoda onto the grass, and into the hugs and congratulations from our special people.

Snap snap snap

— 10 —

The First Dance

Between the Victorian villa and the pagoda, there was a pad of concrete with an archway covered in beautiful winter vines winding their way up the trellis…a perfect place for family photos. Before Eric and I stepped away for more photos of just the two of us, we made sure to take pictures with everyone and then left the group with canapes and aperitifs.

The reception area was on the other side of the pagoda and pond in a separate permanent structure. It was a beautiful large space, yet with draped fabric from the center of the ceiling to the tops of the walls, the space felt quite intimate.

Feeling delighted with how the day had gone so far, I took a deep breath and looked around the room. Some of my most special people were there. Our guests chatted excitedly while finishing up their cake and sipping wine, beer, or coffee. A Lady Antebellum song, "Need You Now," played in the background.

To my left, my new husband was connecting with my childhood friend, Lindy, and David, her husband. I'd known Lindy since I was ten. Even though we didn't see each other for years at a time, it was like we still lived down the street from each other, and we always picked up where we left off.

To my right was Bella. Her eyes were big and round as she reached for a second helping of wedding cake.

I set down my glass of champagne and looked over at my DJ brother. It was time.

He saw me and nodded to give me the heads up that he was ready for us. I reached for Eric's hand and told my friends I was whisking him away to the dance floor.

Hand in hand, we walked from the bride and groom table to take our places for our choreographed dance. In his booming baritone voice my little brother announced, "And now, the first dance of the new Mr. and Mrs. Leseberg!"

My world came down to that moment with him…my love, my beloved, my lover, my Bebe, my new husband. We swayed, both of us together as one, and with Eric supporting me from behind, I allowed my eyes to close. I turned toward him, and we pulled apart and began the gentle push and pull of the Nightclub Two-Step.

As I look into your eyes
I know the reasons why
My life's worth a thousand skies

Sway to the left, the right, and then the grapevine. Eric forgot for a moment which way to go, and I gently pulled him to his left. He executed the grapevine beautifully, in perfect time to the beat. Then, the leg lift at the end of the grapevine…and we both did it!

My baby you
Are the reason I could fly
And cause of you
I don't have to wonder why
Baby you

The merry-go-round was next, and we held each other's hands and spun around, our heads thrown back like kids loving that feeling of going around and around, slightly out of control.

How do I explain that smile
And how it turns my world around
Keeping my feet on the ground

We stepped to the left, to the right, elegantly easing our way out of the merry-go-round move, and focused on the next tricky steps.

There's no more just getting by
You're the reason I feel so alive
Though these words I sing are true
They still fail to capture you
As mere words can only do

The rhythm, the beat, Marc Anthony singing, "My Baby You" for us, the disco lights reflecting the kaleidoscope of colors all over us and the dance floor. Just us and our precious dance together, moving as one.

Next came the deep dip. I spun out and back into his arms, and he held me and supported me, as we had practiced. He dipped me beautifully, and we held the moment for an extra split second. The deepest of dips, my beloved supporting me and holding me lovingly.

I will soothe you if you fall
I'll be right there if you call
You're my greatest love of all

Click click click click click
Click click click click click
Click click click click click

The three photographers were clicking as fast as their cameras could capture the precious moment, which, as it turned out, was the money shot.

Then came the final choreographed element. I rose from the dip, Eric spun me gently out, back in, and supported me as I slowly sank onto his bent knee.

Arianna...I feel so alive

The dance was wonderful, and exactly as we had envisioned it. Just me and my gorgeous man. The big love of my life.

I was ecstatic to have married my beloved that day.

It was an absolutely perfect day.

— 11 —

The Wedding Night

Our wedding day was nearing an end.

I was hot and sweaty after dancing all evening and took a moment to catch my breath away from the dance floor. I pushed the hair out of my eyes and dabbed my slick face with a napkin, not concerned about how I looked at that point, as the photographers had long stopped clicking and angling for the right shot.

I looked around the room for my new husband and saw him chatting animatedly with Shelley and Karen, twins with whom I've been friends since our early twenties in Auckland.

I sidled up to him and took his hand, whispering in his ear, "It's time."

We did the rounds, hugging our people goodbye.

It was our time now.

Bella was delighted to be taking a break from her mommy and new daddy, as she loved being surrounded by her New Zealand family. When I had told her we were leaving her for a week-long honeymoon, she said in her best grown-up voice, "It's okay Mommy; family is everything to me. I can't wait to play with the twins and have sleepovers with Ma and my cousins."

Eric and I held hands and started down the path. We didn't have far to go as the beautiful Victorian villa that housed our wedding night room was right next door.

As we walked by the fountain, my new husband pulled me in tight, put one hand on each side of my face, and whispered, "This was the best day of my life. I married the woman of my dreams, and I promise I shall always be here for you, and I'll always *always* be your biggest cheerleader."

We kissed passionately in the light of the full moon, standing in front of the beautiful fountain, lit from below and above.

He helped me and my big dress up the stairs, and I didn't worry that my love couldn't carry me over the threshold into the bedroom. After all, in his words, my 6'1" frame "supported 180 pounds of pure goddess." Ha!

We paused at the door, and this time I took his face in my hands.

"I promise to love you madly, deeply, forever and ever…always."

I grinned and added, "And make wicked love with you as long as we both shall live."

He laughed out loud, spun me into the room, and started freeing me of my wedding dress, its job done. He took his time, starting at the top buttons, and worked his way down one by one, pausing to nuzzle my neck. There was no opportunity for me to change into my white lacy honeymoon night ensemble, as we wasted no time setting about consummating our marriage.

We had met and matched, literally and figuratively. We were lovers together like neither of us had experienced before.

After making love, I lay there feeling happy that I had married my beloved Eric. My new husband started lightly snoring, and I rolled into him, delighted that not only had our day been dreamy, but I had just married my forever guy.

— 12 —

The Honeymoon on Lake Taupo

My new husband and I spent our one-week honeymoon at a friend's holiday home in the popular tourist destination of Taupo, in the middle of the North Island of New Zealand. The home was in a great location, within walking distance of the lake and a quick drive to restaurants, grocery stores, and enticing boutiques and gift shops.

After running around like crazy for the wedding, it was lovely to have some time to ourselves. It reminded me of our first week together in Hawai'i, when it was just us. We let ourselves in the front door, looked around to get the lay of the land, and made a beeline for the bedroom. We dumped our bags and crashed on the bed.

Eric kissed me all over and our heavenly honeymoon began. We enjoyed making out and making love like we were decades younger and age didn't matter.

We went on long morning walks along the lakefront and checked out the boats at the harbor. We strolled leisurely around the quaint town, and we either cooked at home or ate delicious food in the town's cafes and restaurants. We sat with local treats at a picnic table near the lakeshore, looking on as tourists tried to hit a hole-in-one onto a tiny island in the lake.

We went to see the stunning Huka Falls, not surprisingly the most visited and photographed natural attraction in New Zealand, and drove around the lake and up into the snow. We had lunch at the gorgeous lodge, The Chateau, reminiscent of a lodge in the French or Swiss Alps.

We soaked and made love in natural hot springs and took selfies by the stunning lakeside and beaches, looking rather bare in the winter months.

One evening, Eric cooked a delicious dinner of vegetables and New Zealand lamb chops, spiced with my favorite herb, rosemary. After we ate, we retired to the couch. I snuggled into my new husband, and he ran his fingers through my hair, gently massaging my scalp. I heard him take a breath before he said, "I love and appreciate everything about you, the new (and final!) Mrs. Leseberg. I love and appreciate the way you planned and executed a fantastic wedding for us…it was absolutely perfect. I love and appreciate your sexiness and sensuality, and I'm so excited to have found you after my life-long search." He bent forward and kissed the top of my head.

It was my turn next, "I love and appreciate that you are YOU, and I'm thrilled that you are my new and forever lover and husband. I celebrate that we finally found each other. I love and appreciate that we adore each other, and that we share a level of respect and freedom I've never experienced."

It was a magical honeymoon, and as much as we didn't want our week together to end, after seven days of bliss, it was time to head back to Bella and the rest of the family.

Before leaving New Zealand, we spent a week visiting with family and friends. We made the best of the cool, wet, wintery weather, playing the family card game "Foo," (like gin rummy but with a twist), visiting the forests, walking the beaches, and eating most of our meals in. When it was time to leave for our flight to the U.S., we made our tearful goodbyes and drove to Auckland.

We flew back to Seattle to start our married life together. Eric and I as Mr. and Mrs. Leseberg, and Bella at her new middle school with new friends and a new daddy. Life was indeed grand.

— 13 —

The First Snow and Summer of Boating

We settled into a routine in our new life together as a family of three, and Eric and I developed a sweet married rhythm, grateful that we got along so well.

Being able to swim in the pool and live and boat on the lake helped Bella and me transition from being in or near the ocean like we had been for most of our days in Hawai'i.

Eric had purchased a 24/7 Malibu Wakesetter boat a few years before meeting me, custom-painted in bright yellow. He loved that boat and was either in the captain's seat speeding fast or being towed behind on a wakeboard or sky ski.

With the boat docked on the property, we loved being able to fall out of bed, throw on swimsuits, grab some snacks and drinks, and head out. The three of us went out regularly. When Bella invited her friends, we enjoyed the sound of squealing girls as their raft went flying in the air while Eric whipped the boat around with crazy donut maneuvers.

Eric and his friends often made good use of the calm surface early in the morning for wakeboarding. Later in the day, the wind and boat traffic would typically pick up and make it harder to wakeboard. In time, Eric taught me how to drive the boat with enough finesse to pull him up on his wakeboard, which is a bit of an art.

He was very patient teaching Bella to wakeboard, and I was amazed how quickly she picked it up, not giving up until she could do it. I have tons of photos and video footage in my computer archives of the two of them wakeboarding with big wide grins, throughout the summer.

Even in the winter, living on the lake was a divine experience. Eric and I could lie in our bed and look out over the eastern side of Mercer Island. When covered in snow, it was a spectacular sight, a winter wonderland.

I recall the priceless look on Bella's face when she saw her first snowflakes fall in Washington. She was wearing a purple and white puffy winter jacket, with matching hat and gloves. She had finally transitioned to sneakers, after wearing flip-flops every day from her first eight years living on the Big Island, and now to boots for the snow.

She looked at the snowflakes with such wonder and pulled off a glove to feel the flakes on her hand, excited as they touched down and melted quickly on her warm bare skin.

Lucky for us, life together in Washington was falling into place, and we felt incredibly blessed and grateful.

— 14 —

Eric's Dream Job at Microsoft

In our first year of marriage, I uncovered something I didn't know about Eric. He was a worrier.

Being a Leo, he liked being the breadwinner, and it was a source of pride for him to provide for the family. He would lie in bed for hours on end, worrying about things—our finances, mostly. Having lost a fortune in the first tech bubble, and after working his way back to solid financial health, only to lose another seven figures with a recent failed real estate investment, he worried harder. On top of it all, the six-year period where Eric was a co-founder of a tech start-up took a huge toll on his emotional, financial, and physical health.

After making it out relatively unscathed and having taken the summer off to get married and take some time with his new family, he decided to head back to Microsoft in the fall of 2010. He had worked there since the nineties and was glad to get back after his six years with the start-up.

After an initial job as a technical writer, he found his way into a position he loved, one that made good use of his strategic brain. It was in the Office of the CTO (Chief Technology Officer) at Microsoft Consulting Services. Things were looking up for my beloved and his career. It was hard work, but he was up for the challenge. He was all in.

Almost five years later, in the latter half of 2015, Eric was offered a dream come true at Microsoft. He was given *carte blanche* to choose an industry to work with, one that aligned well with strategic planning. The CTO tasked Eric with finding a way to disrupt a complete industry vertical by shifting Microsoft's relationship with their clients, from trusted advisor to more of a critical and entwined partner. Eric landed on the shipping industry and got busy working on a project that had global ramifications for significantly improving logistics and providing huge cost savings across the entire globe. He spent time preparing for worldwide travel, submitted paperwork for "Global Entry" and all American and Canadian security fast-track programs, and was on the verge of scheduling trips to Panama and South Africa.

Eric was ecstatic that his love for his work and his desire to travel were coming together, especially as we had been building up our financial strength and had held back on travel in our first several years together. So when these international travel opportunities for Eric's work were coming to fruition, I had visions of joining him and experiencing the local scenery, adventure, and culture while he was working. After all, one of the elements of our initial attraction was our desire to travel together.

Little did we know what was just around the corner for Eric; not only would there be very little travel left for us, but our lives were about to change, forever.

PART TWO

— 1 —

Thanksgiving 2015

I t was Thanksgiving, November 2015, our sixth one together, and we had twenty people in our home.

I took a deep breath, inhaling the delicious aroma of the turkey just out of the oven, and delighted in the animated sounds of our close friends chatting, laughing, and excitedly anticipating the holiday meal.

I watched as my husband graciously broke away, picked up the electric turkey-carving knife, and started cutting the meat. I walked over to him and gave him a peck on the lips before spooning the side dishes into their respective bowls.

After a few minutes, he whispered to me that he had some pain in his upper back and was having difficulty carving. I grabbed the nearest guest and recruited them to finish the job.

We didn't think too much about it and went on to have an unforgettable, fun Thanksgiving, with an abundance of delicious food, oblivious to what was happening in Eric's spine and bones.

— 2 —

It Started With a Niggle

W hat had started with a niggle that Thanksgiving Day, an annoying ache in his upper back, grew progressively worse over the next few weeks. We didn't take it too seriously, as we had both experienced sore backs over the years, including long periods of pain impacting typical daily activities and often requiring time off work.

Right after the holiday, Eric took himself to our local, dedicated chiropractor, "Dr. Chiro," my nickname for him.

He performed his usual clicking and cracking and didn't sense any need to get updated x-rays, as he'd taken them the year prior. Eric went back every few days in the hopes of feeling some relief. However, the doctor told my husband that he didn't feel he was making progress and recommended that Eric explore other avenues to find out what was causing the pain. Eric wasn't ready to change treatment plans yet and continued to see Dr. Chiro until one day, when he was working on his upper back, the pain from the adjustment was so bad, Eric yelled out, "Fuuuuck! I think you just broke my back!"

A friend referred us to another chiropractor in Redmond. By the time we saw the new "Dr. Young Chiro," a few days after the incident with Dr. Chiro, Eric was starting to have trouble walking. So, I had to wheel him from the car into the treatment room in a wheelchair borrowed from their office.

At the first appointment, the young and inexperienced chiropractor worked on Eric's hips, not realizing what was taking place in the bones under his hands. It seemed to help a little and my guy was able to walk out of the office. In a subsequent visit, Dr. Young Chiro tried to get Eric to perform a series of exercises, including rolling on the floor on a hard spongey roller, directly on the area of pain in his upper back. He scratched his head when my beloved screamed out in pain.

We didn't go back, as Dr Young Chiro seemed to be making things worse.

By mid-December, Eric started using up vacation time and stopped going to work at the Microsoft campus in Redmond. He could barely sleep and was popping painkillers like candy. He began to stay upstairs all day, and I brought him his meals and drinks. When it became too painful to get to the toilet, he started peeing in a cup. We still didn't take it seriously enough, and Bella and I even took a video of him wearing a back brace and crawling around upstairs on all fours.

We celebrated Christmas Day at a friend's condo in Bellevue. My beloved shuffled from the parking lot into the building and up the elevator to the twenty-fifth floor. Once inside, he gingerly lowered himself onto a loveseat trying to find a comfortable position. It was a seat designed for one, and our friend came bounding across the room, practically jumping on Eric's lap. As soon as he screamed out in pain, she leapt up in apology.

He made it through the holiday, barely. It became one day at a time, with the hope that the pain would start to subside at some point.

Since I was working during the holiday period, Eric's best friend of twenty years, (Andi with an "i," short for Andreas, from Germany), offered to take him to a local urgent care between Christmas and New Year's. The doctor sent him home with painkillers and muscle relaxants. They tried again a few days later at a different urgent care and came home with more of the same.

On the evening of January 11th, 2016, Eric's pain had become so intense, he moaned with every slight movement. I was incredibly worried about how bad it had become, so I called 911.

I asked for an ambulance to come and take my husband to the ER at the local hospital in Kirkland. The two paramedics didn't have a good solution to get Eric down the stairs and waited until a couple firefighters could join them. Shockingly, the four of them still couldn't figure out how to get him downstairs and suggested he walk to the stairwell and down the stairs...all the while, in agonizing pain. Little did they know that Eric's back was literally at a breaking point.

The doctor on the ER floor late that night was clearly tired, and it was obvious she didn't want to be there. I don't recall her last name, but it began with K. As he was lying on the hard bed, "Dr. K" performed her usual routine of poking and prodding. Halfway through her examination, Eric screamed out in pain, and she requested the nurse push more painkillers into his IV and left the room. Eventually, after I tracked her down myself, she returned to complete her assessment. I inquired whether she would order an MRI so that we could find out the source of his intense pain. But instead of imaging, she prescribed more medication and sent him home.

The next day, I was beside myself. I didn't understand why it was so hard to get a friggin' MRI! I was now on a mission, determined to find out what was going on. We heard about a back pain specialist in Redmond, and I called and begged them to find a space in their schedule. They did, and I readied Eric for another painful journey.

I made a bed of pillows in the back passenger area of Eric's big yellow Tonka truck. As he lay behind me, writhing in pain, I drove him to the back specialist. Unbeknownst to us, this doctor only gave steroid shots, and then *only if* the patient already had x-rays and an MRI. We had been so desperate for an MRI, we didn't think to check before we made the appointment. When the doctor told me, I was livid and asked how the heck we could get one. He shrugged his shoulders and recommended we go to see Eric's general practitioner.

Before this, Eric barely needed a GP as he was fighting fit and rarely sick. But I was done chasing treatments that clearly didn't work. I drove him straight to his GP without an appointment, and struggled to get him out of the truck and into the doctor's office.

My beloved laid across several chairs in the waiting room, hoping to find a comfortable position while I marched up to the check-in desk. Not only were there no appointments available, but the doctor couldn't see him for another three days! I was almost in tears and asked what we could do to get an MRI. The sweet receptionist leaned forward and quietly recommended we go downstairs to the ER, and off we went.

This ER doctor was bright, alert, and looked me in the eye as I stood up to my full six foot, one inch height, and told her that we were NOT leaving until MY HUSBAND HAD AN MRI!

"Dr. Bright" sprang into action, and two efficient male nurses got him undressed, into a gown, and rolled Eric away for an MRI within minutes.

I was so relieved; I sank down onto the plasticky cushion of the chair in the ER, alone, holding my head in my hands, tears rolling down my cheeks. I was frustrated and angry, disappointed and sad. I cried for Eric and all the pain he had endured. I cried for not getting him there sooner. I cried for the tired and uninterested ER doctor the night before. And I cried for the medical system that purports to be the best in the world, yet makes it so damn hard to advocate for what our loved ones need.

— 3 —

The "C" Word

Eric was wheeled back into the same ER room, and we held hands awaiting the results. We didn't have to wait long though, as the radiologist, upon glancing over the images, saw a pathologic fracture.

Dr. Bright clearly and calmly explained that there was a fracture in his spine, and that the bone had been weakened by some sort of mass or tumor. She looked at us directly and said the one word we were absolutely NOT expecting to hear.

"Cancer. Mr. Leseberg, it appears you have a cancerous tumor, which is the underlying cause of your fractured vertebrae."

We sat quietly in shock.

"Cancer?" Eric finally asked.

"Yes. I'm recommending that we send you to our sister hospital in Seattle for surgery, to remove the tumor," Dr. Bright said.

A thousand questions were swirling around us, but there was no time to ask them. The hospital staff moved into high gear making arrangements for Eric to be transported to the trauma hospital in Seattle.

Somehow, we held it together in those next few minutes, not yet processing what was happening. I leaned in and gently hugged and kissed my guy goodbye, and told him I would follow closely behind.

Before they wheeled him away, still not having begun to comprehend the severity of his situation, Eric gave me a list of items to bring from home: laptop, power cord, charger, power strip, T-shirts, underwear, and long shorts.

I smiled and had to remind myself to keep breathing. That was so Eric, still adding items to his list as he was being wheeled away for his ambulance ride to the hospital for emergency surgery.

— 4 —

The Drive Home Alone

No, no, no, no, no! *This can NOT be happening!*
It was only a niggle in his back forty-nine days ago.
What do they mean there's a cancerous tumor, and it fractured his spine?
What the fuck?!

I was driving home alone and hadn't called anyone yet. I needed to process the last several hours, so I carried the weight of the news alone. I didn't try to stop the flow of the tears that came, nor wipe them away. This was my time, just me driving Eric's yellow truck, slicing through the fog on that cold January afternoon.

It was hard news to process.

My mind was racing, wishing I had pushed harder, earlier, for an MRI.

Breathe in.

Breathe out.

Don't focus on what could have been.

Eric was always reminding me not to dwell on the "coulda, woulda, shoulda's." I needed to stay in my body and be present for my guy.

But, hell no no NO!

This cannot be happening.

Girl, get back in your body!

Stay present. Breathe.

Stay present. Breathe.

I drove home on autopilot and was only there long enough to grab his electronics, clothes, and toiletries. I selected the same for me, stuffed everything in a bag, and ran back down the stairs to my car. As I was driving to the hospital, I made a call to arrange for Bella to stay with a friend for the evening. I told her that her daddy had to have surgery, and assured her that he was going to be okay.

He would be, wouldn't he?

— 5 —

Finding Eric in the Hospital

The only parking space available was deep in the bowels of the underground hospital parking lot. Around and around and down I drove, winding further and further beneath the earth. I finally found a spot, parked the truck, grabbed our bags, and took the elevator up to the first floor. I politely asked the man sitting under the large question mark where I could find Eric Leseberg.

He pointed me in the right direction, and I started out on what would be many hundreds, possibly thousands of walks through hospital corridors over the coming year...walks where I regularly wanted to shout out about the horrors of the cancer journey. This time, though, right at the beginning, I calmly put one foot in front of the other and kept my big voice small and contained. Soon enough we would learn the language and rhythm of this place, the people, and the system.

Miraculously, I located the correct hospital wing, elevator bank, floor, and room number, and I found my husband.

There he was, looking adorable in his one-size-fits-no-one hospital gown. He looked up at me, and I noticed the gray and blue of the gown intensified his deep blue eyes. He smiled, and I ran. I ran into his arms and held him as tightly as I could—this man, my beloved, with a cancerous tumor in his spine. Of course, I wanted to shout, "*No, no, no, no, this CANNOT be happening!*" But I swallowed my fighting words and sat with my guy, focusing on staying present and calm.

In just a few short hours my Bebe would undergo urgent surgery.

— 6 —

Meeting the Surgeon

Memory is a funny thing. I had almost forgotten a tiny detail of that day.

I'm not sure what I could have been thinking, but a small part of me must have wondered whether my guy would make it through his surgery the next day. I don't remember making the phone calls, yet I must have because suddenly I was looking around Eric's hospital room, and it was full of people. They were all talking at once, and the surreal thing was that they were chatting amongst themselves and ignoring the man in the bed.

I had reached out to Eric's only biological daughter, Alison, as soon as I knew something was up. I told her that her dad was in the hospital, about to have surgery, and awaiting a cancer prognosis.

She and her five kiddos came in right away and became regular visitors both at the hospital and once we were back at home.

I must have called someone to bring in our bewildered Bella, and I recall that at least two of the three Long brothers, Eric's long-time friends, were there. There must have been others too, but I don't recall who.

Then, as suddenly as they appeared, they all disappeared, wishing Eric well in his big surgery the following day.

Breathe, remember to breathe!

Breathe in. Breathe out.

Thank goodness everyone has gone.

Breathe in! Breathe out!

I sat down by the bed, took Eric's hand, and apologized for having an impromptu party in his room. He shrugged and said it was fine, that he appreciated where my heart was.

Neither of us had begun to process the diagnosis, the elephant in the room. The "C" word.

Is my Bebe going to be okay?

Is he going to survive this?

Are we going to lose each other, having just found one another seven years ago?

What…the fuck…is…happening?

I sat thinking about the big plans we had.

Eric had long dreamt about sailing in the tall ships around the South Pacific, and we both imagined walking hand-in-hand on the white beaches in the Seychelles and photographing elephants, lions, zebras, and giraffes on safari. *So much to do, yet how much time did we have left together to do it?*

We looked up as a huge presence came striding into the room, his coat flapping behind him. Tall, striking, and of European origin, he looked like he had just walked off a shoot for the January issue of the *GQ* Surgeon of the Month Magazine. This gentleman turned out to be my beloved's doctor and surgeon, "Dr. GQ."

He pulled up a hospital folding chair and sat at our level, his intelligent blue eyes a match for Eric's. Captivated, we listened as he shared what was going to happen—before, during, and after the surgery.

He said that if they had discovered the source of the pain earlier, they would have radiated the tumor in his spine first. But they were out of time, and my beloved would require two surgeries. The first surgeon would make an incision at the top of Eric's leg, by the groin, go up the vein to the T8 vertebrae, and cut off the blood supply to the tumor.

The second surgeon, Dr. GQ, would open up Eric's spine, remove the cancerous tumor, and most likely his severely damaged T8 vertebrae. They expected to replace it with a titanium cage.

Remove a piece of his spine?

Isn't that dangerous?

A titanium cage!

What the fuck?

They were going to come soon and wheel my guy away to perform a full battery of tests throughout the night, including additional MRIs to obtain more images of the tumor.

After he was done speaking, Dr. GQ asked Eric to sign a bunch of consent forms. Eric played devil's advocate for a moment, asking what would happen if he didn't sign the stack of papers. Without hesitation, Dr. GQ told Eric that he wouldn't have long and that he was very lucky to have made it this far.

Breathe in. Breathe out.

A gangly, aggressive, nasty, bloodsucking tumor had taken residence in my beloved's spine!

What the fuck?

What the actual fuck!

Breathe in. Breathe out.

My mind was screaming, but I held on tightly to my guy's hand and kept my inner voice inside.

We stared after the surgeon as he left the room, his white coat disappearing along with his six-foot-six-inch frame.

We held tightly onto each other and shared our gratitudes with each other, our daily habit. "I love and appreciate that you are here with me at the hospital and that you will be here when I wake up from my surgery tomorrow," he said quietly. I squeezed his hand and replied, "I love and appreciate that you are in good spirits and that you are taking this unexpected development calmly and positively."

Our GOCs were cut short, as they came to wheel him away for the long night of tests.

We held hands…until we couldn't.

— 7 —

GOCs and Getting Wheeled Away to Surgery

I was alone in the hospital room for much of the night as Eric's spine was getting its picture taken, thousands of times, in minute, tiny slices.

I lay down on a hard cot beside the window and drifted off into a dreamland where Eric and I still had a whole health-filled life ahead of us.

After hours of tests, they wheeled my beloved back to the room to await the first surgery. We held onto each other for dear life, not knowing the outcome of the next twenty-four hours.

The last sixteen hours had been both a blur and slow motion. Time had passed in a flash and then slowed, as if we were moving through a room filled with thick gel.

I reached out for my Bebe's hand and started with my GOCs first.

"I love and appreciate that you are taking all this in your stride, with no complaints, and that you're just getting on with it. I love and appreciate you, and I am so glad I winked at you on that memorable day on April 20th, 2009. I love and appreciate what an amazing daddy you are to our daughter, and that you take her on fun daddy-daughter dates to get Chinese food and thick shakes."

Oh God!

What the heck?

What's going to happen now?

Would Eric be able to walk, or will he be paralyzed?

Would this be the last time we did GOCs together?

Is it really, truly, cancer?

Maybe that aggressive, nasty, bloodsucking tumor was benign and not malignant after all?

Help! Please help!

Eric squeezed my hand and gathered his thoughts for his GOCs.

"I love and appreciate that you are right here with me and dealing with all this calmly. I'm grateful you're not panicking, but just rolling along with everything that's happening. I love and appreciate that you gathered our special people in the room last night, including my two daughters. The truth is that we don't know what's going to happen, and I'm glad I saw everyone."

I snorted and then cried a little, but we were out of time. They came to wheel him away for the first of the two surgeries.

Time slowed to a standstill with the words of our last gratitudes, and our hands pulled apart.

"I love you, Bebe! See you in a few hours," I shouted as Eric, my beloved, my Bebe, my guy, my lover, my husband, my everything, was being wheeled away into the great unknown.

"I love you back, Bebe!" he croaked, with the first sign that he was feeling the enormity of what was happening.

— 8 —

The Mother of All Surgeries

It was 8 a.m. on the morning of January 13, 2016, and Eric was in surgery. I sat on the window seat with my knees pulled up to my chin, trying to process what was happening.

My mind wandered and explored some of the *what-ifs*. *What if he was paralyzed during his surgery?* That would mean a serious adjustment, but I figured we could manage. *What if that was our last gratitude session? What if that was the last time we held hands? What if that was the final chapter of the Phillipa and Eric love story?*

There's a fucking tumor in his back!

Cancer?!

How did this happen? How did we not know?

Shit!

What the fuck?

Breathe in. Breathe out.

Breathe in. Breathe out.

I looked outside. It was a dull, gray day, and the view across the courtyard was of a dirty orange-colored brick wing of the hospital. I allowed the tears to flow, processing the significance of this new development in our lives.

Later, I glanced up as a nurse bounded into the room with a smile on her face. The first surgery had gone well. The blood supply had been successfully cut off from the tumor. I felt like leaping off the window seat and grabbing her in a huge snotty-nosed bear hug to celebrate the good news. But I didn't. I smiled politely, dabbed my eyes, and thanked her for the update.

Now it was time to wait for the outcome of the second surgery. The big one. The mother of all surgeries, and it would take several hours.

I spent those hours distracting myself, reading, wandering, calling and chatting with close friends and family.

Breathe in. Breathe out.

Breathe in. Breathe out.

He's going to be fine.

The big surgery is going to go as planned!

Breathe in. Breathe out.

Breathe in. Breathe out.

— 9 —

The Titanium Cage and Cancer-Killing Cement

I must have fallen asleep, yet sensed a presence in the room. I opened my eyes, and Dr. GQ was standing there. He sat down on a folding chair and looked me in the eye.

The surgery had gone perfectly to plan, like "textbook surgery," he said.

I didn't find out until afterward that this was a relatively new surgery and that there weren't any textbooks on this one yet. If I recall correctly, there was a team of eighteen medical professionals in the huge operating room, as big as a small apartment.

They had successfully extracted the tumor, removed Eric's T8 vertebrae, and replaced it with a titanium cage. They had also observed cancerous cells in T4, scraped those away, and filled up the area with a kind of cancer-killing cement. I later heard that Dr. GQ had gotten himself into a legal situation by using that cement stuff, as it hadn't been approved by the FDA. But I didn't care, as long as it worked. Besides, I was aware of discussions around FDA approvals and some of their rulings made absolutely no sense to the layperson anyway.

I gulped back tears of relief and managed to whisper my thanks to Dr. GQ. He asked if I had any questions.

Yes, a million.

But wait, I can't think of even one!

I shook my head, and with a nod of acknowledgment, he stood, spun on his heels, and left.

— 10 —

He Made It Through!

The nurses warned me that Eric would look a little weird when I next saw him. They said it was because he had been lying on a downward angle for seven hours with his head in a vice and his spine completely immobilized for the surgery.

When he was wheeled in, his face was indeed extremely puffy. But that smile! It was huge and went from ear to ear.

The surgery had been a resounding success, and he was happy to be alive. I rushed over to him, squeezed his hand tightly, and leaned in for a kiss.

I was so grateful he had survived the surgeries and was able to talk and smile and wiggle his toes.

We didn't know what was ahead. However, we figured that as the way forward became clear, and we had our target in sight, we could find a way to slay that fucking cancer dragon.

Facebook Post—January 20, 2016
So incredibly grateful to the team of world-class surgeons
who replaced a part of Eric's spine with a titanium cage last
week! Our world tilted just a little more with the cancer
diagnosis a couple of days ago. Thank you to all those who
have shown up in our lives in all sorts of magical ways!
Blessings and prayers most graciously accepted for the
right path for Eric lighting up!

~ 11 ~

Eric's Hospital Stay and a Poem by Bella

It had been a huge cutting-edge surgery, and even under normal circumstances, it might take several months for the healing to take place. The added complication for Eric was that he was going to need to start cancer treatments at some point, and sooner rather than later.

In those post-surgery days, the initial issue for Eric was the management of his intense pain. The doctors prescribed a ton of medication, including Oxycodone, Oxycontin, another med to help him sleep, another for constipation (just in case), and so many others that I lost track. Thank goodness Eric and the nurses were on top of his meds.

Then there was the question of what type of cancer Eric had. No cancer treatment could begin without knowing what they were dealing with. A tissue sample taken from his spine had been sent to the lab for analysis, but they were having difficulty figuring it out.

The days progressed without a prognosis. There was talk that it was bladder cancer, but they really didn't know.

As we waited for an accurate read on the type of cancer, Eric healed slowly from his surgery. I didn't leave his side for exactly one week. I slept in the cot beside his bed, working remotely from the hospital room.

A daily hospital routine developed in that time.

Right on schedule, every couple of hours, the nurses, wearing comfy sneakers and scrubs in all the colors of the rainbow, poked their heads into the room.

They pumped the hand sanitizer by the door before checking on Eric and selecting his medication from the locked cabinet. They scanned his ID bracelet and asked him his name each time they gave him meds. They had to confirm it was really him. A different technician would draw blood and take his temperature and blood pressure. *Tap tap tap*, they efficiently recorded every drug and every test result in the bedside computer.

Our week was punctuated with visits from some of our special people who came in with food, clean clothes, and other supplies we needed. We warned them that when they came, anything could be happening in the room and to be prepared. Eric might be sleeping, sitting on the side of the bed trying to pee into a container, or he might be walking around the room with his monitors—a black adhesive strip covering his recent spinal surgery, and his butt exposed! But no one was bothered by any of it. They were just glad to spend time with us.

While Eric and I were at the hospital, Bella stayed with friends and came in to see her dad as much as possible. Our girl was turning into an amazing young poet and wrote poems for Eric that she read aloud on her visits. She even wrote him a song and sang it to him one afternoon, something she rarely did. The nurses popped their heads in or gathered by the door to listen to Bella sing. There wasn't a dry eye as she sang a song she had just written.

Not another Goodbye
by Bella Christian

I have never before lost a soul to this prison,
So with the time that we have, I pray I'm forgiven.
For I cannot seem to find the right words in my throat,
No redemption or expression, a simple synthetic quote.
I wish I could speak all the thoughts fogging my head,
Or the things that keep me awake at night in my bed.
I have learned and know that I am afraid,
Of what to expect, the panic and the rage.
Some revel in pain, others cry until worn,
Some yell and they scream when broken and torn.
I hope for the best, but prepare for the worst,
Because I have never had to deal with this cancerous curse.
But there is a difference between being optimistic and real,
Something to dream of and another to feel.
You have so many people but not enough hands,
We will hold you in our arms until the very end.
We bow down to you and the power you will lead,
For the people you've met and the credit you'll receive.
A father, a husband, a brother, a son,
A granddad, an uncle, a fighter who's won.
Do not be afraid, we know that you're strong,
There is always darkness before the light of dawn.

— 12 —

The Big Conversation with Bella

The hospital staff had Eric up and walking, right from the day after surgery, to help with the recovery process.

He was progressing to plan, and after a week they sent us home. Soon after we got home, Eric called Bella into the bedroom with us. She sat in a chair by the bed, not sure what was happening.

We had struggled with how to go about this and ultimately decided to keep her in the loop as much as possible. Now was the time to talk. But, how do you tell your fourteen-year-old daughter her daddy might be dying of stage-four bladder cancer and that he may not have much time left?

Oh God!

Is this really happening?

This is a lot for our Bella-girl to process.

This is so fucking unfair!

Why, oh why, do we have to have this conversation?

Oh God, here it goes . . .

Eric reached out, picked up Bella's hand, and spoke directly to her.

"I don't know how much time I have." He swallowed a big lump in his throat. "I feel like I've had a great life, lived some wild adventures, and am ready to go, if that's what it's coming down to. I love you very VERY much and would be so sad if I wasn't around to watch you grow up and be there for your life's big events...like seeing you graduate from high school and college, walking you down the aisle, and being a grandad again."

He trailed off, as if the thought of not being there for our girl was too much.

Bella sat there with tears pooled in her eyes, looking blank. She squeezed his hand and said, "You'll be fine, Daddy. I know you will be." Then she got up and left the room.

I didn't blame her. I mean, how *does* a fourteen-year-old process that her father might be dying? The truth is, they don't. They tuck it away and wait to deal with it on another day, month, or year. Just like the rest of us. Thankfully Bella continued putting her words on paper to help process the enormity of the situation, and that was okay. For now.

Late at night a few days after the talk, the results came in. Finally! We were lying in bed and put the call on speaker so we could both hear what "Dr. Uro-Onco" had to say. He told us he had good and bad news. The bad news was that Eric did indeed have stage-four cancer.

No shit!

We sort of figured that much out on our own!

The good news was that the cancer wasn't bladder cancer, it was Non-Hodgkin's Lymphoma, (NHL), which was purportedly easier to treat. He explained that treatments for lymphoma cancers in recent years had come a long way, yet there still weren't many great solutions for bladder cancer patients.

Oh, yay?

After we hung up, we snuggled tightly, each lying there with renewed hope.

In the ensuing days, there was a tug of war around when to start chemotherapy. One party, Dr. GQ and team, wanted to wait as long as possible to allow the cells to fully heal around the wound and titanium cage in Eric's spine. They recommended four weeks minimum.

The other party, the oncologists, wanted to get started on cancer treatment immediately.

The decision was out of our hands, and it remained to be seen who would win out.

— 13 —

The Role of Food in Eric's Recovery, or Not?

It was about a week after we had returned home from the hospital, and I saw it there. In the bathroom. Untouched. The green smoothie I had made for my beloved an hour earlier.

I had poured all my love, hope, and healing energy into that smoothie, made with organic kale, ginger, lemon, parsley, pink coconut water, a banana, frozen blueberries, hemp protein, flax seeds, and a raw/organic protein mix. I had added ice, upon my Bebe's request, as he liked his drinks chilly cold.

It was a defining moment, a fork in the road of his recovery. I realized we might have a problem, a clash in our beliefs around food and nutrition, and I wondered what changes my guy was willing to make in order to heal. He could choose to take the left path or the right, the blue pill or the red, or in my mind, choose life or death.

I picked up the glass and walked across our bedroom to the bed. Eric was awake and watched me, looking a little sheepish when he saw what I held in my hand.

He said, "I'm so sorry, Bebe. I can't do it. If it doesn't taste good, I just can't." Roughly translated, if it didn't taste like his favorite thick shake, made with ice cream and laden with sweet syrups, he couldn't stomach it.

I had made the assumption that because my guy had been diagnosed with stage-four cancer, he would jump at the chance to change his diet to include better food choices. I figured he would eat or drink anything, *do anything* to give himself a better chance at surviving this thing. I hoped he would be motivated to make any necessary changes to support his body's healing.

We both knew his situation was dire, but it seemed apparent he may not be able to make the transition to healthier options.

We were really close, my husband and I. We hardly ever argued. On that day, we argued. We argued about food and its role in potentially healing him, or at the very least, helping him to diminish the damage about to descend on his body with the imminent chemotherapy treatment.

I begged him to consider making better choices and help save his own life. But he just couldn't do it, as it turned out. He opted for whatever food tasted good to him, and that included thick shakes, mint chocolate chip ice cream, and chocolate chip cookies...even while in the hospital *and* with the blessings of the people in the white coats.

Although this was *our* journey, it was Eric's body.

With as much grace, love, and kindness as I could muster, I committed to supporting my beloved and his decisions.

And so it was, I said yes to my husband.

I said yes to his choices that were not my choices.

I said yes to this man I loved deeply and madly.

I said yes to quieting my inner voice.

— 14 —

Finding the Cancer Center in Seattle

We felt like nervous newcomers visiting a foreign land. First, we couldn't find the entrance to the parking structure, and, frustrated, we circled around the block several times in the heavy Seattle traffic.

Although we didn't know it at the time, before long our cars would practically drive themselves to this cancer center. But, on this day, even after we finally found the right parking structure, we still had to navigate from the parking lot to the office location at one of the big Seattle cancer facilities.

This was a place dedicated to members of the club, albeit a club no one willingly joins—the cancer club. As we were entering, others were leaving. Sadly, we could instantly identify who was visiting the club for treatment by their headscarves, pale skin, thin bodies, shaved heads, and tired eyes. By process of elimination, we could tell who were friends and family, there for support and encouragement, or perhaps just transportation.

It struck me in the gut that we really were a part of the club now, something I would never in a million years have imagined for us.

My first impression of the Seattle cancer center was that it was BIG.

With so many people on a cancer journey—almost two million new cases of cancer every year in the U.S. (as stated on the American Cancer Society website), there was clearly a huge demand for these services. The hospital network was prepped and ready to supply the hundreds of professionals necessary to handle all the cancer cases showing up at their doorstep.

One of our close friends, Hilary, had been on her own cancer journey for the last year, including spending time in Mexico exploring alternative treatment offerings. She had coached us the evening prior, sharing with us some good questions to ask in the session and what to expect. Thankfully, she had offered to join us to meet Eric's new oncologist. We saw her standing by the elevators, and after hugs all around, we went up to the third floor.

We checked Eric in, and the three of us waited in the reception area, sitting on the brand-new blue, gray, and silver modern reception furniture. The seating was a little hard for my taste, and my overall sense was that even with the massive renovations taking place, this was still a sterile doctors' reception lounge. I had rarely seen such high-end doctors' offices, though. There was obviously money in cancer.

I wondered, with their huge budget, why they couldn't design it to be more welcoming with warmer tones and more comfortable seating.

Ugh!
Here we go! Eric's seeing an oncologist!
Oh boy!

— 15 —

Awaiting the Oncologist's Arrival

We were eventually ushered down the long corridor to a small office, my black leather, chunky-healed mod boots clomping on the shiny hard floor.

It had a rather uncomfortable bench, a small desk, a computer, and a few folding chairs. There was no sign of a lovely, warm interior design in here either.

The three of us sat on the hard bench, and I put Eric's hand in my left hand and Hilary's in my right. I looked at Hil, and she nodded. "You've got this."

Oh God! Oh God!
Eric's seeing a friggin' oncologist!
What the heck?
How did that happen?
Ugh, he's going to jump on board the traditional therapies, I know he is!
I wish he would consider going to that place Hilary told us about in Mexico!
This is it! We're about to have THE chemo cancer treatment conversation.

We heard footsteps, and the door started to open. A young brunette with a big smile, sparkly eyes, and a white coat peeked into the room. This was Eric's new oncologist. My nickname for her: "Dr. Smiley."

Hilary had warned us about this part, and she was right. It was overwhelming, sitting in a small sterile office, across from a cancer doctor wearing the proverbial white coat. It's not that she was intimidating or that I didn't like her. In fact, she was very nice, clearly smart, and open to patiently fielding the myriad questions we asked her. It's just that the topic of conversation was intimidating, in and of itself.

The "C" word typically instills fear. As soon as most of us hear the word cancer, we often jump to the worst-case scenario, thinking that this is the end and that a long horrific journey and intensely painful death is imminent. Many people hang on every word the cancer doctor says and jump on board, with no questions asked, when they inform us there are only standard options for treatments available. I was afraid we would be pushed and encouraged to jump quickly into a treatment plan without considering what else was out there.

Oh God! Ugh!

This is it! We're having THE cancer conversation.

— 16 —

Asking the Big Questions

If Hilary hadn't coached us in some of the important elements to cover, I'm pretty sure I would have been a blubbering mess, unable to think clearly or ask any of the necessary and difficult questions.

I had been holding my breath while Dr. Smiley went over the basics, and I consciously exhaled and started going through the questions I'd written down to ask. The first was, "What is Eric's percentage chance of surviving this thing?"

Her eyes scanned over all three of us, and she said, "He has a really good chance of surviving with this type of cancer, say eighty/twenty. There is solid research in the Non-Hodgkin's Lymphoma field, and we've made really good strides in treatments in recent years."

Okay, okay.

We could work with that. Eighty percent is good, right?

Next, I asked, "How did Eric get cancer?"

Dr. Smiley shrugged her shoulders ever so slightly and said in response, "We have no idea how Eric got cancer, or in fact, how anyone really gets cancer. It's a host of different factors, like stress, diet, environment, genetics, and such."

We both asked the next question simultaneously, "What now?"

"*Weeell,*" she replied, "We'll need to start you on chemotherapy as soon as possible, but since you're still healing from your surgery, perhaps sometime in the next few weeks."

Eric and I took in a collective breath and sat with that for a long moment.

"How will we know if it's working?" I asked, not being happy that chemotherapy was the only option being offered.

"We'll test every few months to see whether the cancer has subsided, using a PET scan," she replied.

Shit. Fuck. Shit.

Chemotherapy!

PET scans!

I can't even.

"Will I feel sick? Will I be able to work?...Will I lose my hair?" Eric asked his three big questions all at once.

"*Weeell,*" she responded, "Everyone is different, but yes, one of the common side effects is that you might feel sick. You can work as much or as long as you like, and you can figure that out with your company. And yes, a lot of our patients lose their hair. It's a common side effect."

Eric, as always, playing the devil's advocate, asked, "What if I don't do anything?"

She looked at him directly in the eyes and said, "You will likely not make it."

Breathe in. Breathe out.

Shit! Fuck! Shit!

"Aren't there any other options? Anything healthier you can offer? I heard high-dose IV drips work well," I implored, already knowing what her answer would be.

"No, I am not aware of any healthier options."

My last-ditch attempt, "What about high-dose Vitamin C drips? Anything?"

Dr. Smiley answered, "I don't know anything about the Vitamin C drips, and there's no research to support using Vitamin C. I did hear once that there was a case where Vitamin C impacted the efficacy of a lung cancer treatment, and it's not recommended."

Did she just roll her eyes? What the heck?

She heard one story about a lung cancer patient, and that's it?

What about all the other peer-reviewed research out there?!

Shit. What's up with this?

Surely there's something natural that they can bring in to at least "complement" the more chemical-laden treatments?

I kept my big inner voice inside and asked, "What about Eric's diet; should we change it completely?"

She responded, "No, just keep doing what you're doing. Diet doesn't really have much of an impact on the cancer."

What? Did she just say that?

Diet doesn't impact the cancer?!

That CANNOT be right.

I came back to one of the big questions for me, "What about sugar? I heard that it feeds the cancer?"

"Tuh!" And she leaned forward and did the downward wrist gesture. "Tuh! If sugar gave us cancer, we'd all have cancer!"

What the fuck?

What the actual fuck?

Hasn't she read the data recently?

We practically all have cancer!

What's a PET scan anyway, if it isn't where you drink radio-active liquid sugar and take x-rays of the cancer lighting up as it hungrily gobbles up the sugary substance?!

She said that her staff will be reaching out to schedule the next appointment, with labs, the following week.

With that, Dr. Smiley asked if there were any further questions. When we all looked at her blankly, she stood, wished us well, and left.

— 17 —

Traditional Treatments It Is

We tend to put doctors on a pedestal. We trust them and make the assumption that they know all the answers, and know how to heal us. We assume that because they're smart, they will not only be doing the right thing for our loved ones but can also perform miracles.

That is just not the case, sadly.

Our doctors are human, and I believe we, as patients, are working with a deck that is stacked against us from the start, especially in the cancer arena. The fact is that our doctors are not trained in how to heal us, but rather they are trained to treat our symptoms, essentially only with pharmaceuticals.

I have observed over the years that in the U.S. and other developed countries, we have a "symptom care" system. A "health care" system would focus on achieving and maintaining great health from the get-go. Early signs of something going whacky in our cells, like inflammation, would be taken very seriously. Doctors would be taught that what we eat and drink is critical and that diet is one of the key contributing factors to good health. But as the system is, the question becomes—how much can doctors really learn in their four hours of nutrition classes at medical school? And on top of that, because they give pharmaceuticals so much attention, how much do they objectively know about nutrition and its impact on the body and our health?

If you think about it, when you talk to people about their miraculous healing stories from cancer, they often credit changing their diet and lifestyle. With the billions of dollars that have gone into cancer research every year for decades, only limited progress has been made in finding cures and understanding causation. Research money has typically been funneled into pharmaceutical drug research, and this trend will likely be forever ongoing because cancer is *still* out there. Per the American Cancer Society's website, it's the number-two killer in this country, second only to heart disease by a couple of percentage points: twenty-three versus twenty-one percent of all deaths in the U.S.

What I learned in that first meeting with Dr. Smiley was that she truly believed there were no complementary treatments available. She stuck to her wheelhouse, prescribing chemotherapy and related drugs to deal with the various side effects we have all heard about. She had zero interest in alternative treatments, or what had worked for other patients elsewhere if it wasn't related to the traditional triad of surgery, chemotherapy, and radiation.

Later, I began to understand that even if she was curious, she was simply not allowed to recommend or offer anything that fell outside the "Big Three." She could, in fact, be potentially disciplined, discredited, and even lose her license if she started to recommend alternatives.

"Seriously, Eric?! Are you sure? Just look at the data. Chemo practically kills more people than it saves. Bebe, please, let's go down to that clinic in Mexico!" I implored when we were at home.

But Eric was sold, hook, line, and sinker, and made the decision to go the traditional route.

We had a few more heated discussions about this, arguing back and forth about the pros and cons of either side. I had several friends reach out to me, encouraging Eric to go the natural route and not to do chemotherapy. One offered a CBD oil program for ninety days. Another recommended *The Truth About Cancer* docu-series as a good resource to check out. Many sent links to all sorts of different therapies out there in the world, and our friends Hilary and Karla, both on their own cancer journeys, were more than happy to share their experiences at a place called Sanoviv in Mexico.

It was pretty overwhelming, and I knew which direction I would have chosen if it was my body.

However, it wasn't my body, and Eric needed a solid and clear path, and the urgency that Dr. Smiley had instilled won out.

Traditional treatments it was.

— 18 —

Things Take a Turn for the Worse

A couple of weeks later, Eric's second visit to the oncologist didn't turn out as expected. He was in bad shape, and since he couldn't hold his own weight, we brought in a wheelchair from home.

As with all his onco-doctor appointments, he had his blood drawn on a different floor of the cancer wing. An hour later, the oncology appointment was scheduled so the doctor could see the results and make decisions on how and when to move forward based, in part, on the labs.

First, Dr. Smiley was surprised to see how much Eric's physical body and motor skills had deteriorated since the initial visit. Second, the lab results were not great, and she called for a hospital bed to get the liquid therapy started right away. She presented the protocol she had landed on, nicknamed R-CHOP, the acronym for rituximab (Rituxan), cyclophosphamide, doxorubicin hydrochloride, vincristine sulfate, and prednisone.

After explaining the R-CHOP protocol, she gave Eric a thick packet of forms to sign, absolving her, her staff, and the hospital from any adverse reactions, including, but not limited to risk of infection, anemia, nausea, vomiting, constipation, organ failure, death, and of any possible liability further to the administering of said chemotherapy.

Eric wasn't happy about this and jokingly pushed back. But what could he do? By that point, he had already made the decision to move forward and go the traditional allopathic route.

As soon as he was done signing the documents, the nurse showed up and accompanied us to the cancer wing, across the causeway and above the busy Seattle street to the hospital.

He was admitted to one of the many dedicated cancer floors, and the chemotherapy drugs were ordered from the onsite pharmacy in the basement.

I was feeling shellshocked, with no idea what to expect, never having seen chemotherapy up close. In fact, until Eric's cancer showed up, I didn't fully understand what it was. I researched and learned that to destroy cancer cells in the body, chemotherapy uses anticancer or cytotoxic drugs, to literally poison living cells.

With Eric's type of cancer, his chemotherapy treatment was going to be administered systemically, meaning the chemo drugs would travel throughout the bloodstream to reach and kill the lymphoma cells all over his body. Unlike other types of oral chemo or chemos that are infused into the body through IVs during outpatient visits, his would require a hospital stay for up to a week for each session.

It was freaky for me to see the nurses specially trained in working with the toxic chemotherapy drug protocols wearing their hazmat gowns, gloves, face masks, and shields, hanging the double-wrapped dark burnt-orange bags marked with something akin to a skull and crossbones symbol.

If any of the nurses got this stuff on their skin, there'd be hell to pay.

If they couldn't get even one drop on their skin, it was hard to conceive what this stuff was doing to my husband's insides, and what impact it had on the healthy cells as well as the cancer-ridden ones. I recalled reading somewhere that chemotherapy is to the body like Napalm was to Vietnam (as distasteful an analogy as that is).

You kill the good with the bad.

Chemotherapy is like that. The healthy cells are obliterated, along with the cancerous cells. And, for added measure, the immune system is often completely destroyed in the process too.

Oh boy!

Facebook Post—February 5, 2016

A room with a view. The journey has begun, and Eric is determined to kick this cancer to the curb! I am on board and holding the space for a complete recovery! Join me in seeing Eric absolutely 100% sur-thriving!!!

— 19 —

Let the Liquid Therapy Begin

And so, the liquid therapy began. It started off smoothly, and we did what we often did…our GOCs.

I began, "I love and appreciate the way you got clear about what you wanted to do with your treatments, and you're handling the start of your chemo in good spirits. And I love and appreciate that grin of yours…it makes my heart melt."

Eric said next, "Bebe, I so love and appreciate that you are with me, as much as you absolutely can be…and you're holding down the fort at home with Bella, your webinar role at Microsoft, and you're still finding time to see real estate clients and closing on houses. I love you and appreciate you…so much!"

Truth be told, we were terrified. Yet, we wanted to believe the traditional treatment protocols could work miracles. We swallowed our fear, determined to slay this cancerous dragon courageously.

Interestingly enough, the whole chemo cocktail is not administered at once. The oncology nurses started with the steroid and then moved on to the others in the cocktail, one or two at a time. When the Rituximab was administered, I noticed that one of the nurses stayed close by.

Per the brochure they gave us, Rituximab is a "chimeric monoclonal antibody against the protein CD20, primarily found on the surface of immune system B cells." Cell death occurs when it binds to this protein. Here's the kicker: the antibody is made by combining genetic one-third material from a nonhuman source (in this case, mice!) with two-thirds genetic material from a human.

Eric and I joked with the staff that they were giving him minced-up mouse nuts! Honestly, we figured we ought to find things to laugh about, because what was the alternative?

One of the many side effects of this drug was severe chills and/or fevers, and a few minutes after the nurse left the room, all hell broke loose. Eric's body went taut and literally began jumping off the bed with chills and uncontrollable shaking. I called the nurse back and she handled the situation quickly and efficiently, by administering another drug, previously okayed by the doctor in the event of such a reaction.

It took an hour or so for Eric's symptoms to fully subside, and when I read up later on other possible reactions, I realized it could have been worse, much worse. He could have suffered any one or more of the following: cardiac arrest, tumor lysis syndrome (causing acute kidney failure), progressive multifocal leukoencephalopathy (PML), pulmonary toxicity, and/or bowel obstruction and perforation.

Wow, I guess Eric got off lightly. For the time being anyway.

After a week of the liquid therapy, Eric was more than ready to come home. I had been coming and going to handle home life and work, and when I arrived to pick him up, he was dressed, sitting up, his items stuffed into a plastic bag, ready to slip into his wheelchair and get wheeled out of Dodge.

Facebook Post—February 13, 2016

Best Valentine's present ever! Eric is back home from his trip to the hospital. Never ever, in a million years, would I have thought I would be so grateful for the custom-chemo cocktail that Eric received over the last 7 days. It literally saved his life! Round 1 down...5 rounds to go. We're ever so grateful for all your prayers, blessings, and healing energy. They played a big part in his progress. Keep 'em coming!

— 20 —

Sharing Our Story

Many folks, when learning of a new cancer diagnosis, fall so deeply into fear that they jump on board whatever treatment plan they are offered first. In most cases, this would typically include one or more of the traditional surgery, chemo, and radiation programs. No questions asked.

Understandably, many also clam up and go inwards, simply trying to survive the ups and downs of the experience. They often shut out the outside world, and unless people in their sphere reach out directly, their pain and their journey often remain private... certainly not something to put on social media for the world to see and comment on.

However, I discovered that social media was a tool that helped sustain me and literally kept me going on the days I thought I might lose it. Thank goodness for both friends, Hilary and Karla, unafraid and unapologetic to articulate their respective cancer journeys on social media.

Encouraged by their willingness to tell their stories openly, I also started to share on Facebook occasionally, and later in the journey, as things intensified, daily.

In the beginning, being a very private person, Eric insisted on reading my comments before I posted, so he could approve the verbiage. At times, he asked for an edit here and there, or for elements to be removed altogether. After each post, we both enjoyed reading the encouraging comments from our Facebook family and quickly realized this was an awesome opportunity to send and receive love and support in real-time.

As the journey continued, I noticed everything. I read every word and acknowledged and appreciated every comment, like, heart, sad face, caring, or wow emoji, text, phone call, voice message, card, and email.

I shared with everyone, often, how grateful we were that so many friends and our Facebook family truly got the message that we welcomed hearing from them and that they kept it up.

Facebook Post—February 27, 2016

It's that time again...another 5 days of liquid therapy for Eric. It's good to remember that a cancer diagnosis isn't necessarily a death sentence. For us, at least in part, it's been a phenomenal opportunity to get to know each other on another whole level...more love, joyful moments, understanding, appreciation, forgiveness, and gratitude. Here's to a full and complete healing for this amazing man! Thank you all so much. Every little thought and prayer is most appreciated!

— 21 —

Methotrexate Damages Eric's Kidneys

Following the second of the six major planned chemo sessions, Eric's doctors became concerned that there was cancer present in his spine and came into his room to explain. Eric was in bed, and I was sitting next to him, with my back to the window and holding his hand, when Dr. Smiley explained, "If this is the case, it could spread to your brain by crossing something called the 'blood-brain barrier.' "

The Physician's Assistant (PA), elaborated further, "The brain is shielded by a cell layer around blood vessels, keeping out harmful substances and retaining helpful ones, though it's not foolproof and can be affected by conditions like cancer."

While they didn't really *know* that there *was* cancer present in the spine, they did decide to add into the overall protocol an additional three to six treatments (each with three to five days of hospitalization) of a drug called Methotrexate, *just in case!* This was another chemotherapy drug that's used to treat Lymphoma cancers, among other illnesses, by halting the metabolism and rapid growth of cells. The difference is that this one had to be injected directly into the site. In Eric's case, his lumbar region.

After our conversation with the doctors about the additional treatment, we jumped online to check out the side effects. They included liver damage, ulcers, a condition creating a predisposition to infection, nausea, abdominal pain, fatigue, fever, dizziness, inflammation or scarring in the lung, and kidney failure. There was also a growing awareness of possible neurological damage and memory loss, which may result from the drug crossing the blood–brain barrier and damaging neurons in the cerebral cortex.

People with cancer who received this medication often nicknamed these effects "chemo brain." We joked about this, but in fact, it really wasn't funny at all.

The journey took on a surreal quality a few days later, when I was sitting beside Eric's bed, chatting with him and stroking his arm. His P.A. waltzed in with a smile and stood towards the end of the bed. He addressed both of us with, and I quote, "Hey, that Methotrexate chemo treatment has seriously injured your kidneys. But don't worry, the damage was in a part of the kidneys that regenerates." Eric and I looked at each other, incredulous.

I asked, "What does that really mean? What do you mean his kidneys have been damaged but don't worry, it'll be fine?!"

He responded that he'd be checking in with Dr. Smiley to figure out the next step. As it turned out, Eric's kidneys were so badly injured with this one chemo session, Dr. Smiley had to consult the kidney specialist to figure out a plan.

At this stage of the treatment, we realized there was a fair amount of guesswork going on. In Eric's case, it was a game of hit or miss. "If that doesn't work, we'll try this. If this doesn't work, we'll try that!"

I couldn't stop the barrage of thoughts swirling around my head whenever one of the doctors suggested something new.

O. M. G.!

These guys are operating from guesswork!

Why did they inject methotrexate into his spine if they didn't know cancer was present?

What the heck?

They almost took out his kidneys for a "just in case" scenario!

Seriously! What. The. Fuck?

After some time and lots of energy and resources, eventually Eric's kidney levels came back into range enough to start the next full-strength chemotherapy session.

Number three. Of six.

Facebook Post—March 18, 2016

Good morning, Seattle! Eric and I had a date night in his hospital room last night! And, we ordered in pizza! We started watching an old James Bond movie, but both promptly fell asleep…so I guess you could call it a sleepover date. Beautiful way to wake up though, watching the different shades of blue, purple, and orange over Mt. Rainier, our local 14,000 ft. beauty. Have an awesome day/night everyone!

— 22 —

Eric Loses His Hair

J ust before big chemo session number three, Bella and I took Eric to the hospital and helped him get settled in. We put his extra bag of clothing in the cupboard and laid his Seahawks blanket out for him to use if he got cold. We sat in chairs on either side of the bed. I held his hand, and Bella had her hand on his arm.

Eric grinned, reached up to his head and literally pulled some hair out. Even though we all expected him to lose his hair at some point, it was a little shocking to see it happen. We figured that he may not have too much time left with his thick head of hair, and decided to capture the moment with a selfie.

She had the longest arms of all, our Bella girl. With an incredible wingspan exceeding six feet, she put her arm's length to good use as the designated selfie-taker. Our three pairs of eyes followed the camera this way and that, until she figured out the best angle.

"Smile!" she instructed, and the three of us did.

Click.

"Okay, duck lips!" she instructed.

Eric and I did our best with that one, as teens seem to be innately born with some sort of weird duck-lip talent. We were able to scrunch our mouths into a sort of pout, but I don't think anyone would've called them duck-lips.

Click.

That ended up being "the shot," the photo I liked the best. My lips didn't really show the lines I had accumulated over the years, and Eric looked adorable with his lips protruding.

"Just like a duck!" he joked.

It was a light moment, and we laughed together.

Bella and I planned to leave Eric alone at the hospital that night, as we needed some mother-daughter time. When we hugged him goodbye, I ran my fingers through his gorgeous locks, not realizing it would be the last time I ever touched them.

My guy had an enviable head of thick blond hair. But chemo-bloody-therapy changed all that, as we knew it would. As soon as Bella and I left the hospital that day, our beloved Eric decided to have his hair all shaved off, and talked one of his favorite nurses into doing the deed for him.

At home, later that evening, Bella was watching a movie in her room, and I was lying alone in our big bed, reading a book, when the text came through. I reached for my phone and was shocked to see a selfie of Eric completely bald.

As I often did in these moments alone, I allowed the tears to flow. There he was, brave and smiling. I wondered whether he, too, had some tears for the deeper meaning of the milestone—the loss of his hair and what that meant.

It was a stark reminder that we weren't just imagining Eric had cancer.

Fuck this fucking cancer journey.

It's really happening.

This is not in our imagination!

Eric has lost his fucking hair!

Oh, my darling Eric...I'm so sorry that you had to lose your beautiful head of hair!

I kept my inner voice to myself and smiled and hugged my guy when I saw him the next day. Bella did too. We tried our best to take it all in our stride. If I was struggling a bit, I found myself wondering about Eric and how he was *really* doing.

"Are you okay with your new hairstyle, Bebe? How do you feel with it all?"

"I'm okay with it, I guess. I knew it was going to happen, and I quite like my new look," he grinned. "Besides, I didn't really have a choice. It was either let it come out in clumps or shave it all off."

It was too late to save his hair. It was too late to take back the chemo treatments. It was too late to go back in time and live a more stress-free life, eat healthier food, cut back on his five or six cups of coffee a day. It was too late to not spray gallons of Roundup on the weeds on his property on Lake Sammamish.

It was too late for all that.

So, we all followed along with the program. We just kept moving forward, one day at a time.

Facebook Post—April 5, 2016

Our wee family...loving Eric and having a family dinner date in Eric's hospital room. We kinda like Eric without hair.

— 23 —

Those Who Showed Up and Those Who Didn't

Sometimes I just sat and watched life go on all around me. People at the hospital or in the stores, everywhere I went, running this way and that in all their busyness. I wanted to shout out, "Don't you know that my husband has cancer? He might be dying...we just don't know yet. How can you keep living your life?! Stop!"

I acknowledged that most others in our world were continuing their life as usual. Unlike us, their lives hadn't taken a turn for the worse after an ER doctor introduced the C-word into their vocabulary.

As the partner of a loved one dealing with cancer, I realized I just couldn't do it all. I eventually got used to reaching out to ask for help, and I was grateful when people showed up, and moved and shifted priorities in their day to help us.

What was interesting was that the people I thought might offer to help, didn't. And people I didn't think would reach out to volunteer, did.

I say this with no judgment. We knew it took effort for our friends to make time in their busy schedules to take Eric to and from appointments. I can think of many times in my life when someone I cared about was struggling, or their loved one was having medical issues, and I didn't put myself out to help. Looking back, I feel bad, but I totally get it.

There's also the mental and emotional aspect. Some of the people in our lives found it difficult to deal with the situation, and to even be around Eric. Perhaps he became a mirror to their own mortality?

Regardless, some didn't show up at all.

Facebook Post—April 12, 2016

Hey Seattle and Eastside peeps...is anyone available to take Eric to a medical procedure in Seattle tomorrow, (Wed) 2-6pm? Please private message me if you could do one or two ways, Kirkland/Seattle. Sorry to ask, but his ride fell through for tomorrow. Prayers and blessings needed more than ever, as he is halfway through and not feeling great. Thank you all soooo much! Your messages help keep us buoyed up! xxx

— 24 —

The PET Scan at the Three-Month Mark

We all wondered, but no one knew. The strategy was to R-CHOP and methotrexate the cancer to death with the treatments for the first three months and then wait and see. The daily labs were one indicator if anything was amiss, but no one knew for sure if the whole treatment protocol was working.

And if Dr. Smiley and her team didn't know, we certainly had no clue.

Only after three months, and the all-important PET scan, would the doctors know the degree of success, or lack thereof, of their treatment plan. In the interim, the answers to almost any question about Eric's progress were, "We really don't know," "I'm really not sure," "We won't know until..." and "*Weeell...*"

Eric had had a PET scan before, at the beginning of all this, and we knew they were like all-over body x-rays, but we really didn't know much about them. The day before Eric was scheduled for his next one, we asked his P.A. to enlighten us more about what was going to happen.

He was used to questions from us and knew that we were genuinely interested. So, he stood at the end of the bed, took a breath, and said, "PET, or positron emission tomography, is similar to a full-body X-ray but uses a radioactive tracer instead of contrast dye. It creates detailed 3D images by tracking tracer accumulation in organs and tissues, highlighting areas with increased cellular activity, which can indicate cancer and provide info on blood flow, oxygen, and metabolism."

We just stared at him, trying to take all that in. But I was curious, and asked, "Why three months?"

The P.A. responded, "Good or bad, that's the time period the medical insurance companies are willing to pay for a PET scan."

When he left the room, Eric and I looked at each other. We had already researched the cost of these and they're several thousand dollars each. I said to my beloved, "Well, there you go. Reading between the lines, the insurance companies like to keep tight control over how often their policy holders are allowed to receive the results of their pain and suffering."

Eric nodded. It was a lot for him. Although he was feeling nervous about the scan, he was excited to know if the chemo was working. His eyelids started to get droopy, and I watched as he fell asleep.

I sat there, trying to process it all. Of course, I wanted to know if this stuff was working too, but on another level, it was extraordinary to me that there aren't better ways to measure our loved ones' progress, without being injected with radioactive tracers. There must be other options to check on the shrinking or growing of tumors. I wondered about the offerings in countries like Sweden and New Zealand, where healthcare is social, and it's in the interest of the government to uncover cancer cases as early as possible. A girlfriend had recently shared with me that Sweden has equipment much like an ultrasound but with a detection software/chip that can detect cancer and inflammation in its earliest stages.

There's a PHD researcher from Sweden who has one of these machines in the U.S., and I called her that afternoon to ask about the technology and about her experience with it. What shocked me to my core was that the practitioner shared that, in Sweden, it's rare to be diagnosed with cancer in the third or fourth stages because they're monitoring the body with prevention in mind. She reiterated that, in the U.S., the reason there are so many cancer diagnoses in the later stages is that they're focused only on symptom-management. By then, it's often too late, or there's a lot of catch-up work to do.

I didn't even want to think about the possibility that we could have found out about Eric's cancer at stage one or two, as it was too painful to consider lost opportunities. But, one might wonder why these machines aren't available all over the U.S.? I know I did.

Facebook Post—April 22, 2016

Eric's getting a little radioactive today...having a PET scan, and the good news is we'll get a visual soon showing how much his tumors have reduced. Yay! Fingers crossed! Prayers, healing energy, and blessings all gratefully received!

— 25 —

This Shit Really Works?

We had gone back home between the PET scan and Eric's follow-up appointment a few days later. Back at the hospital again, we were sitting in one of the sterile waiting rooms, feeling nervous, yet excited, when Dr. Smiley walked in. It had been a while since we'd seen her happy face, and I suspected she too had been holding her breath. Judging by the size of her smile, we figured the results had to be good.

"I have great news," Dr. Smiley beamed. "The tumors have all but gone. Come and take a look."

Eric looked at me with a huge grin and wheeled closer to the screen. I peered over his shoulder as she pulled up the results on the computer. It was surreal. The previous PET scan had big bright spots over multiple organs and bones, indicating there was cancer present in several locations. Surprisingly, the Christmas tree lights that had previously showed up were no longer shining.

Well, I'll be.

Seriously, this shit really worked?

Holy hell!

Eric asked, "So, what does this really mean? This is awesome news, right?"

"Yes, it is great news. It means that the protocol we landed on worked, and we may even consider using the same treatment plan for the next three months. I'll confer with my colleagues, but it seems likely we'll go that route."

On the drive home, Eric was animated and chatty, "Can you believe it Bebe?! It's really working. The cancer has reduced so much!"

He squeezed my thigh as I was driving, and I responded, "I know, right? It's hard to believe it, but it looks like the chemo cocktail did its thing!"

Eric leaned his head back into the headrest and sat in quiet thought, and although I was trying to be as supportive as possible, I still had my doubts. To me, it seemed that the doctors congratulated themselves for a job well done, breathing a collective sigh of relief that the R-CHOP, combined with the methotrexate, had worked. And since the first round of the major treatment protocols produced the desired results, it looked like they were about to agree to do an exact repeat, in the event their luck might continue for a subsequent three months.

I wasn't filled with confidence in the doctors or the "cancer machine," the whole system that funnels patients into these treatments. But what could I do? I advocated for Eric when he was feeling sick, too afraid or shy to speak up, or too weak to have an opinion one way or another. Yet what could *he* do? He was on board and literally trusted his oncologist, her crew, and the system, with his life.

— 26 —

The Good Days and the Bad Days

The doctors did indeed agree to continue with the same chemo cocktail for the ensuing three months, and Eric had completed two of the three main rounds of R-CHOP, when we went out on a date to celebrate.

It was a decent evening with the temperature in the mid-sixties, and I pushed Eric along the Kirkland waterfront. He loved everything about boats, and we enjoyed just sitting there and taking in the view over the multitude of boats in the marina. I liked boats too, but I loved sunsets even more. I hugged him from behind and watched as the sun set at around 8:30 p.m.

We came home around 9 p.m., and as I was helping Eric get ready for bed, he told me he wasn't feeling well. I kept a close eye on him for the next hour or so, and leaned in to feel his forehead at one point. It felt hot to touch, and I went searching for the thermometer.

"Good grief Bebe, your temperature is 103°F. I think we need to get you to the ER right now," I said.

I thought, *Yay, just what we need…a long wait in the ER when my Bebe isn't feeling the greatest.* But that night it was a relatively quick wait, and at two hours the nurse brought him back into one of the dozen or so emergency rooms. The doctor took one look at his chart, ordered a few basic tests and not long after, had the nurses start the admission process.

The hospital staff got him registered and checked into the ward and into his new bed for the next few days or so. I pulled up a chair, grabbed his hand, and asked how he was doing. He closed his eyes and took a breath.

"I just want to feel good again. I'm so sick of feeling sick."

I leaned in to kiss his cheek and sat back. I stroked his arm and sat quietly. After a long night, he was feeling the effects of the drugs, and I watched as his eyes fluttered and sleep came quickly.

I considered that this comment was the closest my beloved ever came to complaining. Throughout his journey, he almost never whined. He spoke up if he was in pain or had various symptoms, but he never got irritable or cranky. He just took it all in his stride and kept hoping for the best. He had never grumbled about using a cane, transitioning to a walker, and then into a wheelchair. He just got on with it.

As I tried to get comfortable in the visitor cot beside Eric's bed in the early hours of the morning, I thought about the cancer journey. It can be a game of good news, bad news, good days, bad days—at least until they were all good or all bad.

There were days where his test results looked promising, and the outlook seemed rosy. There was hope and excitement that the hideous journey would end sometime soon, with light at the end of the bleak tunnel.

Then, there were days when a test came back with a negative outcome, and the docs would admit things were not working as they had hoped. A fresh round of fear would infuse our minds and bodies, until we took an opportunity to keep it in check, and keep marching forward.

One day at a time, was my final thought early that morning, as I was finally falling asleep.

Facebook Post—May 31, 2016

This cancer journey is not an easy one! I was just about to post how well Eric was doing and that we're almost there... with just one more main chemo cocktail. But, alas, now we're back in hospital and Eric has a fever of 103°F...not typically life-threatening, at least not unless you've had your body napalmed to pieces and your immune system is completely shot. Thanks everyone for your prayers and healing energy, it absolutely helps! Keep 'em coming!

— 27 —

The Promise of Summer

At the beginning of June, we calculated that my guy would be done with his final treatment before June 21, the official start of summer.

The relaxed laughter of the summer months was our favorite. We dreamed of having a phenomenal season ahead, with endless days of hot, dry weather and blue skies...filling them with delicious barbeque food, salads, summer berries, friends, wine, boating, wakeboarding, and wake-surfing.

Those who knew Eric well weren't at all surprised to hear that he was figuring out ways to get back to work full-time. He loved being useful and, of course, enjoyed putting his strategic brain to good use. After summer, we agreed he could work again. After summer.

Life was good, and our beloved Eric was going to live and be there for all the little and big milestones. We were almost at the finish line.

Facebook Post—June 11, 2016

We're almost done with the final chapter of this cancer journey! My beloved husband is back in the hospital for what we hope to be his final phase of liquid treatment! This photo of Eric looking happy and healthy was taken a couple of years ago, and I wanted to repost a pic of my husband/lover/best friend, looking and feeling fit and in great health! Prayers, healing energy, and awesome visualizations are welcome for my beloved.

— 28 —

The Ringing of the Bell

"Ding, ding" went the sound of the bell in the cancer ward. But, to be honest, after six months of chemotherapy, the ringing of the bell in the oncology ward was a bit of an anticlimax for us.

We had visualized that when the time came, we'd have our special friends present, maybe some of his family would fly in, and it would be a huge milestone—one of celebration, progress, and life!

Sadly, it was just another busy day at the hospital, with nurses flitting back and forth, peeking in on their dozens of patients.

Machines dinging and donging and beeping and trilling. Visitors coming and going, some with heads held high and hearts filled with hope, and others with eyes red and heads hanging low, all hope lost to the cancerous curse.

Dr. Smiley wasn't there, and the nurses on the shift were not ones we recognized. It was nothing special at all, the ringing of the bell. Yet, we did it anyway.

Eric was in his best shirt, and for posterity, I videoed the occasion. I recruited visitors and professionals nearby, and these strangers kindly pasted on a smile and applauded as best they could. I wondered if perhaps they knew something we didn't. Did they know that the chances of this really being the final ringing of the bell were slim? Did they see beyond our dreams for a fabulous end to the summer, with a knowing that perhaps all was not well in the body of my beloved?

Either way, we breathed a huge sigh of relief.

Eric was done with the sixth big, and we hoped *final* round of the R-CHOP chemo cocktail. We figured we were through the end of the tunnel and that we could get back to living and being a family without the endless hours on the road to and from hospital visits, doctors, PAs, nurses, NPs, tests, bloodwork, biopsies, surgeries, CT scans, X-Rays, MRIs, PET scans, needles, IVs, medications galore, ports, fevers, infections, vomit, dry heaves, constipation, diarrhea, and the ominous burnt-orange hanging bags marked with the skull and cross bone hazardous symbol.

Done.

We were done.

It was time to celebrate life! It was time to celebrate love and good health! It was time to enjoy summer!

— 29 —

A Day of Boating and Friendship

It was a gorgeous day at the end of July, and I was standing on the end of the dock.

In anticipation of jumping in the lake, I had my black-and-white polka dot swimsuit under my floaty summer dress, and a big floppy hat to keep the sun off my face. I had a cooler at my feet filled with sliced up watermelon, grapes, deviled eggs, carrot and celery sticks, hummus, and organic chips and salsa. To drink I had water, beer, and Mike's Hard Lemonade.

I had called ahead to let Eric know that I was done with work and ready for him to pick me up. I stood there enjoying the sounds of summer—boats starting and stopping, and laughter and happy voices coming from across the bay.

I squinted into the distance and could see our yellow boat do a wide circle. Someone was being towed from behind, wake-surfing on the big wave the boat generated.

As they came closer, I could tell it was Niclas, the younger of Andi and his wife Bea's two sons. Andi and Bea were Eric's closest friends and had been for about twenty years, ever since they moved from Germany to start a new life in the U.S. Having known Eric their whole lives, their two boys thought of him as their uncle, and they were in their teens before they realized that he was an uncle of the heart, not of the blood.

Niclas let go of the rope and Eric expertly circled around to pick him up.

My Bebe slowed to a crawl as he got closer and edged toward the dock. He masterfully touched and reversed, allowing me to jump on without having to tie up.

"Here she is!" Eric shouted out. "The working girl and quick-change artist!"

After I hugged my hellos with Andi and Bea, Niclas (wet from his wakeboarding session) and Bella, Eric reversed back out and off we went.

We motored leisurely out beyond Juanita Bay, dropped anchor to slow our drift, and set up to eat and drink.

I loved being out with my favorite people, listening to their stories, and enjoying their laughter.

I sat close to my Bebe, holding his hand and leaning into his bony shoulder. I was grateful he was here, still with us, and I desperately wanted to believe he was not just in remission, but cancer-free. He was still too weak and fragile to get back behind the boat at this point, but he loved being out, driving, and participating.

I closed my eyes and sent my thanks to the Universe for this day, for my guy, for the kids, Bella and Niclas sharing an earbud, listening to music, for our friendship with Andi and Bea, for the boat, the sunshine, the lake, and this awesome summer experience.

What could possibly go wrong?

Facebook Post—July 28, 2016

Yep, it's definitely summer in Washington! Been working today, and waiting for the boat to come and pick me up from the dock! Life is indeed good! Livin' the dream on Lake Washington! Nothing like the sounds of summer and the kiddos laughing and having fun on the lake! Great day!

— 30 —

What's With the Candy in the Blood Cancer Reception Area?

Eric's face screwed up into a ball as he chewed on a piece of steak, and I wondered if he was going to spit it into his hand or on the plate.

"It tastes like a cross between eating cardboard and licking an ashtray," he said.

I was bummed for him, as steak had long been one of his favorite foods, and he had barbequed it for that evening's dinner. The salad, made with love by Bella and me, elicited the same reaction.

However, I didn't let up on Eric's food and nutrition intake, with or without functioning taste buds. Sadly, as soon as the liquid poison treatments had begun in February, one food at a time lost its taste and any temptation for him. Food that might taste delicious one day had no appeal the next. Even his favorite seasonings didn't seem to help.

I kept up on my research even after ringing the bell, and I devoured information on alternative treatments for cancer. Eric wasn't ready to go there yet, so I read, listened to podcasts, and watched documentaries on my laptop whenever I had an opportunity. I was intrigued, yet saddened and shocked by stories shared by real people.

There was the story of the parents who had their child taken away from them because they didn't want to do chemotherapy. There was the teen who was handcuffed to the hospital bed, and although he didn't want to have a port inserted into his artery, the doctors started him on a chemotherapy protocol anyway, with neither his nor his parents' consent.

Thankfully, I found hundreds of success stories for people healing without the typical allopathic treatments, but unless you search for these, most people would never know or acknowledge there are other options out there.

One of my favorite stories was of an eighteen-year-old diagnosed with a rare, aggressive, and inoperable form of brain cancer. The doctors presented her with a grave prognosis, and since they had nothing to offer, they literally sent her home to die. She researched like crazy and ended up healing herself with a change in diet and by using essential oils. She breathed in the oils, she bathed in them, she rubbed them into her skin. Who knows what the deciding factor was for her, but she not only survived—she thrived, with the tumor completely gone. She went back to her medical professionals to share the phenomenal news and guess what? They didn't want to hear about it. They weren't even the slightest bit curious.

In my perfect world, everyone would have access to it all. Those who opted for an allopathic route could go do that. Those who chose a natural path would be free to do so. Individuals who preferred a mix of the two could without fear of retribution or repercussion. I wished that all medical doctors were trained in the importance of food and how it can be used as medicine to heal ailing bodies or, *at the very least,* to encourage our loved ones to complement their other treatments with healthy food.

I would wave my magic wand and ensure that doctor offices didn't offer candy to patients as soon as they walked in. Each time we walked into Dr. Smiley's reception, we saw the large glass bowl filled with colorfully enticing sugary hard candies. By offering this in a clinic catering to people with blood cancer, it seemed to me to normalize candy consumption.

I had read about "eating the rainbow," but the phrase referred to the bright yellows, reds, and greens of peppers and crispy apples; the dark purples, deep reds, or soft greens of grapes; the various shades of green in lettuces and leafy greens; and the oranges, whites, yellows, and reds in carrots.

This is a far cry from the brightly colored candies offered, without discrimination, to everyone who walks into the doctor's office in the lymphoma clinic of the very large cancer institution in Seattle.

Facebook Post—July 15, 2016

What's with the candy in the doctor's office? Took Eric for a check-up and bone marrow pull today...just to be sure there aren't any little random C cells hiding out in his body. I'm continually stunned and amazed at how slow the medical profession is in linking dis-ease to nutrition, or lack thereof. At the very least, the food we eat is a contributing factor to the health of our bodies. Gotta love Hippocrates, 'Let thy food be thy medicine, and thy medicine be thy food.' He knew a thing or two! That's my rant for the day. Thank you!

— 31 —

Our Sixth Wedding Anniversary

I woke up on our anniversary morning to a massive bunch of flowers on my bedside table. There were roses, carnations, gerbera daisies, tulips, and lilies, in shades of intense pink, deep purple, and white for contrast. There was a card leaning against the vase, and I felt Eric stir as I reached for it.

"Happy Anniversary, Bebe," he said in a heavy sleep-filled voice, reaching for me.

I left the card where it was, for now, and turned into his hug.

"Happy Anniversary, Bebe! You did it! You made it to our sixth wedding anniversary, and you somehow managed to sneak a massive bunch of gorgeous flowers into the bedroom while I was sleeping. Thank you, I love them."

I squeezed him tightly, lying with as much of my body against his as possible. We laid there for a long while feeling the love cycle back and forth.

My mind wandered back to when I said YES to being Eric's wife and life partner on July 24th, 2010, having known each other for only fifteen months. As most do, we had assumed that the proverbial "so long as we both shall live," referred to a lifetime together.

Now, here we were on this day, July 24th, 2016, and it was indeed a day to celebrate!

Eric cleared his throat and started on some early morning GOCs.

"I love and appreciate YOU! You are the best thing that ever happened to me, Bebe. I am grateful you winked at me, and that I came to meet you in Hawai'i."

He was on a roll and continued.

"I love and appreciate that you married me six years ago today, and that we have made it through...the best of it all, and the worst…we did it! I love and appreciate that you never gave up on me, and that you were with me…loving me, supporting me, getting me what I needed, and advocating for me when I couldn't. There were a few moments in the hospital when I didn't know if I would make it, and I'd open my eyes and there you were, sitting beside me, or lying on the window ledge, sleeping in all those weird places, to be close to me. That meant everything to me. I know I wouldn't be here now if it wasn't for you."

I sniffled a little into his shoulder and armpit and shared mine in return.

"I love and appreciate that you introduced GOCs into our lives. For our seven-plus years together I've felt so appreciated, so heard and so loved. I love and appreciate that you asked me to marry you and that you came to New Zealand six years ago so we could get married in my birth country. I love and appreciate that you've worked so hard on your healing and kept a positive attitude to thriving and living a long and healthy life together."

Afterward, I ran downstairs to make a tray of breakfast goodies. As his taste buds were far from recovered, I found it best to offer a range of items and he could pick at whatever looked enticing.

I carried the tray upstairs, and Bella brought the bouquet I had put together the evening before. My flowers for him were bright yellow sunflowers, tulips, roses, lilies, white hydrangeas, and I added matching yellow happy anniversary balloons.

I had also planned a wee surprise for Eric and suggested he come over to the bedroom window and look down to the lower deck.

There it was, a Traeger barbeque, with a big yellow bow on top! This was something he had always wanted, and I figured there was no better time.

He stood there for an extended moment and turned to hug me tight. I could tell he was surprised and delighted.

"How did you get it up on the deck without me seeing? Those things are heavy!"

I touched my nose, the universal sign for that's only for me to know.

We canceled our anniversary dinner reservation and Eric tried out his new BBQ. He was chuffed with his gift, and I was delighted to have surprised him on that day.

Facebook Post—July 24, 2016

Happy 6th Anniversary to my best friend, my big love, my life partner, my husband, my sounding board, my life coach, my travel mate, my Bebe! I am so excited we made it to 7+ years together...literally through thick and thin! So happy to have him by my side for the rest of our lives.

— 32 —

Off to Canada for a Summer Getaway

Eric continued to struggle with sleep, pain management, and getting around, and although we had started planning to travel abroad to celebrate his progress, we agreed that Europe would be too much, too soon. We decided instead to go on an adventure much closer to home. We had heard of a fabulous resort on Pender Island in the Canadian Gulf Islands and began researching.

We booked a package starting the following day at Poet's Cove Spa and Resort. Since Bella was happy to stay with a friend, we were good to go.

Eric was in heaven driving us up to the Tsawwassen Ferry Terminal in Vancouver, where the British Columbian ferries operated a regular service to Otter Bay on Pender Island. It was an hour or two on the ferry, and we sat holding hands and enjoying the views from the inside seating.

The resort staff were friendly and welcoming, and our spacious room overlooking the bay and marina was fabulous. The resort lived up to its reputation for world class spa treatments and delectable food. The water temperature was just right and we spent hours in the pool talking, laughing, cuddling, and floating. The water helped support our bodies, and I loved lying weightless in Eric's arms.

Back in the bedroom, we were a long way from having raunchy sex again, but that didn't stop us from fooling around a little. Everything had changed for my Bebe though; his feelings and nerves were all jumbled. He shared with me that it just wasn't the same anymore, and that made us sad.

Moving around the resort, Eric started to massage his right hip and leg, and I could tell it was getting harder for him to stay upright. He actively started looking for seating wherever we were, rather than standing for long periods.

Eric was likely in denial about the real reason for the discomfort in his body and told me on several occasions that his bones were just healing and growing back in after the cancer treatment.

Looking back, I can see that that didn't make any sense, but I wanted to believe that story as much as he did.

Facebook Post—August 10, 2016

Phew! Found my passport, just in time to be whisked off to the Golf Islands in Canada! There's an incredible view from our suite at the Poet's Cove Spa and Resort, Pender Island! Wahoo! It's time for some rest and relaxation with my Bebe! I think we deserve some time away, don't you?

— 33 —

Eric's Birthday in Hospital (again!)

I was worried about my guy and discreetly asked the manager for a wheelchair for the remainder of our stay.

In typical Eric style, he didn't complain. He just settled into the wheelchair and allowed me to push him around.

"I'm so sorry you have to get back into a wheelchair, Bebe. How are you feeling?" I asked and leaned down to kiss him lightly on the top of his head.

He reached for my hand and replied, "I don't know what's happening, and I'm afraid something is going on in my hip. It's probably better to be safe and have me in a wheelchair, but I am feeling bummed and disappointed that I can't stand and get around easily."

We had been looking forward to celebrating his 55th birthday at the resort and had reserved the best table for a romantic dinner and sunset overlooking the marina. Sadly, his discomfort continued to grow, and we made the call to leave early.

I was so concerned, we booked ourselves on the next ferry. As soon as we were back on the mainland, I drove straight over the border and directly to an ER in Redmond. They recommended we go immediately to the Seattle sister hospital, and as soon as we arrived, he was admitted.

Facebook Post—August 20, 2016

Happy Birthday to my wonderful husband! My heart breaks that you are back in the hospital, and awaiting results from yet more tests! Not the best birthday present, but I'm so proud of you, your courage, and willingness to just take it one day at a time!

— 34 —

So, the Chemo Hadn't Worked After All?

The doctors suspected that they had been too quick to say Eric was in remission and that the cancer hadn't gone after all. To be sure, the doctors ordered an urgent MRI to see what was happening in Eric's right hip.

What?!

The cancer hasn't gone?

He's not in remission?

Looks like we rang the bell too soon!

What is going on?

What the fuck?

The medical professionals could see that the bones in Eric's right hip socket and femur had disintegrated to the point of being completely unstable. They consulted with an orthopedic surgeon and decided to operate the following day. They needed to insert a metal rod into his femur for stability and support.

How is the cancer still eating into Eric's bones?!

I don't understand how we got a clear PET scan?

What is going on?

What the...actual fuck?

"I'm so sorry that it looks like the cancer is still doing its thing and that you need surgery. Are you okay with all this, my love?" I asked quietly, reaching out for his hand.

"Yes, Bebe. I don't really understand what's happened, and I just want to be able to walk again and feel good. I'm taking it one day at a time."

If he was thoroughly disappointed that the doctors had offered false hope at the three-month and six-month marks, while being uncertain how best to treat him, he didn't show it.

He was exhausted after our trip, and glad to be horizontal again. He slowly closed his eyes, and I heard his breathing even out as he slipped into sleep.

I sat there holding his hand and wondered what his cancer was doing. On one hand, it didn't seem that smart, particularly if its plan was to continue to overtake his organs and eat through his bones. If its goal was to kill the host, what was the point in that?

On the other, it appeared to have an innate intelligence, morphing and changing, adapting to the toxic poison designed to target and kill it.

I pondered how on earth Eric got a clear PET scan after the first three months, only to have the same chemo cocktail be completely ineffective after the subsequent three months of infusions. Not only that, how did the cancer morph and grow into something potentially more aggressive and deadly?

If I didn't think it was crazy, I might be in awe of this enigma…cancer.

Facebook Post—August 23, 2016

Enjoying the view from the penthouse floor of Eric's Seattle hospital room! Surgery tomorrow. Prayers, healing energy, and blessings most gratefully received.

~ 35 ~

Our Friend's Wedding on Bainbridge Island

To give Eric more stability to the cancer-ravaged site in his right hip, the doctors inserted a rod extending from his hip bone into his femur. The surgery went according to plan, and he rested quietly in his hospital bed over the next forty-eight hours.

A few days after his surgery, I arrived to pick Eric up at the hospital. When I walked into his room, he was showered, dressed, and ready to attend our friend's wedding, as unbelievable as that may sound.

With a big grin, he said, "Hi Bebe! It's time for my jailbreak!"

I kissed him on the cheek and said, "Well then, let's go! I have our wedding outfits in the car."

I was amazed the surgeon and onco-docs had allowed him to leave the hospital so soon after his surgery. However, Eric is a tough negotiator, and as long as he promised to come right back, they gave him the green light.

I rolled him out of the hospital, got him into his big yellow truck, and headed for the Bainbridge Island ferry terminal. Eric was animated during the forty-minute wait and chatted about anything and everything. I was so happy for him and our big adventure.

We had lunch at a quaint island restaurant, with delicious food and outdoor seating. After we ate, we went to the bathroom together to change into our wedding attire. I helped Eric out of his blue jeans and into his black dress jeans and shirt, and I slipped into an off-the-shoulder cobalt blue dress, black strappy shoes, and added gold jewelry for the final touch.

The location was fabulous—a small boutique winery, with a quaint 1920s villa on the property, overlooking the ocean. We had a great time at the wedding, as our friends' families were lovely people and graciously accepted us into their midst, hanging out with us between the proceedings.

At one point, our newly married friends stopped by to visit. Someone offered to take a shot of the four of us. In the photo, I'm sitting next to Eric in his wheelchair, the newlyweds, Georgia and Noah, are leaning over us from behind. We're all smiling big, wide, happy smiles, and it was my favorite shot of the day.

We didn't know it at the time, but this would be the last wedding Eric would ever attend, his last ferry ride, and sadly...his last fun adventure.

Facebook Post—August 27, 2016

Eric cracks me up. He has very sharp negotiation skills! He just had surgery a few days ago, yet persuaded the surgery and oncology teams at the hospital to let him out for the weekend, to attend our friends' wedding on Bainbridge Island! So glad we were able to go. Beautiful couple, amazing and welcoming friends and family, and we were so honored to be a part of their big day! Congratulations Georgia and Noah!

— 36 —

Let's Get (Yet Another) Chemo Party Started

By now we knew the drill. The process from earlier in the year repeated itself and another hospital visit was scheduled by Dr. Smiley's office.

We packed a bag at home with long, baggy shorts and loose T-shirts, toiletries, a miniature speaker, and computer electronics.

I bundled my love into the wheelchair, rolled him down the ramp in the garage at home, and helped his fragile body into my SUV. I folded the wheelchair and put it in the back. I no longer needed the GPS, since Eric, my car, and I were regulars there.

Despite the number of times we'd been here, when we checked in at the lab, they recognized Eric by sight but not by name. We did the prerequisite wait for the required blood tests. Once his blood was drawn, I rolled him up to the third floor and into the reception area. Even after the many dozens of visits, they still needed to see his ID each time, just in case he was impersonating someone with stage-four cancer eating away at his bones and damaging his organs.

I glanced over to see if the candy was still there. It was. *I guess it will always be.*

We waited the customary wait time, me on the hard seat and my Bebe in his wheelchair. Eventually, we were let in to wait, yet again, in the small cold room for Dr. Smiley. She showed up, eventually, and we went through the same routine.

"The cancer is still there. Your readings are (blah blah blah). You will need more chemotherapy. We're also working on a plan for a stem cell transplant."

What the heck is a stem cell transplant?

The only difference in the chemo routine this time was that she told us what new combo they were planning to use: RICE, with the hopefully winning blend of Rituximab, Ifosfamide, Carboplatin, and Etoposide Phosphate. I asked her how she arrived at that chemo cocktail and, aside from running it by her counterparts, she didn't have a good answer. The chemo recipe was apparently a guess, albeit their best.

Then, off we went. I knew the way and wheeled Eric on the pedestrian over-the-street bridge, into the cancer ward.

History was repeating itself, only this time it was a new cocktail they were mixing in the hospital basement to drip into his body, and a new piece of word art, with a neutral backdrop and big brown letters, had been hung in the ward. We stood/sat looking it over and taking it in, both nodding in agreement.

Cancer is so limited,
It cannot cripple love,
It cannot shatter hope,
It cannot dissolve faith,
It cannot destroy peace,
It cannot kill friendship,
It cannot suppress memories,
It cannot silence courage,
It cannot invade the soul,
It cannot steal eternal life,
It cannot conquer the spirit.
— Dr. Robert L. Lynn

I wheeled Eric into his room. A different one. Weirdly, it was always a different room.

"Okay, Bebe," I said, "Let's get this chemo party started!"

Facebook Post—October 1, 2016

Apologies for not doing more regular updates, but Facebook isn't always my top priority. At the same time, I'm very grateful for the platform providing a way to send and receive so much love all at once! Eric is just done with another period in hospital, receiving more liquid therapy. Now, it's a month of daily trips to the hospital to get injections in preparation for his upcoming stem cell transplant. Thank you ALL once again for your continued prayers, healing energy, kind words, food showing up on our doorstep, and healing sessions offered out of pure love!

— 37 —

Prepping for the Stem Cell Transplant

The doctors inserted three massive tubes into Eric's neck to make it easier for the daily blood draws necessary for the collection of cells, in readiness for his stem cell transplant.

"Ha ha, I look like a freak! I don't need to dress up for Halloween. I look scary enough as it is. I'll just go to Alison's Halloween party as myself," Eric joked to me one day.

I chortled back, but we both knew it wasn't really funny at all. There's nothing humorous about tubes sticking out of your neck and a stem cell transplant.

These types of transplants can offer significant benefits for cancer patients, especially those with lymphoma and other types of cancer. In Eric's case, the doctors hoped for a cure, especially as his cancer proved to be aggressive, and he had relapsed after initial treatments. They'd hoped that the new stem cells could help eliminate residual cancer cells and restore the body's ability to fight cancer.

They prepared Eric for an autologous transplant, where the cells would be harvested from his own bone marrow. This type of transplant has little to no risk of rejection, compared to the alternative, where a donor's cells are used for the procedure. The basic premise is to replenish the body with healthy, normal blood cells to replace the defective cells damaged by cancer.

The daily injections (at a cost of over $5,000 per day) required Eric to go into the hospital every day. He was determined to drive himself most days, being the stubborn man he was and desperate for a little independence.

That was approximately a thirty to forty-five minute journey each way. There and back, every day.

The month of daily blood draws was very tough on Eric, taking its toll on his weary mind and body, with an already weakened immune system. I wondered if even the simple act of drawing so much blood each day was enough to negatively impact his immune system. He kept up his sense of humor though, and quite enjoyed freaking people out with the large protruding plastic tubes sticking out of his neck.

Thankfully, the sum total of cells from the one month of blood draws was successful in terms of the sheer number of stem cells collected. In fact, Eric was proud that he was an overachiever and produced way more cells than necessary.

Now it was a waiting game to confirm that everything looked good and the stem cell transplant was a "go."

Facebook Post—October 13, 2016

Eric texted a friend, 'Just completed my second stem cell collection. They think they collected another 4 million cells, so that totals 8 million collected, compared to the required 5 million. Today, the technicians were fascinated because the numbers showed that I had a total of 63 million stem cells circulating in my body, and the usual is 20-30 million. All well on my side, Eric.'

— 38 —

The Month-Long Blood Draws Were a Waste of Time?

We had so much hope for the stem cell transplant. We believed this was precisely what Eric needed to advance his progress toward good health. But there was so much we didn't know or understand about the risks involved, and it turned out that in cases where the underlying condition was not completely eradicated before the transplant, there's a risk that the disease could come back.

We were sitting at the island in our kitchen, having a snack, when Dr. Smiley called. She casually mentioned, "So, we have some bad news. There is cancer present in the cells we collected from Eric."

We looked at each other, trying to grasp the enormity of the news.

Fuck! Fuck! Fuck!

I spoke first, "So, what does that actually mean, in layman's terms?"

"Weeell," she responded, "It means that Eric's cells are unviable and cannot be used for the transplant."

I looked at Eric, and his head was hanging low. I responded, "So, are you saying that the one-month-long process of injections and collecting cells was a complete waste of time and energy, because there is cancer present, and you can't use his cells?"

"That is correct," she responded quietly. Then she told us she had to run. "I'll have the staff call to make another appointment." And with that, she hung up.

What. The. Actual. Fuck!?

I mean, seriously? Why wouldn't they check, as the month progressed?

Why did they wait until the end of the intense, exhausting, (and expensive!) thirty days of blood draws to figure out that the daily effort and collections was a complete and utter failed attempt to prepare for a stem cell transplant?

I wondered how much of this was about the revenue his month long blood draws had generated, totaling $175,000?

Fuuuck!!

I walked over to Eric, enveloped him from behind, and kissed him on his bald head.

"How are you doing Bebe?" I asked quietly.

He responded, "I'm not really sure...just trying to process it all. I guess I'm a little in shock...disappointed...sad."

I was livid.

I had observed the toll this process had taken. I'm not a doctor, but I couldn't believe they were surprised that cancer cells were present, and I didn't understand why they didn't check first before putting Eric through this month-long injection and collection process. It just didn't make any sense to us, on any level, and impacted the last vestiges of trust Eric had in the medical professionals.

Facebook Post—October 15, 2016

Sometimes I just shake my head at the occasional extraordinary turn of events. We found out today that the stem cell transplant is no longer a viable option for Eric. So sad for my Bebe, and we're trying to process what this means for him.

— 39 —

I'm Sorry, but There's Nothing More We Can Do

The day began like so many those days. We started getting ready three hours earlier than the appointment time at the doctor's office in Seattle.

I brought coffee upstairs for my guy, first thing. Organic half and half, no sugar. He pulled himself higher in the bed so he could drink the creamy goodness without spilling any. After his coffee, he rolled and flopped out of bed and wobbled with the walker to the bathroom. He liked to be independent but was not afraid to ask for help if he needed it. As always, he used the restroom on his own, but I made sure I was close by, just in case.

It was hard for him to stand in the shower, so I ran a bath and helped him in and out safely.

Together we managed to get him into his once-too-tight, and now big-and-baggy blue jeans. His white T-shirt, with a nod to his favorite musician, Peter Gabriel, hung loosely on his frame. He lifted his arms high, and I slipped his comfy navy sweatshirt on him.

He sat on his butt and went down the stairs one at a time. Since he didn't have good motor function in his right leg, I lifted the jeans on the right side, and he scooted down to the next step. I helped with the left leg, and then the right again. It was slow progress, but I helped Eric into his wheelchair at the bottom of the stairs, wheeled him down the ramp to my SUV and off we went, yet again.

We waited the prerequisite half an hour at the cancer center lab and were ushered in for his blood pull. I rolled Eric out and up the elevator to the third floor. We waited in the blood cancer reception area, alongside fellow patients, some covering their heads with scarves, hats, and wigs.

For the first time in the nine month process, we were ushered into a room with a window, a view to the outside world. I sat on the plush window seat, slipped off my shoes, hugged my legs, and stared through the window. Eric rolled up close by and I reached out for his hand. We chatted and chuckled as we often did.

I'm pretty sure that neither of us had thought through where we were on his journey, and we certainly didn't realize the significance of the quiet knock on the door.

It was Dr. Smiley, and she was not smiling.

The news was not good. Not good at all.

There was no big build up, nor apology. Perhaps an, "I'm so sorry, we did everything we could," or even, "This is the end of the road," might have been appropriate.

Nope. She just pulled up the lab tests as she always did. She chatted about what she saw in the results.

None of that was important. What was important was the little slip of paper she grabbed. She proceeded to scribble down some bullet points, numbered them one through four, and passed it to us.

Still not realizing the significance of the moment, we looked it over together.

1. Radiation to help with the pain in the right upper leg and hip
2. Try to get on the Car T-Cell trial at our competitor network
3. Research any other trials for stage-four NHL
4. Palliative care (and there was a name and number written next to it).

My beloved Eric and I looked at each other. We probably should have guessed that this was it. Afterall, the stem cell therapy was no longer a possibility. The doctor was not aware of any trials within the walls of her network. There was the Car T-Cell trial taking place at their competitor network, but she didn't know much about it.

That left palliative care!!
Oh God! I know what that is!
Oh shit! No! No! NO!
Seriously? There's nothing more you can offer him?
Oh my God! Is this it for my Bebe?

After a long pause, Eric addressed the elephant in the room head-on and asked the two-million-dollar question, "How long do I have?"

Dr. Not-So-Smiley looked down, and then back up with sad eyes, and started off as she often did, "*Weeell,*" she said, "at the aggressive rate your cancer is growing, I would say six weeks."

My inner voice was going fucking bonkers.

Oh shit! Oh fuck! No! No! No! No!
Seriously?
Is this truly the best you can do?!
Oh my Bebe! Oh no!!

I stood quickly, pulled my handbag strap up on my shoulder, put both hands on the back of Eric's wheelchair, thanked her, and started to leave.

Eric shouted over his shoulder, "Did your staff call in the Oxy prescriptions?!"

"Yes," she said quietly.

And that was the last we saw of her for quite some time.

Oh, my fucking god!
What the heck did they do to my beloved in the last nine months?
Now, they're just giving up? Sending him home to die?
Fuck! Fuck! Fuuuuuck!

I marched Eric down the hallway, parked him by the restroom door, and went inside. I lost it for a minute and allowed my tears to flow freely. Then I dried my face, quieted my inner voice, went back out the door, grabbed the handles on the wheelchair, wheeled Eric to the car and drove us home.

— 40 —

Prepping to Leave the Country

This time we both agreed it was time to seriously consider the clinic in Mexico as a workable and perhaps the only option. We found the number for Sanoviv and called.

They asked us a series of questions about Eric's health status, and requested his latest test results.

It was a Thursday when we called, and thankfully, they told us they could admit us that Sunday.

We didn't ask too many questions, as we figured this was Eric's final chance at life.

For the next few days, Eric devoured some of the natural treatment information I'd been researching since this all began. He absorbed any and all information on the alternative options available that he had not been willing to acknowledge—until now. He also half apologized for not listening to me when he was first diagnosed, but I hugged him tight and said that it didn't matter. We were where we were, and we had to do something, *anything*, to get a different result.

He finally acknowledged that allopathic medicine had failed him.

The doctors had tried every trick in their limited tool kit. They did the nine months of chemotherapy, (the two by three-month sessions of R-CHOPs, the one three-month session of RICE, who knows how many methotrexate sessions), and countless medications. They had performed the three surgeries, (the big one and two smaller ones). They completely and utterly destroyed his immune system. And they sat by and watched him get hooked on opioids.

But, even after all of that...*none* of it moved the dial on Eric's cancer.

It. Simply. Didn't. Work.

I know it does for some lucky and blessed people. But not for Eric.

It was time to leave the country to get the care he needed.

This was it. All or nothing. Life or death.

PART THREE

— 1 —

Leaving the Country to Save Eric's Life

We went to bed that last night in Seattle full of hope. In the days before cancer invaded my husband's body, I loved snuggling closely with my face on the squishy part of his chest. I would lay my head on his pectoral muscle, lose myself in his heartbeat, and hide away from the big wide world. But my special spot was different now. The fat and muscle had long since melted away, and my face was uncomfortable on the stretched skin and exposed bone.

When I dreamed, I visualized a different outcome for my beloved...a healthy, adventure-filled life.

We left Seattle in the wee hours of the morning, winging our way to Mexico with Eric's walker and just one carry-on between us. The purpose of the trip was to save my husband's life, and there was no need for additional baggage.

We were picked up in San Diego by a sweet, talkative driver from the healing center who drove us straight through the border into Mexico. Eric and I sat staring out the window, holding hands, taking in the shocking sights of poverty, the overcrowded makeshift homes, yet observing the vibrant colors and upbeat people milling about.

As the road followed the coast to Rosarito, our driver shared some useful information about our destination. Roughly translated, Sanoviv means "healthy and vital long life." The clinic had been open since 2000 and was the brainchild of an extraordinary man, scientist, and researcher Dr. Myron Wentz. He wanted to create a center where the best possible nutrition and the latest science-based therapies could counter chronic and degenerative disease. Essentially, it is a world-class healing and research facility utilizing a functional approach and offering a unique blend of conventional, alternative, and integrative programs.

Dr. Wentz originally considered San Diego, but, purportedly at the time, the American medical authorities pushed back on approval for him to create his facility in the U.S., so he left the country to build his dream clinic in Mexico.

After about an hour, the van slowed, and we drove through tall iron security gates onto the grounds of the healing institute.

"This is it, Bebe," I said softly. "The place that can turn your health around."

Eric grinned and squeezed my hand. He had no words.

We had many unanswered questions and high hopes that the team of professionals there could reverse Eric's dire health prognosis.

Facebook Post—October 23, 2016

What would you do if you were told by your doctor that you only had six weeks left to live? Well, I don't know about you, but we're saying, 'screw that!' We've packed our bags and we're heading down to a fantastic clinic in Mexico. Please join me in visualizing Eric happy and completely transformed in health.

— 2 —

Settling into the Five-Star Medical Facility in Mexico

At the stunning five-star health clinic on the Baja California Pacific coast, where every room has an ocean view, Eric was treated like a whole person from the very first moment.

We entered through the custom double-glass doors etched with dolphins and were welcomed by name and with huge smiles. The staff checked us in without delay and gifted us each a welcome pack with cream-colored organic sweatpants and shorts, a choice of organic baby blue and pastel yellow t-shirts and tanks, Birkenstock leather sandals, refillable water bottles, and a brush for a daily dry skin-brushing routine.

The staff requested we wear the clothing and sandals while on the grounds of Sanoviv to avoid passing on viruses from the outside world, and the laundry service would collect the clothing worn each day and return it the following day, laundered and folded.

We were provided with a schedule for the remainder of that day and the next. Sundays were typically quiet, and we were happy to take our time to settle in and get a sense of the place.

As soon as Eric sat in their basic-model wheelchair, he wished he had brought his more comfortable version from Seattle. But, in classic Eric form, he didn't moan or whine; he just got on with it.

I wheeled him to the elevator and up to the sixth floor to settle into our suite. We passed between the two twin beds, through the French doors, and out to the balcony overlooking the sparkling Pacific Ocean.

I pulled up a chair next to my husband, picked up his hand, and laid it in my lap. We took in the palm trees, the pools, the cloudless sky, the sound of the crashing waves below, and for a moment we imagined we had arrived at a five-star resort for a fun and relaxing vacation in the sun.

It wasn't until afterwards, when we were back in Seattle, Eric shared with me that in that moment he had considered that this wouldn't be a bad place to die.

Facebook Post—October 24, 2016

An exciting start to our medical adventure and life-saving mission! We are happy here and have a strong belief that Eric can do it! I'll keep you updated as the events here in Mexico unfold for my wonderful husband...so, stand by. In the interim, all prayers and blessings and healing energy gratefully accepted.

— 3 —

An Unbelievable First Forty-Eight Hours

The light had begun to ease the dark of night when I awakened. I looked over at Eric's outline—his jaw was slack, his mouth open, and he was gently snoring. I quietly opened the sliding door to the balcony and stepped outside into the cool morning air.

Leaning against the railing, I breathed in the magic of this place.

We heard that this parcel of land was previously owned by the wealthy Strauss family. They built a mansion here with marble floors, hallways as wide as rooms, and massive banks of windows overlooking the ocean. It has powerful energy ley lines, (believed to be invisible threads that weave through the Earth's ancient landscapes, connecting sacred sites and natural wonders), that run through the land with some of the strongest natural healing energy in the world. Even NASA had been interested in purchasing it.

If there was healing magic at this place, we were open for miracles.

Leaving Eric to his deep sleep, I slipped out quietly to power walk around the property. There's a little stone track that skirts the edge of the cliff overlooking the ocean, with a view along the spectacular Baja coastline. My walk doubled as fitness and walking meditation, and I drank in the pinks and golds of that first spectacular sunrise with every step.

At Sanoviv, each day starts early with a ringing of the bell at 6:30 a.m. Everyone is invited to a room in the mansion where fresh organic lemons are provided. They believe that a glass of freshly squeezed lemon juice in water with a dash of cayenne pepper, on an empty stomach, is the best way to wake up the organs for each new day.

Not surprisingly, the water from the faucets was triple filtered and run through a reverse osmosis process. We could also choose from a selection of organic herbal teas, and for the coffee lovers, there was no coffee available to drink anywhere on the property. There are many reasons they don't offer coffee, like the heavy use of pesticides on the crop and the acid-forming properties that can change the body's natural pH balance.

Back in the room, I helped my beloved get dressed and wheeled him down to the main gathering room. There, I witnessed something I thought I'd never see—Eric having a wheatgrass shot. I chuckled as he made a funny face and struggled to get the first sip down. I threw mine back and drank another of the pungent, ultra-healthy liquid.

There was a class or meditation each day at 7 a.m., typically delivered by one of the staff. Doctors and medical practitioners teaching about spirituality and meditation is something you don't see much of in the U.S., if ever. During that very first morning class we found the doctor's delivery so passionate and his meditation so powerful, we were both moved to tears.

Next came the golden milk, made from scratch (almond milk, honey, turmeric and cardamom), and a delicious breakfast with angel eggs (as opposed to devilled eggs), and cooked vegetables.

Eric had a full complement of tests and assessments scheduled for the first three days at the clinic, and he was scheduled to see his medical doctor daily.

Sitting in a comfy office, holding hands, we only waited a few minutes for Eric's new doctor to arrive for the first appointment. He was a smart young man, oozing with kindness, and looking like he had stepped out of the Latino version of GQ Magazine. His smile was as big as his heart, and from the very first moment he was 100 percent present with Eric.

I nicknamed him "Dr. Kind."

He looked at Eric, started asking questions, and listened intently to the responses. He wanted to learn everything he could about Eric's childhood, family circumstances, relationships, marriages, parents, where and how he had lived, his passions, his work history, and more.

He explored what made Eric happy and what his stressors were. He asked about his years in the Navy as an engineer on nuclear submarines and the serious car accident in his early thirties.

Dr. Kind specifically asked what Eric had been doing eight to nine years earlier. Eric and I looked at each other, a little stumped, but did the math. We figured that this was when he was fighting with the local city authorities and experiencing permitting issues on his newly purchased waterfront property on Lake Sammamish, Washington. He spent weeks spraying gallons of Roundup to kill the overgrown vegetation and clear the land in preparation for building his 10,000-square-foot Mediterranean-style dream home.

This brilliant young doctor intuited quickly that Eric was a daredevil, thinking himself bulletproof, in this case from chemical exposure to Roundup all those years ago.

I could barely comprehend what I was witnessing. A doctor who was not only asking Eric about all aspects of his life, but one who truly believed this information held vital clues for his current health predicament.

We came away amazed. The contrast between the U.S. medical system and doctors to our experience in Mexico was astonishing: the comfortable and personable rooms, no waiting periods before and between appointments, the questions asked, and the amount of time allocated for each session.

Eric was treated as a human being, not just a number on a bracelet in a cancer ward in a hospital where they ask your name every time they dispense a pill, draw your blood, and deliver your food.

It seemed to me that in Mexico there appeared to be no medical authorities outlawing natural and alternative healing therapies, supporting mostly allopathic protocols. The stranglehold of the pharmaceutical corporations on the treatment of cancer either doesn't exist or is not as powerful.

I wheeled Eric to have his blood drawn at the lab, but this was a draw with a difference. We were fascinated to see his blood through a microscope. Where there should be clear and healthy boundaries around the edge of each circular cell, we could see big holes, weird shapes, and scary faces staring back.

Next was the dentist, and not just any dentist, a *bio-dentist*. One who focuses on alternative approaches and uses healthy materials in her craft. She figured that the significant dental work—as a result of his car accident, the bone grafts, bridges, and implants—may have been a major factor in his developing the dreaded disease.

Even having conversations about contributing factors to his health crisis was music to my ears. When we asked the U.S. doctors how Eric got cancer, they would shrug their shoulders and admit they had no idea. They'd mumble something about diet and stress, but they really didn't have a clue. They didn't even appear curious.

After the dental appointment, I pushed Eric to the chiropractor at the facility—not one who clicks and cracks and makes Eric scream out in pain but touches gently and intuits with kindness what is going on at a deeper level.

"You're focusing on the past and worrying about the future. We're going to work on bringing you back to the present and deepening your breath," he told Eric at his first appointment.

Then I wheeled him to the Quiet Room, a room full of energy machines that can both diagnose and treat. Between all the machines there are several thousand programs covering every possible health scenario. The energy in that room was extraordinary, and we couldn't wait to find out more.

Finally, I dropped Eric at the spa. When I walked in later, I saw him getting his toenails buffed. He looked up at me, grinning from ear to ear. It was his first-ever pedicure, and he was delighted with his shiny set of polished toenails. Ironically, it took a close call with his mortality for him to open to the joys of nurturing spa treatments.

Each night, after dinner, they played a movie or documentary. That evening it was about the dangers of genetically modified or engineered food. I already had a sense of this, but the movie reiterated there is nothing good or helpful with modified foods.

We slipped into the hot tub and soaked for an hour.

"Can you believe this place, Bebe?" he asked quietly as he reached for me. "I'm really sorry it took me a while to realize that I needed to come here."

Sitting with my legs weightless over his lap, I replied, "Oh, my love, please don't apologize. You needed to believe a place like this could help and even heal you. And, I know…it's truly phenomenal! I'm only just beginning to process it all. I'm so glad we're here. You're going to be okay. I know it."

Facebook Post—October 25, 2016

So far, Eric has met up with his amazing young doctor, the chiropractor, the bio-dentist, had his vitals taken, looked at his blood under a microscope, sat in the "Quiet Room" amongst the healing machines as they measured and recorded his energy field and organ health, enjoyed a pedicure, and a lesson on breathing and meditation. He drank freshly juiced green organic vegetables, wheatgrass shots, golden milk, and fresh coconut milk from a real coconut, and he has eaten from the wide range of delicious food available. All this, in just the first forty-eight hours!

— 4 —

A Reality Check with Dr. Kind

I stood on the clifftop and gazed out over the ocean. I looked down closer to the shore and marveled at the power of the waves as they rose up and curled under, creating the perfect tunnel for the surfers living their bliss.

I looked toward the mansion, taking in the people milling about, and spied my love sitting in the sun. He had taken off his shirt and was slouched in his wheelchair. His eyes were closed. He looked relaxed, albeit a little gray, but even from this distance I could see a slight smile.

Although I saw a skeletal version of my once-healthy husband, I truly believed that this place could breathe some life force and vitality back into his broken body. I saw him open his eyes, broaden his smile, and raise his arm to wave at me.

His smile was a magnet, and as I started walking over to him, I caught some movement in the bush behind his wheelchair. It was a tiny green and brown hummingbird, hovering silently above a flowering Bird of Paradise. I snapped a photo of this extraordinary scene, and in the frame was Eric's discarded T-shirt and Birkenstocks, the bright orange and green of the bird of paradise plant, the tiny bird lingering mid-air, and the intense blue of the ocean beyond.

Eric happily shared that this was his long-departed grandmother, visiting him in the form of a hummingbird. I sincerely hoped she didn't see a different outcome for Eric, that perhaps his time was running short, and she was there to usher him home.

After our break in the sun, we got a serious reality check. Dr. Kind told us that Eric's hemoglobin number was so borderline, had it been one point lower, he would have been sent home. He also confirmed his bone marrow was too depleted to survive another round of chemo, at least in his current weakened state.

We discovered that Sanoviv was not afraid to use a mix of conventional treatments in conjunction with alternative and complementary ones, and as it turned out, Eric would require some radiation. When we met with a radiotherapy specialist, he estimated Eric would need at least five sessions to help with his intense pain and slow the growth of the large tumor in his right hip.

After our meetings with Dr. Kind and the radiation specialist, Eric began his treatments. We were blown away by how many they squeezed into one day.

Although some of the treatments were either banned in the U.S. or not covered by insurance, a handful were sneaking in through chiropractic and naturopathic doctor offerings. For example, Eric had a regional hyperthermia treatment where, in a carefully controlled environment, the medical practitioner turned up the heat over one of his bigger tumors to 107°F. On alternate days, they planned to heat up his whole body. The idea is to kill off the unwanted cancer cells and tumors that can't survive in the adverse conditions created by the high temperatures and to stimulate the immune system to work harder.

Like the pedicure, Eric also experienced reflexology for the first time at Sanoviv. I watched as the therapist used her hands and thumbs to massage the bottom of his feet, designed to simultaneously heal and regenerate other areas of his body. She explained that reflexology is good for stimulating nerve function, eliminating toxins, and boosting circulation. I don't think he heard what she was saying though, as I saw his eyes flicker and close.

Additionally, Eric had two IV drips. One was Vitamin C which, when administered in high doses by intravenous (IV) infusion, is known to kill cancer cells. The other was Transfer Factors, essentially small immune messenger molecules produced by all higher organisms. I asked someone about this and was told they're an ancient part of the immune system and represent "an archaic dialect in the language of cells." So much for modern medicine. I wondered if it was about awakening the cells to a language of long forgotten healing potential.

After his IV treatments, I wheeled my beloved to get a green juice, customized with ingredients to help his anemia. The ever-changing, personalized treatment from his nutritionist was extraordinary. What a concept! We also devoured a delicious pea protein shake with homemade nut milk and probiotics. We ate nut butter with celery and carrots as a snack, and had a lunch of organic chicken with cooked vegetables and a mound of raw and organic salad, representing all the colors on the spectrum.

After the treatments and delicious food, Eric fell asleep back at our suite. In the late afternoon, I gently awakened him from his deep slumber and wheeled him outside to catch the sunset and have dinner.

We sat quietly and watched the bright gold ball as it dropped below the horizon and set for the night. Eric pulled me into a hug and whispered in my ear, "Thank you, Bebe. For everything."

Facebook Post—October 26, 2016

Another day in paradise is ending. The perfect location on the planet to heal. This place has confirmed over and over that there is not only hope, but life.

— 5 —

Thursdays, a Liquid Day at Sanoviv

In his pre-cancer days, Eric and I used to weave ourselves around each other in bed, needing the closeness of our bodies like we needed air to breathe. In the years we were together, I don't recall us ever sleeping in separate beds. Until now.

He had never been a good sleeper, so I enjoyed watching him sleep soundly in the twin bed across the room. Sadly, I heard him shout out in pain during the night, as he inadvertently rolled onto the wrong side. The tumors had been growing fast and furious on his right side, and there was a big one reaching from his hip, deep into his femur.

Leaving him to his precious sleep, I snuck quietly out of the room for my exercise hour, and was blessed to witness the peninsula of Baja California wake up. It was a stunning sunrise, with creases of light slowly appearing above the coastline, manifesting into a full blanket of every conceivable shade of pink and orange. I stood in awe at the incredible sight.

When I returned, Eric was snuggled up in his comfy Seahawks blanket, gifted by a thoughtful colleague. His first words of the day were, "Morning, Bebe. I think I'll pass on the sound meditation today."

"Not a chance," I quietly responded.

Several minutes later I was wheeling him to the nurses' station for his vitals and then to the auditorium for the sound meditation. I figured that he was offered so many phenomenal healing opportunities here, he ought to do it all. One never knows which combination of treatments and healing sessions could be the exact one to kick cancer to the curb.

The sound meditation teacher was a lovely young man who also doubled as the Doctor of Psychology, "Dr. Heart." He started the session with deep breathing exercises, meditation basics, and moved on to sound bowls, tapping and running the cloth-covered stick around the top. He then suggested we keep our eyes closed and listen to the sounds he made as he walked around the room with various instruments.

My favorite sound came from an instrument that sounded like shells running over a sandy beach as the tide gently rolled them back and forth. I opened my eyes to peek at what was creating the magical sound and saw it was a cross between a long kaleidoscope and an aboriginal didgeridoo.

At the end of the session, Eric was slumped over in his wheelchair. My sweet man had been transported back into the world of sleep, and I hoped that the sound mediation was at least healing for him on a deeper level.

Later that morning, I walked in as Eric was finishing up his regional hyperthermia treatment. There was a round metal cylinder heat lamp in the center and infrared by his feet. He had been at 104°F for fifty minutes and felt well-cooked by the time I arrived. That treatment was rough, but he knew it would help the efficacy of the upcoming radiotherapy, so he had persevered.

It was a Thursday, also known as a liquid day at Sanoviv. A once-a-week day of freshly juiced vegetable juices, protein shakes, and soups, designed to give the digestive system a rest from solid food. However, the nutritionist decided Eric was an exception, because of his anemia and weight loss, and recommended he have buffalo meat and vegetables for lunch. To avoid any questions from the other guests, we ate lunch in our room.

After our lunch date, we left the compound to go to the radiation center in Tijuana. At the impressive state-of-the-art facility, the staff staged Eric in readiness for the radiation that would take place daily, the following week.

I sat with the radiation technicians and watched the monitor as they ran him through a Computed Tomography (CT) scan. They pointed out where the tumor had eaten into his hip socket bone and the top of his femur. I was shocked to see gaping holes and honeycomb shapes where the bones should be solid, and thought about how freaky it was that Eric's body created a massive tumor monster, eating through his bone.

Upon returning, I took my beloved to his first hyperbaric oxygen therapy session, where medical use of oxygen is at a higher pressure level than our atmosphere. The treatment takes place in a chamber that uses 100 percent oxygenated air at an elevated ambient pressure. It is designed to increase blood flow and circulation, increase oxygen levels to the body's tissues, boost the white blood cell count, and generally kick butt to the typically low-oxygen environments that cancer thrives in.

When I met him later for dinner, he joked that his hyperbaric session was more pleasant than the "Sahara heating session" earlier in the day. I chuckled, appreciating that he kept his sense of humor throughout the pain, discomfort, and setbacks...all of it.

The fish and vegetable soup at dinner was so delicious, both Eric and I went back for seconds. I enjoyed watching my guy as he spooned mouthfuls of healthy soup into his mouth, and with raised levels of happy hormones from my afternoon infrared sauna, everything was good in my world...for now.

Facebook Post—October 27, 2016

This place of healing and stunning sunrises and sunsets, of doctors who double as sound meditation practitioners, is extraordinary. It's sustaining both of us—Eric, to find a way to live...me, to lift me up in support of my lover, husband, best friend, buddy, and life partner. Time for bed for this girl and boy. It's been another big day—life-changing, life-affirming, and heart-opening!

— 6 —

Healing, Gratitude, and Angel Eggs

Early the following morning, I was walking on the path to the mansion when the sound of birdsong stopped me in my tracks. I caught some movement to my right, in the hedge. I peered past a pink hibiscus flower, through the branches, and spied a tiny bird. She stopped singing and sat still for a moment, staring back at me.

She started up again and stayed on the branch singing her little heart out. I was captivated and watched in awe, her chest expanding and contracting, breathing in the cool morning air and turning it into a magical hummingbird song. After she flew off, I took a deep breath, and consciously slowed down my fast-beating heart. I was beyond excited to have had a moment with a delightful little hummingbird.

I continued on to the tearoom, poured a mug of steaming hot tea, and walked outside. Looking back through a large window, I could see the team of professionals sitting in a circle in the yoga/ meditation room. The medical doctors, nutritionist, dentist, body code lady, psychologist, fitness specialist, and chiropractor gathered every morning to discuss developments with each and every patient. This, I believed, was what truly personalized care looked like.

After they completed their session, fellow guests and their companions started gathering for the 7 a.m. session, eager and ready to learn and meditate. I chose my spot, sat down and saw Eric arrive in his wheelchair shortly after.

I smiled and waved at him, closed my eyes, and listened to the sound of crashing waves, birds singing, and the barking dogs next door. I sincerely hoped we wouldn't have to name this session "barking dog meditation," but thankfully the dogs quieted as soon as we got started.

The session was about energy psychology postures, and we learned about energy meridians, did a little tapping, and focused on five main postures: calming, energizing, focusing, balancing/ mind clearing, and gratitude.

One of the calming postures was great for anxiety and easy to remember. You cross your arms in front of your chest and dig your fingers into the soft flesh under your armpits, pushing in hard to find the sore spot on each side. It's something easy to do, even in public, as it looks like you're just crossing your arms.

After learning about the postures, we were guided to lie on the floor or sit on the chairs for our own meditation. The recommendation was to focus on one word. I initially chose "healing" but kept coming back to "gratitude." It made sense, as I have a strong belief that gratitude is the precursor to manifesting what we want in our life, including healing.

The light stretching class in the gym was the next and final activity scheduled before breakfast that morning. When we arrived,

I grabbed a large exercise ball and found a spot in the almost-full class.

Eric stayed in his wheelchair and picked up two light hand weights to get his arm muscles working. He hadn't been able to exercise much all year, and his muscles had atrophied terribly. It was fun stretching and watching my guy with his weights in the mirror. At one point, I saw that he was hunched over to one side of his wheelchair, sound asleep, looking adorable and still dutifully holding the hand weights.

After a delicious breakfast of local organic "Angel" eggs topped with a vegetable puree and cooked vegetables, Eric experienced his first-ever colon hydrotherapy session. The practitioner confirmed it's best to poop one to three times a day, otherwise there are too many toxins sitting in your body, often creating all sorts of health problems. He had another session scheduled for the following day, and we joked that after a few more weeks of this he would be squeaky clean.

Rather than meeting Eric's doctor in his office next, we sat in the garden to go over his progress and strategize how best to move forward. He recommended Eric continue with it all: the oxygen, heat, psychology, colon hydrotherapy, chiropractic and nutrition sessions, IVs, healthy food and liquids, massage, reflexology, and all the various biofeedback and energy machines in the Quiet Room.

At this stage, it looked like Eric might stay for an additional three to four weeks. I would stay as long as I could, going back and forth to Seattle, depending on my Microsoft and real estate work schedules. We would make the final determination later as we saw how my beloved was progressing, and as we learned what portion of the treatments would be covered by our medical insurance company.

We rounded out the day with an educational documentary, *Happy*, on the science of being happy. We learned that the body can produce happiness hormones on its own. Endorphins essentially help us deal with stress and reduce feelings of pain. Serotonin acts as a mood stabilizer, giving us feelings of well-being and happiness. Dopamine is responsible for allowing us to feel pleasure, satisfaction, a sense of achievement, and motivation. The main message made total sense. It's much better for your health if you are, or can train yourself to be, happy.

Back in the room, Eric fell asleep right away, and I enjoyed lounging around and journaling on the couch in our suite. It was a beautiful spot to write, with the constant sound of the waves racing and crashing on the shore. I felt only gratitude and happiness as I wrote my daily missive, and I figured they were the themes for the evening.

Cheers to gratitude and happiness.

Facebook Post—October 28, 2016

I just love this place. They offer some form of meditation teaching and practice every morning. The healing power of meditation cannot be underestimated. To find it offered as part of the daily program in a healing center and taught by doctors, nurses, specialists, and surgeons is just mind-blowing to me.

— 7 —

Phillipa Makes a Hummingbird Friend

It looked like I had a new friend in the pink flowering hibiscus hedge. The wee hummingbird was perhaps only as big as my thumb. Her body was an intense velvety green, and the shade changed as she moved and caught the light from different angles. I named her Cerise, because her head was a deep pink, and just like the green hue, the color changed as she moved.

I became a regular visitor to what was coined by Eric and some of the others, "my Hibiscus Hedge," and she became known as "my hummingbird," because it seemed she only appeared for me or if I was present with someone to point her out.

I looked for Cerise several times a day, and my heart beat a little faster when I saw her. She seemed to have a sense of humor too. On one occasion, I asked her telepathically if I could take a picture and video of her. In response, she lifted off the branch and hovered, at least until I picked up my camera to take the shot, and then she promptly settled on the branch behind a leaf. She repeated that a couple of times, and eventually she sighed, lifted off, and floated long enough for me to take a picture and get some video footage.

I bid goodbye to Cerise and went to find Eric and go to breakfast before his first session of the day. I was pleasantly surprised to find him sitting with a small group of guests, huddled over a low table, engrossed in a giant hummingbird puzzle. I rarely saw him disengage his busy brain long enough to spend time on a puzzle, and I enjoyed watching as he picked up a piece and focused intently on the search for its home. He grinned with a look of achievement when he was able to place it in its rightful place.

At a breakfast of delicious homemade granola, made-from-scratch nut milk, chopped strawberries, blueberries, and cinnamon, we sat with some fellow guests also going through a cancer journey. They were extraordinary people with remarkable stories, most also having experienced a similar disillusionment with the medical profession in general.

A chap from Oregon started talking about Roundup and the dangers of the main ingredient, glyphosate, for our health and for the planet. He had been a landscaper for many years and his daily use of Roundup was likely the main contributing factor to his lymphoma. He shared that to obtain your pesticide licensing in Oregon, you had to learn it was safe to drink up to 8 oz of Roundup.

What the fuck?

Seriously?

Who in their right minds would drink the nasty stuff?

I told them I had read that chemicals in pesticides can trigger cancer by disrupting hormones, damaging DNA, inflaming tissue, and turning genes on or off. There's even research to support that glysophate is now present at detectable levels in seventy-five percent of air and rain samples, worldwide.

After that shocking group discussion, we had a little free time and made our way down to the lounge chairs by the lap pool. We laid under the banana trees, and enjoyed the killer view south along the Baja coast. I was delighted to see Eric get into relaxation mode reading *Everybody's Got Something* by Robin Roberts, a book about her personal cancer journey.

His first session was major autohemotherapy/ozone with UV. This is where they take your blood, mix it with medical ozone, and drip it back into your vein. The treatment is known to improve circulation, ease pain, lessen inflammation, and boost the immune system. I learned about many treatments offered here, like this one, that are rarely available in the U.S. I found that profoundly sad.

Next, at his colon hydrotherapy session, the practitioner added wheat grass to the water to replace the flora in his colon. The day prior it was organic coffee to draw out the toxins from his body. The fact that the only coffee available at Sanoviv was for enemas appealed to Eric's sense of humor, although he did miss his morning coffee routine, truth be told.

His spa treatments that afternoon were a second reflexology session and a lymph node massage, designed to help the body effectively cleanse from unwanted toxins. It was exciting to see how much my guy was thoroughly appreciating these healthy, nurturing treatments, and he wished he had taken advantage of them decades ago.

Being a Saturday night, our dinner was accompanied by a mariachi duo, and the two sweet elderly gents played and sang with everything they had. The meal was a delicious paleo bread dish with pickled beans, onions, and a green salad, followed by a raw dessert—a weekly treat on Saturdays.

Kicking back, enjoying the music, I reached out for Eric's hand. He turned to look at me and grinned. He was relaxed and, just for a moment, we could almost believe all was well in our world.

Facebook Post—October 29, 2016

Today felt like a vacation, replete with my hummingbird in the hedge, a puzzle, meeting awesome like-minded people, reading books in the sun, nurturing treatments, a mariachi band, and dessert with dinner! Once again, I find myself in gratitude and awe for this place, the staff here, and the love with which they treat us and prepare the food.

— 8 —

Sunday, the Closest Thing to a Day Off

I reached down and adjusted the chaise lounge sun chair by the pool. It was Sunday, the closest the patients got to having a day off. I looked over at Eric, relaxed and tanned, lying in the sun, holding up his book to block out the glare.

I took a moment to reflect on how he was progressing. Overall, he was doing well. He was a different person from the guy who felt duped, shunned, and let down by the traditional medical system just one week earlier. He was humbled and grateful to be here, his spirits were high, and he was hopeful he would not only survive this chapter but go on to thrive.

On the flip side, he was experiencing intense pain in his right hip and couldn't put weight on that leg. He was completely wheelchair bound, and grunted with pain when he inadvertently hit his leg or caught his foot in the wheelchair.

Even though he was a little apprehensive about the radiation treatment starting the following day, he was looking forward to the pain reducing and hopefully dissipating altogether. He had long discussions with the doctor and understood that if he didn't take the radiation option, given the aggressive nature of the cancer, it would literally eat right through the femur bone, essentially destroying its host.

Although he knew there was still a chance the treatments here would not work in time, he acknowledged that he had done and was doing everything possible to save his life—with *both* the traditional and non-traditional routes. It wasn't easy, but we talked about our finances, the kids, his will, the boat, the truck, our two investment properties, and even computer passwords and bank account access, in the event he didn't make it.

We each sat alone in deep thought, and at other times we cried, hugged, and clung to each other in intense emotional pain. We giggled together at fun memories and decried the craziness of what he'd been through. We experienced the whole gambit and felt strongly that it was better to be open about what was going on for each of us, rather than keeping it hidden away. We didn't know how much time he had and figured that by discussing the many possible outcomes, there would be no surprises.

As soon as Eric completed his only scheduled session that day, a three-hour IV, we played Foo. I joined in on the group puzzle, and we met some of the new guests who arrived that afternoon, chatting with them over dinner. They came from all over the world, most searching for the ideal integrative approach to whatever ailed them.

One couple we met, Angelina and her husband, was from Canada. After years of debilitating headaches, she had been diagnosed with cancer of the brain and had been told by the Canadian medical professionals that they would need to open up her face in a twenty-four hour-plus surgery to remove the tumors. She thanked them for their treatment plan and came to Sanoviv to explore other options.

Later that evening, Eric opened up about crying in his recent session with Dr. Heart, when recounting two events. One was a night about ten days prior, when we were cuddling in bed at home in Washington, and he told me that he felt quite comfortable that I could take over as head of household, taking care of myself and Bella. Eric had told Dr. Heart how important it was for him to know I would be okay, and he bawled when sharing his feelings on the topic.

The other was when his eldest daughter and four of her five kiddos were saying goodbye the evening before we left for Mexico. He had almost lost it as we were all chaotically getting into place for a family photo, and although he held it together, he blubbered when he recounted the moment with the sweet young doctor.

I told him that it would have been okay if he "lost it" in front of his daughters, grandkids, and me because that's being real. I'm sure we could have benefited from a really good cry.

— 9 —

A Day of Oxygen, Radiation, Hyperthermia

Early the following morning, I stayed to support Eric and watch through the hyperbaric chamber camera monitor, since he had panicked during his last treatment. I appreciated that they were teaching him how to visualize his body healing during these treatments, envisioning oxygen flooding every cell and ushering out the cancer.

We picked up our lunch-to-go after his session, and our driver took us to Eric's first radiation treatment in Tijuana. As he was lying on the cold hard table in the all-white sterile room, a robot moved over him, directing the radiation from four different angles and with passes of ten to forty-five seconds each.

After it was over, he reported it was like being in a bank vault with its massively thick doors and walls made of lead. He said that lying completely still on the hard surface was like having a sword stuck in his hip, with someone twisting and turning the blade. My heart hurt when he shared that the pain was excruciating and not knowing how long he was going to have to endure being completely still, he had started crying.

We hoped his pain would reduce significantly by the time the five sessions were over, and now that he knew how long it took, he believed he'd be able to handle it better.

When we returned to Sanoviv, I dropped Eric off for his regional hyperthermia session, timed again to enhance the efficacy of the radiation that week. He was looking forward to his spa treatment afterward with a back massage to round out his treatments of the day.

"How are you feeling with everything right now, my love?" I asked as we were finishing up dinner that evening.

"It's a lot. The radiation was intense, but I'm glad it's going to help my hip pain, and I'm happy we're here. Of course we still don't know what the outcome will be for me, but this is the best place for us to be. Thank you again Bebe, thank you," he said as he pulled me in for a hug.

Facebook Post—October 31, 2016

Today my guy was flooded with oxygen, had a burn-gun targeting and radiating his hip, was heated up into hyperthermia, and massaged to complete the day. Other guests and companions have begun to notice how much more alive (pun intended!) he's looking. They're commenting unsolicited, and this is great validation that they're seeing what I'm seeing. We are strong in our belief and visualizations, and are delighted he is making huge progress daily.

— 10 —

Tapping, Breathing, Death & Dying, and an Inwards Smile

I t became harder for my beloved to move his right leg and getting into his sweatpants in the mornings proved to be difficult. Given time, he could still dress himself, and although he liked being independent, he wasn't afraid to ask for help.

After dressing and his daily labs, Eric joined me in the education center for a session on tapping exercises and acupressure points. We tapped between our eyebrows, on our temples, above the lip, and on the top, front, and back of our heads. We put pressure on the point in the webbing between our thumb and index finger and massaged for a few seconds, taking slow deep breaths. These simple exercises can have an immediate, powerful effect, relaxing the body and keeping anxiety levels manageable.

Dr. Heart led us in a thirty-minute guided meditation and asked us to come up with a person, place, or thing that we associated with an "inward smile." We visited different regions of the body, following along with the directions.

Eric said afterwards that he went out of body and didn't recall a thing. Honestly, I never thought I would see him relaxing like that, or learning to meditate, and I was impressed how willing he was to try out new modalities to save his life.

Later, while Eric lay in the sun getting his immune booster and anti-cancer IVs, Dr. Heart sat with him, delving deeper into how his diagnosis had impacted him and others. My beloved reiterated he now felt ready for whatever his path would be for himself and for me as his wife. However, he said he did not feel ready to say goodbye to his daughters, if it came to it, and they chewed on that for the rest of the session.

Dr. Kind and the nutritionist also joined him outside for his consultations. We appreciated that if you couldn't get to the medical professionals, they came looking for you.

Then we picked up our lunch and were driven off to Tijuana again. Thankfully, the next radiation treatment was a little easier for Eric, and there were no tears.

When we returned, he went straight into the Quiet Room, where a machine ran electrical impulses up and down his spine. He loved it in that room, yet had no words to explain why. Interestingly, it was the one location on the property that the companions could not accompany their person.

We had both listened intently as our driver told us that this was the room that seemed to be the biggest threat to the American authorities who, even after sixteen years, were still trying to exert their influence over Mexico City to have the medical institution shut down. Thankfully for those of us seeking alternative approaches, Dr. Wentz persevered, and we could enjoy the full benefits of the place—Quiet Room and all.

After a jam-packed day of treatments and travel, we crashed straight onto Eric's bed. Soon after, his breathing quieted and softened into sleep. I stayed in his arms, allowing myself to feel deep sadness over all the things cancer stole from us.

Apart from the obvious things like good health, vitality, work, and freedom to schedule our lives, cancer treatments had also screwed with the nerves in his feet and hands, and greatly impacted his libido. Gone were the days when we made easy and wonderful love daily. I struggled to recall the last time we had sex and thought it was perhaps several months ago. We both lay on our left sides in our king bed, and my lover boy spooned me from behind. Instead of Eric experiencing a climax, it was an anti-climactic moment for him. The chemo saw to it that his nerves and feelings were all jumbled and mixed up.

While he wondered whether he would ever get *that* climactic feeling back, I wondered whether I would ever get my whole and complete husband back.

I would, wouldn't I?

Facebook Post—November 1, 2016

Today, Eric tapped, pressed, smiled, breathed, meditated, and was massaged into better health. IVs filled him with volume to reduce inflammation and actively target those monstrous cancerous cells. He talked about death and dying and that, although he felt ready to go if it was his time, he feels like he still has some additional emotional work to do.

— 11 —

Thalasso Pools, the Power of The Body Code, and Forgiveness

The following morning, I heard a knock on the door and opened it to see a stunning woman with silver shoulder-length wavy hair, big blue eyes, and an endearing smile. It was Karen, the body code practitioner.

I was intrigued that many Sanoviv visitors talked most excitedly about their body code sessions. Indeed, they chatted about all their treatments, yet after they had one body code session they couldn't wait for the next. They seemed fascinated about what fears and trapped emotions might be exposed and cleared, or what subconscious beliefs showed up, ready to be rewired.

It was the day for Eric's first session, and since he was feeling nauseous, Karen agreed to come to us. She told Eric the body code system is a powerful natural healing modality and reminded him that his body essentially knew how to heal itself.

I worked in the second bedroom and half-listened in on the session. I heard her begin, gently probing. "What happened when you were fourteen, Eric?" It turned out that Eric had been in a car accident. Although he hadn't suffered any physical trauma, there was significant emotional distress with him believing he had deeply disappointed his mom. Unbelievably, as soon as the driver realized Eric was underage and driving without a license, he exaggerated his injuries and took legal action. Eric felt the injustice of the driver's actions and carried that onwards with an intense sense of helplessness.

"Now tell me about your late twenties," Karen encouraged.

I didn't know how she was intuiting his major life events, because his second car accident was a very serious one at twenty-nine years old. He had been hit by an out-of-control speeding, drunk, and drugged driver and had over two hundred broken bones in his face. His jaw was torn apart on the steering wheel, and his heart stopped twice on the helicopter rescue flight out from the site and once again on the operating table. He told her that this event essentially ended his ten-year military career, and he was deeply disappointed at not being able to fulfill his life goal of becoming an officer in the navy.

"Okay, now what about another event in your late forties?"

He spoke about how hard he fought to save his lakefront property on Lake Sammamish. Eric had battled the city government as they exaggerated the function of the storm water system on the property, designating it a fish system. He was so shocked the city had declared his property a wetland, he took them to court. Although he had won, the permit red-lines and threats continued. He told Karen of the unimaginable stress of having to short sell, losing seven figures in the process, and feeling like there was nothing he could do about it.

Still listening from the other room, I was riveted as Karen brought it all together. She picked up that Eric naturally stepped into the role of being the guardian. Yet, in the three major life events he shared that day, there was no guardian there for him. As he suffered the pain of intense hopelessness and helplessness, there was no guardian for the guardian.

Bingo! There it was.

As soon as she left the room, he wheeled himself to me. He was quiet, in shock, and clearly mind-blown by the session. It took him a while to speak as he was still processing, but said it was one of the most powerful healing experiences of his life.

"Bebe, there was no guardian for the guardian. That's me."

His voice trailed off as he looked down, and I watched a tear slowly trickle down, landing on his chest.

"My love," I said back, reaching for his hand, "I'm so sorry there was no guardian for my guardian."

We left shortly after for his radiation treatment. Since Eric was still feeling nauseous, he was very quiet, and the driver gave him a sickness bag, just in case. Thankfully, he perked up after the third session was over and realized his last couple treatments would be pain-free. I was excited to listen to him chatting to our driver the whole way back from Tijuana to the health center.

The first of his next two treatments was regional hyperthermia, which had become such a walk in the park he read his book during the session. The second was a relaxing reflexology appointment, and he began to attribute this as a major factor in the significant improvement of the neuropathy in his feet and ankles—a huge development.

While Eric was in treatment, I looked for Cerise and found her sitting on a flax bush by the pool on a long leaf blowing madly in the high winds. Her feathers were ruffling, but amazingly she sat quite still on the wildly waving leaf. It seemed she looked at and through me and after a couple of minutes flew off. I wondered if the lesson in that was to remain calm, even when everything around you is in chaos.

Over a dinner of quinoa vegetable burgers, sweet potato baked fries, and salad, we chatted with a couple who had arrived a few days earlier. It was their fourth trip, and they were one of the first groups when the facility opened. Back then, the food was all raw—a tough diet if you haven't eased into it over time. The couple were both there for dental treatments, the wife opting to have her top row of teeth removed, and the husband having all his mercury amalgam fillings removed and replaced with ceramic porcelain ones.

We immersed ourselves in the educational session later that night on forgiveness, which focused on the premise that it's an integral part of the healing journey to learn to forgive oneself and others for all real and perceived hurts. The session was beautifully delivered and my key takeaway: "Forgiveness is releasing all hope for a better past."

Facebook Post—November 2, 2016

I asked Eric today what his highlight at Sanoviv has been so far. His answer was simple, yet profound, "I'm excited to have found a path to life." I love that! He has found a way to live! I'm so happy for him, and delighted for me, for his daughters, and all those whose lives he has touched so significantly.

— 12 —

The Oxygen, the Heat, and the Burn Are a Breeze

I walked by the Hibiscus Hedge as much as possible and caught myself feeling a little disappointed when Cerise wasn't there. It was a reminder to allow those special moments in life to catch us by surprise, because where there's attachment to a specific outcome, there can be pain and disappointment.

It was "Liquid Thursday," and due to Eric's special dispensation to have more substantial food to keep his weight up, the kitchen staff asked him what he'd like for breakfast. He tucked into his custom-ordered scrambled eggs with onions, tomatoes, and mushrooms, and I had two scrambled eggs and a lime, avocado, and raw date smoothie.

I went to work in our second bedroom, and Eric wheeled himself to his whole-body hyperthermia session, where they turned up the heat to 107°F. I peeked in on him in the final cool-down phase, and he looked adorable, all covered in the blue tent-like contraption with his face poking out.

Dr. Kind came to visit us as we were relaxing outside in the sun. He sat in front of Eric, took my beloved's hands in his, and asked how he was feeling. I observed that he constantly explored ways to tweak Eric's treatment plan with the goal to heal him fully and completely. This was in stark contrast to discussions with Eric's doctors in the U.S., where they rarely touch their patients, and because the focus is on symptom-management, it's all a bit hit or miss as to whether any healing actually takes place.

Eric told the doctor that his radiation treatments had become pain-free and that he could stand without support for short periods. Dr. Kind was happy with Eric's progress, particularly that he was able to sleep on his right side, something he hadn't been able to do for several months.

The big personal news for Eric was that his brother and sister were coming from Germany to see him the following week. The three siblings hadn't seen each other in ten years and were looking forward to a sweet reunion. Sadly, I wouldn't be in Mexico for their arrival, as I needed to go back to chilly Seattle for work.

The hyperbaric oxygen chamber, the hyperthermia treatments, and the radiation were all a breeze for Eric that day, and he visualized that he was making good headway with the tumors.

We had some time before dinner, so I wheeled my love to the clifftop in front of the mansion. I leaned forward, slipped my arms around his chest, and we watched in awe as the sky turned every imaginable shade of yellow, gold, and orange.

Dinner was a delicious fish soup, and I delighted in watching my Bebe devour mouthful after mouthful.

Since the evening educational lecture was a repeat from the week before, we played Foo in our room instead. We had one final hand from our last game, and with lady luck on my side, I was ahead. Eric was determined to have another complete game to see if he could turn the tables on his luck. When my guy was determined to see something through, he saw it through.

I loved that about him. He never gave up.

Facebook Post—November 3, 2016

Another fantastic day. Eric is feeling so much better in his time here! He has turned himself around from almost certain death to choosing life. He joked today that he might even get more addicted to healthy living than me, and I laughed and said, 'Bring it on Bebe, bring it on!'

— 13 —

Meeting Like-Minded Souls
and Reading by the Pool

I wheeled Eric in for his early vitals and IV drips. The nursing staff really liked him, and I noticed they started calling him, "My Eric." If I had to guess, I would say it was because he enjoyed engaging and listening to stories about their lives, families, and passions.

I shared breakfast with a sweet thirty-three year old woman from Canada whose mom was with her as her companion. I bit into a delicious crepe wrapped around soft-cooked vegetables and eggs, with avocado on the side, and listened intently to their stories. The conversation took a shocking turn as the daughter shared that she discovered a lump in her breast seven years earlier. The doctor assured her repeatedly she was too young to get breast cancer and insisted it was just a cyst—nothing to worry about. Eventually, still concerned, she switched doctors and bam, stage-three metastasized breast cancer.

The only option they gave her was the traditional chemotherapy route, and she was simply not willing to put her trust in the same medical system that misdiagnosed her in the first place. Unwilling to allow them to poison her body with chemo drugs, she and her mother researched other treatments, and they had high hopes for the options presented at Sanoviv.

We talked about how important it is to take your health into your own hands and to be your own advocate, standing up for what you feel is right. If you don't like what one professional says, go to another.

Eric and I took our mahi mahi and salad lunch to-go on our final radiation run into Tijuana. It was a breeze, and he was glad to be done with the treatments.

As my guy was having a regional hyperthermia session, I finished my work and laid by the pool. The sun was going down, and as the temperature cooled, I slipped into the hot tub with my book.

I felt grateful to have been with Eric for these two weeks and had been amazed that appointments on my work schedule had miraculously canceled or disappeared. I reflected that cancer can be a lonely journey. It's important to have your head in the right place, to truly believe and have faith that you can sur-thrive. It helps enormously if you have your person and your tribe within easy reach. We were in our own world, surrounded by like-minded people in a healing community bubble of love. I was due to leave in a couple days, but exchanged email addresses with many of the others, promising to stay in contact and to share our successes and new treatment discoveries.

We had a common bond. A bond of the cancer club, but with a twist—a deep desire to explore ways to truly heal with customized, personalized, and alternative treatments.

Facebook Post—November 4, 2016

I am so proud of my beloved's progress. He's looking good, with better color and clear eyes. He's looking more like the strong Leo he is, and less like a man who, for a moment, believed the onco-doc when she said he had only six weeks before his bright light was gone.

— 14 —

Eric Begins the Anti-Cancer, Anti-Tumor, Anti-Inflammation Curcumin IV Drip

Two weeks in, Eric told me he wasn't feeling well. We didn't know why; it was just an underlying nausea, and something to bring up with Dr. Kind at his next session. This is one of the issues with the cancer journey. There's so much that is unknown, so many inexplicable aches and pains. We had been hoping he'd constantly feel great at Sanoviv—all the way to good health.

The day came for him to start the bright yellow anti-cancer, anti-tumor, anti-inflammation curcumin IV drip. I sat with him for a while, holding hands and being quiet. I was sad to be leaving the next day, and I knew we would miss each other terribly.

I left him snoozing in the IV chair and went to the spa to heat up the infrared sauna for a detox. I had read up on the many benefits, like detoxing, reducing inflammation, improving blood flow, and boosting the immune system. Since it would take a while to heat up to 130-140°F, I wandered around to the Hibiscus Hedge to say goodbye to my little hummingbird friend. I videoed her sitting still, peeking through the leaves and branches, perhaps sensing my sadness.

I stayed in the sauna for the recommended twelve minutes, showered right after, and dunked fully in the cold-plunge pool. It was so invigorating to go from the heat to the freezing cold, and I felt truly alive.

I looked for Eric and found him resting in the room, having given up on his two sessions. I felt like I could lie down too, and I read and slept for a few hours alongside my guy.

When we woke up, I wheeled Eric down to the pools, and we cuddled and chatted about fun memories of him visiting his two half brothers and sister in Germany in the summers as a teen. They shared the same dad, and Eric had been raised in California with his mom, and his siblings were raised in Germany, with theirs.

Back in the room, I read him the Facebook post I wrote earlier in the day, got the stamp of approval, and pressed submit on the post. In Eric's own words, this past year highlighted terrible medical stumbling and guesswork, and I had full approval to post his daily updates to help share ideas about alternatives to the traditional route.

Facebook Post—November 5, 2016

Eric is ecstatic that the system here in Mexico, 'just makes sense.' He is super grateful that he has the opportunity to heal his damaged and chemo-ravaged body, and is doing just that.

— 15 —

Phillipa Says Goodbye and Heads Back to Seattle

Daylight savings ended the next day, and we snuggled in bed for the extra hour, knowing we wouldn't see each other for a wee while.

I wheeled my Bebe down to the Hibiscus Hedge to say goodbye to Cerise, and the little rascal was nowhere to be seen. I asked Eric to please visit the hedge each day to look for her. I figured it would also give him an excuse to exercise.

Although he was in good spirits and made huge progress in the last two weeks, we had really leaned on each other for moral support. It helped me to know he was surrounded by people who loved and cared for him, and they assured me they would seek him out and keep an eye on him.

I wheeled him out to the van, and when I bent down for a hug, he stood his wobbly self up for a full body connection. I couldn't stop my tears as we hugged and kissed goodbye.

As the van pulled away, I prayed that we had more time and that there were many more chapters yet to come in the Phillipa and Eric love story.

I traveled to the San Diego airport with Maria, a lovely woman who had been diagnosed with breast cancer. A recent mammogram hadn't picked up anything amiss, and she had found the lump herself. She went straight back to the doctor, and it was, indeed, early-stage breast cancer. She had the lump surgically removed and opted to forgo chemo and radiation. She shared something shocking with me: her oncologist told her outright, "It is my job to TALK YOU INTO chemotherapy and/or radiation."

Good grief!

Seriously?

Why and what the fuck?

Shortly after her surgery, and running as fast as she could from her oncologist, Maria came to Mexico to learn about other treatments and to ensure her cancer did not proliferate. Interestingly, she didn't share with her family *why* she was in Mexico, as she knew they would not support her exploring alternative options. She and I hugged goodbye at the airport and agreed to stay in touch.

I was at my gate at the airport before I finally reached Eric on my cell. I wanted to hear all about his day, and let him talk until I was the last person to board the plane. I sent him kisses over the phone and wished him a deep and dreamy sleep.

I couldn't stem the flow and ugly-cried as the plane was taking off. The dear woman next to me, a complete stranger, reached out to hold my hand. No questions asked and no words necessary.

> ### *Facebook Post—November 6, 2016*
>
> Maria and I traveled to the airport together, and like birds of a feather, we talked the whole way. We agreed we are not all made the same, and cancer cannot be treated effectively if we are only numbers, not individuals, and forced into standard protocols and chemo cocktails. One size simply does not fit all.

— 16 —

Karen and Henrik Visit Eric in Mexico from Germany

I reached out for him in our bed the next morning, forgetting for a moment my beloved was still in Mexico.

Later, I received two texted photos from our friend Karla who had just arrived at Sanoviv for her annual check-up. Both pictures showed Eric with his walker and without his wheelchair. She was so excited when she saw him walk into the breakfast room, she cried happy tears and jumped up to hug him.

It was a miracle that after so much pain and bone degradation he was able to walk a little. It was an exciting development, and I got a text from Eric shortly after, "Look Bebe! I'm walking!"

Something magical happened later in the morning, and I squealed aloud in delight. I returned from a run in the cool rain and was stretching on the porch by our front door when a tiny hummingbird came to visit. It was a quick encounter. She hovered several inches from my face for about five seconds, and then flew off.

I finally reached my guy on the phone after dinner.

"Guess what, Bebe?" he said. "I found out that Microsoft will be covering at least some of the medical bills! I've been bugging them every day, and I need to stay on top of it all, but it's looking positive that at least the initial assessment will be covered."

"Oh my God, that's great news! I know how hard you've been working on that," I replied.

"I'm going to soak in the hot pool soon with Karen and Henrik. It's so funny…there was a two-to-three hour stretch when I was in treatment, and I imagined they were relaxing by the pool, but they'd fallen asleep in their room and didn't wake up for hours with jet lag! I love you, Bebe. Talk to you tomorrow!"

"I love you back! Go have fun with your sibs. Talk tomorrow!"

I hung up and the tears came. I cried because I missed my beloved. I cried because I felt so bad I wasn't there with him, even though his siblings were loving him. I cried because the friggin' Microsoft insurance people were dodging answering Eric's questions on which treatments were covered, and why should he have to bug them every day anyway, when he's trying to get the help he needs to save his own life? I cried because of the whole fucking unfairness of it all.

I eventually crawled onto his side of the bed, curling into a wee ball. Just as I was starting to slip away into dream time, two things occurred to me. First, I was so happy Eric's brother and sister were there with him. Second, I wondered if this would be the last time they ever saw him.

Facebook Post—November 9, 2016

My guy is down to 163 pounds. He's been losing and gaining all year (mostly losing), depending on his treatments and surgery recovery time. Dr. Kind wasn't too worried when I spoke to him today, as he believes Eric is just detoxing. But, the million-dollar question remains, 'Are we too late?'

Eric and me on a dolphin swim off the Kona coast, May 2010.

Eric and me, the night we were engaged, April 20, 2010.

Eric and Bella playing and laughing, May 2009.

*Eric and Bella playing in the pool, Waikoloa
Beach Resort, May 2009.*

Eric, Bella, and me on our wedding day,
Tauranga, New Zealand, July 24, 2010.

*Our wedding day, July 24, 2010 - Eric supporting me
as we walked, just as I would later support him.*

Newlyweds!

My favorite wedding photo: the deep dip during our Nightclub Two-Step choreographed dance.

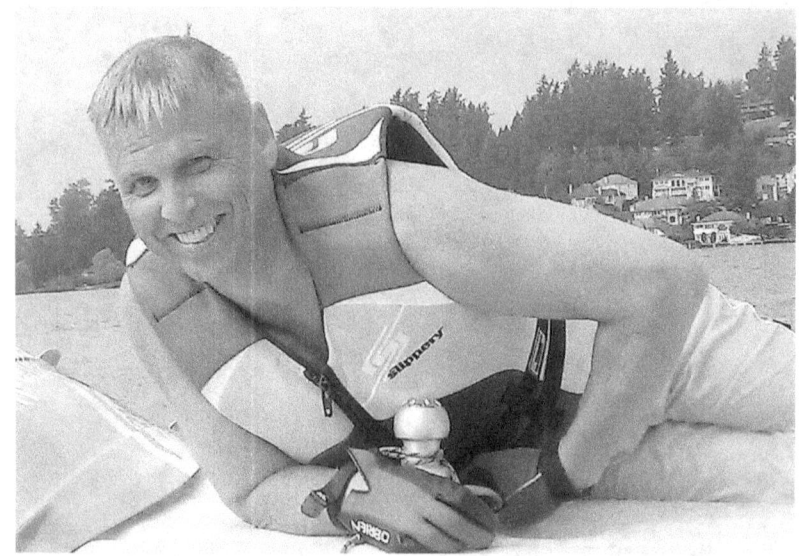

Eric sliding into the boat, post-wakeboarding, July 2014.

Eric and me in Las Vegas, August 2015,
celebrating Eric's 54th birthday.

Eric, Bella, and me at the Juanita Beach Park, September 2014.

Following Bella's direction to make duck lips, just before Eric shaved his head, April 2016.

Eric and me soaking in the hot tub at Sanoviv,
Rosarita, Mexico, November 2016.

Eric sent me a selfie looking like he belongs in the
cast of Breaking Bad, November 2016.

Andi and Bea visited Eric at Sanoviv, December 2016.

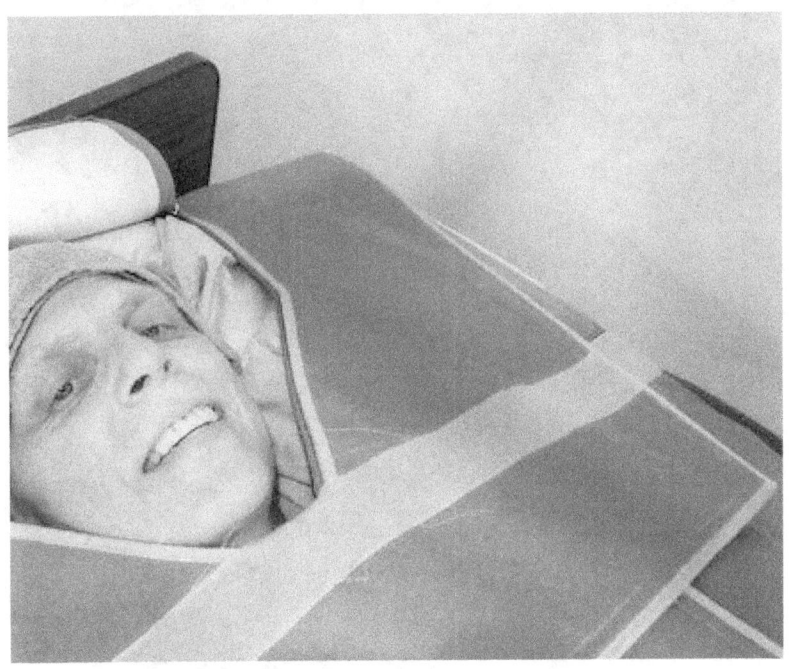

*Eric peeking out from a session of full body
hyperthermia at Sanoviv, November 2016.*

*Me, saying goodbye to Eric as I left Sanoviv to go
back to Seattle for work, November 2016.*

My favorite from the Soulumination photo shoot, December 2016.

*Bea and I visited Eric in the Seattle hospital on
Superbowl Sunday, February 5, 2017.*

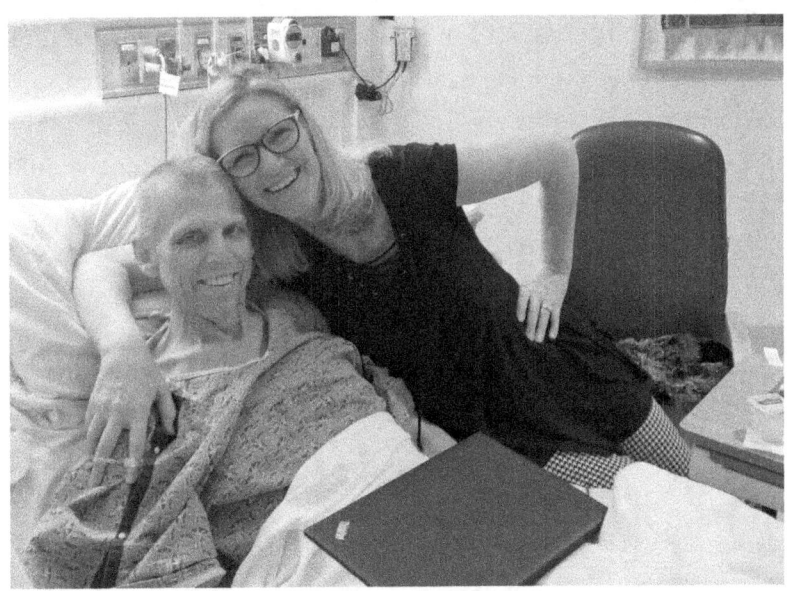

Hugging Eric in the Seattle hospital, February 2017.

— 17 —

Eric Goes Grass Walking and Seeds an Idea

I laughed out loud when I read Eric's text the next day.

"This morning I didn't do a 5km run like you but took my walker downstairs, made it to the grass, and went barefoot. I guess I'm officially now a 'grass walker'! Running off to the whole-body Sahara heat torture coffin now. All in the spirit of getting better! Last night I discovered that a super-hot shower works for my knee pain. Tonight, we will do the pools again in the late evening."

In a later text: "I thought your hummingbird left with you, and only butterflies were hanging in the hedge. But, on my way back from the pool, I saw her for thirty seconds in the bush. Yay, Bebe! I saw your wee hummingbird!"

"Yay!" I texted back, "I'm so happy you saw Cerise. Thank you for looking!"

Our friend Karla, still in Sanoviv, reported that she and Eric talked for hours about big data and the good old days at Microsoft. She said he looked bright and envisioned big plans to help the cancer industry utilizing his technical background and newfound knowledge of complementary/alternative treatments.

Back in Seattle, I was in my happy place, sitting next to my girl watching a favorite Barbie movie from her childhood, *Mermadia*. I liked knowing that Eric was enjoying time with Karla and his siblings, with his dry sense of humor still intact.

Facebook Post—November 10, 2016

I loved that Eric turned around his whole belief system in a matter of days. Nothing like being told you only have six weeks to live to change your mind and viewpoint. I'm so proud of him. He is doing it - he's finding a path to life!

— 18 —

Karen and Henrik Visit Seattle

On the morning of their last day together, Eric, Karen and Henrik relaxed by the mansion, sipping their tea. They enjoyed watching the surfers directly out from the cliff at the well-known surf spot below, nicknamed K38. The German contingent commented that the surf was so huge and scary-looking, they were happy to be observing from a safe distance.

Eric had taught them how to play Foo, and they forgot about the surfers for a while and played their last game. Apparently, Karen was the card shark of the trio and won both games, with Eric in the rear each time.

A brown hummingbird came to visit the Leseberg siblings, and they took that as a sweet send off for Karen and Henrik.

Eric told me that he kept one afternoon session but canceled the other, preferring to spend the two hours with his brother and sister before they left that afternoon. They were coming to stay with Bella and me in Seattle for a few days before heading back to Hamburg.

I was excited to meet them, although it meant Eric was on his own—for now.

A few friends offered to be Eric's companion, but he didn't think it was necessary, as he had the facility and routine down by then. He also liked being independent, zooming around on his wheelchair or hobbling along with his walker.

Facebook Post—November 12, 2016

It's late at night here, and I picked up Karen and Henrik at the airport. We've had a good chat, a snack, and it's time for bed! Goodnight, good afternoon, and good morning to you, wherever you may be. It's great knowing that we have friends keeping up with our journey from all over the world...U.S.A, Canada, Mexico, New Zealand, Australia, England, Sweden, Spain, Hong Kong, Germany, Thailand, and Indonesia! Did I forget anyone?

— 19 —

Eric Slows Down and Has Lessons on Staying Present

E ric told me that while he sat on the clifftop and closed his eyes, he took a moment to just be. He realized that in the frenzy of the Mexican part of his journey—with the pain, nausea, scheduling and rescheduling appointments, calls to the medical insurance company, and trips to Tijuana for radiation—he had not taken many moments to sit quietly and be present.

He had opened his eyes and sat watching the families playing and collecting shellfish in the sand and tide pools on the beach below. With the full moon and ultra-low tide, the surfers were nowhere to be seen, and he picked up on a whole different energy on the beach...family energy.

Later, Eric shared with me another special moment in his day. It was a beautiful sunny day, the temperature in the eighties, and he couldn't resist getting out of his wheelchair to relax on the green grass by the track.

He told me a woman had seen the empty wheelchair and his body on the ground, and rushed over to see whether he needed help. It was sweet of her, and they had a good chuckle when she realized that he was doing fine. In fact, better than fine, he was having one of the highlights of his day.

Sadly, on my beloved's cancer journey, as happy as he was to stay present and enjoy the highs, he still had to contend with the lows. The pain in his lower back and knees had become excruciating.

My heart broke when he shared his tough times with me because I knew if I had been there with him, I might have been able to help in some small way. Perhaps by rubbing his back with essential oils, maybe peppermint, or lavender, or jumping into bed with him to hug and hold him until the pain passed or the pain meds kicked in.

Back home in Seattle, Bella and I enjoyed spending time with Eric's family. We talked about renting a big house on the coast of Spain in the summer to accommodate both the American and German Leseberg contingents. I told Eric about this, and he loved the idea. We all agreed it would be something to look forward to.

Facebook Post—November 13, 2016

Today, the highlights of Eric's day came from two simple experiences. Sitting on the clifftop watching families interacting and gathering shellfish, and lying prone on the grass, in the sun. Maybe it's in the slowing down, consciously breathing, or laughing in the moment and being present, that healing can truly occur.

— 20 —

Eric Gets More Clarity on the Next Phase of His Life's Purpose

E ric had two pieces of exciting news to share the next day.
First, he had transitioned fully from the poison of the *agent orange* to the healing power of the *liquid gold*. He spent six successful hours in the IV room with the gold concoction from one of the most powerful healing plants in the world, curcumin.

Second, although it had been coming in for a few weeks in bits and flashes, he said he had more clarity on his life purpose. It was all about merging technology with people healing naturally.

My guy was a deep thinker and enjoyed his solitude so he could intuit how his new ideas might come to fruition. When he told me Dr. Kind wanted to eventually increase his turmeric IVs to nine hours per day, I figured that should give him plenty of time to think his new ideas into reality.

I told Eric our fun news. Driving away from eating breakfast out that morning, Bella and I spied a glowing neon sign, "Psychic Open. Come on in!" So, we went in.

One of the first three cards the psychic pulled was the death card, and my breath caught for a second. However, amongst other things, she said the card indicates intense change and new beginnings. It signifies a time of deep transformation, likely to be both inner and outward in life. Situations and scenarios will never be quite the same as they once were.

She saw that my beloved's time was not up yet (it's also not appropriate for intuitive practitioners to comment on the timing for one's death they may or may not see), and that he was not finished doing what he came here to do. He had a very powerful mission and was only just opening up to that. That would be his legacy.

Eric liked hearing what the intuitive said about legacy. It tied in beautifully with his eagerness to move through his current healing phase and be able to help others achieve their path to a healthy life, naturally.

Eric updated me on his doctor appointment that day. As always, rather than rushing to prescribe drugs for Eric and get him out of his office so he could see more patients, Dr. Kind took the time to be fully present, to listen and to treat my guy as a "whole" person. Case in point, he had an idea about what might be causing Eric's nerve issue, and he took the time to speak to his colleagues about it. If they were right, and an out-of-whack hormone was the culprit, then it could potentially be treated with homeopathic remedies.

In my mind, Eric didn't need more drugs, especially unnecessary ones.

Facebook Post—November 14, 2016

Bella and I saw a psychic today! She told us Eric was a brilliant and rare being, as old as time. Thank you all for your comments, yet again. They inspire me to keep writing and Eric enjoys it when I read the posts aloud, like bedtime stories of his daily happenings. As our friend Hilda in the UK said in one of her recent Facebook comments, 'I think he's going to make it!' We think so too, Hilda!

— 21 —

The Power of Lymph Drainage and a Two-Prong Fork with Little Balls

A typical day of treatments in the life of Eric at Sanoviv included a hyperbaric chamber session, regional hyperthermia, body code, psychology, a Quiet Room session, a two-hour IV treatment, and a doctor check-in.

The first of the Quiet Room sessions was lymph drainage, designed to help process and remove waste toxins. The other was with a large two-prong fork with little balls on the end, and the practitioner ran it up and down Eric's back. He said he could feel the electrical impulses as they were weaving their energetic magic.

But by 7:30 p.m. that night, Eric was in pain and already in bed. He agreed with the doctor to stay on the homeopathic medicine for two more days before he gave into Oxycodone.

Eric didn't know it at the time, but he was hooked on the "oxys." I was concerned and researched the opioid crisis in the U.S. Apparently, it doesn't take long for the brain's chemistry to change and for the drug to wrap its arms around the brain's receptors, creating a powerful addiction. It was a miracle he had been able to survive the previous three weeks essentially detoxing from the oxys, before the pain became unbearable. He made a deal with Dr. Kind—two more days.

That day, I had some time between meetings, and my mind wandered. I wondered why our special people on the cancer journey are routinely given liquid poison, radiation, and/or surgery? By this time, my husband had experienced all three, and they almost killed him. Being given a death sentence from his oncologist opened him up to seeing that another path is possible. The path of alternative/advanced therapies where organic food, oxygen, heat, botanicals, emotional clearing, meditation, and getting your head in line with your heart can tip the balance towards good health. Perhaps it's as easy as choosing love and life, over fear and death.

I felt incredibly sad that my husband went through nine months of nightmarish treatments, only to find that there are alternative treatments and cures for cancer already out there and readily available, and there had been all along.

I learned that many medical doctors are breaking the rules if they treat with anything other than pharmaceuticals. At times, any particular medical or naturopathic doctor treating with special diets, good nutrition, energy and biofeedback machines, and botanicals can be persecuted, ridiculed, run out of the country, and worse. There's also plenty of material to read about the big pharma companies and how they know about the healing power of botanicals. After all, they have to study them in order to copy, reproduce, and patent them.

My inner activist could go crazy, and I was grateful for the massive amount of material available online and in books and documentaries. Anyone can research big pharma, companies that support GMOs, pesticides, and the demise of bee populations, natural seeds, water sources, and a healthy food chain worldwide.

I don't believe that one needs to focus on doom and gloom, but knowledge is power…especially when it comes to managing the health of our own bodies.

Facebook Post—November 15, 2016

I am glad Eric is willing to face some of the hard truths. It's easy to assume that they couldn't possibly be suppressing life-saving information, and that they surely would only give us the best of the medical advancements available to mankind today. Alas, that is not necessarily the case, and it's up to each of us to do our own research, take care of our bodies, be our own advocate, and potentially save our own lives.

— 22 —

Healthy-Looking Blood Cells and Eric Has His First Facial

There were some signs his health was heading in the right direction. Upon arrival at Sanoviv, a blood test showed Eric's red blood cells were misshapen, clumped and stuck together, and you could clearly see a clear ring of heavy metals around the edge of each cell. Now, weeks later, the technician ran the blood test again and displayed the image from the microscope on a large monitor for Eric to see. He was shocked to witness how much the cells had changed in shape and pattern in a little over three weeks.

"Bebe, you could see my individual cells are rounder, more free-flowing and the ring of heavy metals was almost gone! It was really cool. I wish you could have seen how much healthier my cells look," he said when we talked, super excited.

I responded, "That's amazing! I remember that first time looking at your cells."

He added, "Oh, I almost forgot. I had a facial today! The woman said that my skin looked pretty good, and she couldn't believe I don't use skincare. She said she only had to 'dig in' around my nose, and I guess that's pretty good after fifty-five years of no facials, right?"

"Haha, it's true. You are such a high achiever!"

When I hung up, I continued researching how we might duplicate more of the treatments locally in preparation for his return home. One of my naturopaths confirmed they could accommodate the high dose Vitamin C, regional hyperthermia, colon hydrotherapy, and lymph drainage and massage. Fortunately, her holistic center was close to our home, and they also have an organic, gluten and dairy free café, in addition to a dispensary for the natural healing remedies offered by the practitioners. They didn't currently offer curcumin IV drips, and I asked them to research obtaining the good stuff.

I also found a hyperbaric chamber in Redmond, thirty minutes away from where we lived and five minutes from the Microsoft campus, once Eric went back to work.

Even though some of the treatments were available in Washington, it was a stark reminder that one of the biggest benefits of Sanoviv was that everything was under one roof. No matter what sessions Eric had on any given day, each was only a walker or wheelchair ride away from the next. It takes a lot of energy and effort to schedule appointments and get transportation to and from them all, let alone the cost of the treatments in the U.S. at three to four times the Mexican pricing and most not covered by insurance. I wondered if we might need a full-time driver to manage scheduling and transporting Eric to and from appointments once he came home, since I was still juggling my full-time Microsoft job and part-time real estate.

In my perfect world, there would be clinics like Sanoviv everywhere. Imagine if they were cost effective and/or paid for by our insurance or taxes? I enjoyed visualizing a world where the doctors listened and learned all about us holistically, determined to get to the source of our issues, and not just treat the symptoms. And if only they didn't prescribe drugs *willy nilly* for surface symptoms. I know it sounds like an impossible pipedream, at least in the U.S., but picture if they were knowledgeable about nutrition and recommended healthy food and supplements. What a concept!

Facebook Post—November 16, 2016

We have options to replicate some of Eric's alternative treatments back home in Seattle. They are somewhat close by, albeit significantly more expensive than Sanoviv's out-of-pocket pricing, and mostly not covered by our insurance. But we'll be able to keep the progress going, so all is not lost.

— 23 —

Unfinished Business

As I arrived home the following evening, I heard my cell phone vibrate and saw it was from my beloved, the celebrity of my daily musings of a life-after-a-terminal-prognosis.

We engaged in a lovely, long conversation, and I was excited to hear so much enthusiasm from him. In fact, he had so much to share I couldn't get a word in edgewise. He talked more about his vision for helping the world with natural health, technology, and data.

He was so excited to feel like he finally had something to say, and hoped this would help him get over his deep-seated fear of speaking publicly, by telling his story and sharing his dream.

In true Eric form, he sent me an email with links he'd set up to a new OneDrive location, so we could share information and pictures in the cloud. Seriously, who is so organized they set up a OneDrive on the same day they have a conversation with the psychologist about whether they were ready to die?

Naturally I was curious what his response was when the psychologist did, in fact, ask, "Are you ready to die?"

Eric reiterated to Dr. Heart that he had lived a full life, and he was ready for himself. He also felt comfortable that I would be fine, and that although I would miss him and our deep heart connection, he knew I would work through the pain and eventually move on to live a full, healthy life.

The two people he still had unfinished business with, however, were his two daughters. He loved being a dad and a coach in their lives, helping them through their tougher moments. He wanted to be around for their big milestones…to walk them down the aisle or barefoot along the beach. Hearing this made me tear up, as I imagined what that would be like, not having him there.

Later, I thought more about our conversation. Death is such a taboo subject in our culture. In general, we don't talk about it, imagine it, or dwell on it. I explored letting go of the attachment to a certain outcome and holding on to the only valid and acceptable option—Eric "sur-thriving."

I'm not saying that if my beloved didn't make it I would be *hunky dory*, but it wouldn't be such a shock, knowing what was in each other's heart and mind all the way to the end.

Facebook Post—November 18, 2016
Eric is tickled pink to be the central character in my daily musings. Although it's a kind of life and death scenario, he is so proud of me for allowing my writing to take shape and is already imagining a successful book coming to fruition.

— 24 —

Eric Makes Progress and Phillipa
Prepares to Return to Mexico

The previous night, Eric couldn't sleep. So in the wee hours of the morning he wheeled himself down to the pool area. He managed to get into the hot tub, then the medium temp pool, but getting into the plunge pool he lost his footing on the slippery surface. He landed on his bad hip, slipped into the pool, and shouted very loudly, "Fuuuuuuuuuck!"

I couldn't help it. I laughed out loud when he told me—not at him for hurting himself, but that Eric was cruising around in his wheelchair, helping himself to the pools as everyone else was in bed, sound asleep.

He said that his Sanoviv buddies were noticing that the whites of his eyes were sharper and brighter, compared to a few weeks previous.

I researched why that was and read that fruits and vegetables like carrots, dark leafy greens, apricots, mangos, papayas, oranges, lemons, and pumpkins are rich in the vitamins and antioxidants for healthy eyes. Cutting out alcohol, caffeine, and refined sugars also detoxifies the liver, helping the eyes get whiter.

Karen focused on the source of Eric's continued back pain at his next body code session. She picked up that he had inherited it from his grandfather on his father's side, who had suffered with chronic back pain from an old injury. She helped him clear that energy out of his back, and when I spoke with him later in the day, he said, "Although it might be too early to tell, I've been back-pain free ever since! So far, so good!"

He had an ultrasound treatment on the quarter-inch lump above his knee. As the weekend wore on, Eric noticed it was getting more painful when pressed, and the doctor ultimately decided to schedule a time to remove it and send it to the lab for further analysis.

Eric had requested I go to his former oncologist's office in Seattle to pick up his oxy prescription. Walking in, I noticed the difference in the energy of the place, and I felt a bit sick to my stomach. No one inquired as to how Eric was doing, and they treated me coolly. I looked at the patients sitting around without their hair and their dignity, with their wigs and scarves, and possibly on the track to nowhere fast. I wanted to grab them all up in my arms and march them out of there to somewhere far away, where miracles with health and healing happen every day.

As I was driving away, I got a call from a colleague of one of my girlfriends, following my daily Facebook posts. She wanted to learn about alternative options for two family members, both diagnosed with cancer. She had researched like crazy on behalf of her family members but still hadn't found the right formula for either one. One was given a year to live, and the other was stable and controlling their cancer with a macrobiotic diet. She listened to everything I shared and took notes of my experiences.

Although I was happy to help where I could, I felt sad that so many of us struggle to navigate the system to find anything that isn't just from the traditional menu of treatments. I was astonished with the number of people reaching out to me as if I was some sort of expert. I simply saw myself as a woman whose husband experienced the dark side of the traditional cancer machine and discovered over time many of the wonderful alternatives available. What do I know? Well…a lot, it seems.

I was excited to be heading back to Mexico the following day. I was beyond thrilled to see Eric, the wonderful staff, and of course, my little hummingbird friend in the Hibiscus Hedge. Mostly, I couldn't wait to see how my Bebe was progressing.

Facebook Post—November 21, 2016

Still reeling from the cold shoulder I got at my visit to Eric's previous oncologist's office. It was as if they thought, 'How dare you do not believe our prognosis! How dare you take control of your own cancer care.' There was no, "Hey, how is Eric? How's it going down there?" It makes me feel even more excited to be heading back to the open arms of the incredible and dedicated staff at Sanoviv!

— 25 —

Absence Makes the Heart Grow Fonder

I had Eric's wheelchair with me, and a nice man in security at SeaTac International Airport pointed me to a shorter line. They did, however, perform a very thorough search of the wheelchair. Who knew there were so many hiding places on a wheelchair for unsavory items?

After arriving at Sanoviv, I went straight up to the room to see my precious man, and there he was…standing with a grin from ear to ear. Yes, standing!

I rushed to him for one of our full-body hugs, and I breathed in the smell of him I loved so much. I stepped back, still holding on to his shoulders, and it struck me how much he had improved in the two weeks since I last saw him.

As we say down-under, I said, "You look bloody good!"

We went straight down to the dining room, where a plate of mahi mahi, cooked vegetables, and pickled red cabbage had been set aside for me. Eric had already eaten and enjoyed watching me as I dug in. He knew how much I loved the food there.

After eating, we changed into our swimsuits and went to the spa pool for a dip. We met two single women and had some great conversations around all sorts of alternative therapies. One of the women was quite well-versed in other clinics in the U.S. and Mexico offering alternative treatments, like LifeWorks in Florida, the Cancer Center for Healing in California, Envita Medical Center in Arizona, and The Center for Advanced Medicine in Missouri. In Mexico, there are the Gerson, Hope4Cancer, Immunity Therapy Center and the Oasis of Hope centers.

Back in the room, we snuggled and talked in Eric's bed until we started feeling sleepy. That night, we both slept deeply, happy to be together again.

Facebook Post—November 22, 2016

Made it safely to Sanoviv and was so excited to see my guy with my own eyes. He's looking really good...more 'alive'! Loved meeting more guests at the pool tonight. We appreciated making new connections and talked and talked until late, grateful for the instant connection with like-minded souls.

— 26 —

Phillipa Wonders "What If…"

E ric was in surgery to have his lump removed, and I sat on the balcony gazing out over the ocean, taking a moment to do a reality check.

We knew Eric wasn't out of the woods yet. His doctor echoed there was still a long way to go to get him back to good health, as significant damage had been done from the systemic and local chemos that ravaged his body earlier in the year.

I knew we couldn't turn back time, but I did wonder how we might have handled his treatment differently. Perhaps we may still have agreed to the first three months of chemo, as Eric was in very bad shape when he first presented at the ER.

But if we could do it over, after the first session of chemo killed off some of the cancer cells, I might have brought my beloved to Mexico at that point. Or perhaps if we had even come down at the six-month milestone, when we saw the docs scratching their heads and wondering what to do next, it might have been a better outcome.

Who really knew? No one did. But I did wonder.

I poked my head in from time to time to check on Eric, post-surgery, and he was completely out of it. The surgeon only used light sedation, so I figured he needed the rest.

When he came to, he enjoyed a slow day, a sort of mini vacation from his intense treatments.

We chatted with a couple about to go back home. They shared with us that one of their naturopathic doctors had eventually given up and left the profession altogether. She was so sick of getting hassled at every turn, she couldn't take it anymore. Shockingly, their second naturopathic doctor was threatened by men wearing black and was told he had to destroy his biofeedback machine. That made me sad. And mad.

The couple said that the American Medical Association and the FDA have a term for anyone who offers anything outside of approved protocols, drugs and the pharmaceutical range of products and services. They label them "quacks," and can warn and/or arrest them for performing "quackery." I scratched my head and wondered what century we were in.

Facebook Post—November 24, 2016

I overheard Eric telling Andi how awesome this place is and how amazing the energy is. 'You have to come here to see and experience how wonderful it is. There are no words. I'm changing my diet, and I'm never going back.' It looks like he's realized that simply by changing his diet, and adding in some alternative treatments, he could save his own life.

— 27 —

Eric Is Told to Stay Present and Focus on the Moments of Joy

I reached over and grabbed my beloved's hand. We had pushed our pool chairs together while waiting for the doctor to visit. Tendrils of hair kept blowing in my face, and Eric joked that at least he didn't have to worry about his hair getting in his eyes, as he had long since lost his.

We were chuckling when Dr. Kind showed up.

He had news, and it wasn't what we wanted to hear. The surgeon had taken a peek under the microscope at the lymph node surgically removed from Eric's leg, and it looked cancerous. To be sure, we'd need to wait for the official results in another few days.

"Okaaaay. But what does that mean?" Eric asked.

"We need to step up the treatments. Rather than doing two grams twice per week of the curcumin IV drip over six hours, we'll need to bump it up to three grams over nine hours...every day."

Eric and I looked at each other with wide eyes.

He pulled his chair closer to Eric, looked him in the eye and said, "And I am going to ask you to focus on all the moments of joy."

He looked at me and back to Eric, "For example, really enjoy Phillipa while she's here. Stay in the present moment. We know you are a deep thinker and that when you experience a new pain, you wonder whether the cancer has spread. Remember, all my patients who are successfully beyond the worst part of their cancer journeys found ways to stay present and focus on all the good things in their life. This is very important."

Ironically, I had expected more sympathy from Dr. Kind. Yet, he suggested Eric switch the focus of his energy and thoughts. Quite refreshing, I must say.

The lovely young Canadian woman came to read in the sun and pulled up a chair next to us. She was now alone as her mom had gone back home, and she shared that one of the appointments in Canada she had requested took one year to come through. Even though she had already received treatment from Sanoviv for several months by that time, she had decided to keep the appointment. It was three hours long and the doctor berated her most of the time about her decision to come to Mexico to get treatment. Finally, she raised her voice and said, "What choice did I have?! You misdiagnosed me in the first place, and if I can't get good care here, why wouldn't I go somewhere else?!"

Later in the day, I laid down on the bed and scrolled through Facebook. I had been tagged in a post by our friend Hilary, who had also experienced the same cold shoulder and lecture approach in the past: "Just had the best appointment with my new oncologist. He stayed long after his working hours, for an extra one and a half hours, to sit and talk about everything. First oncologist who has not looked down on me for choosing to do my cancer treatment out of the country. He called me brave instead."

Facebook Post—November 25, 2016

I know people think of Seattle as one of the integrative cancer capitals of the U.S., or even the world, but that wasn't our experience. It was all about the traditional one-size-fits-all approach. If there were practitioners offering the good alternative stuff, they were certainly not offered by the mainstream cancer care institutions.

— 28 —

The Power of Perspective

After breakfast the following morning, I hurried through the light rain to join a half dozen companions gathered in the mansion. One of the women had brought a folder with a choice of mandalas to color and a supply of colored pencils and pens. No surprise that I picked a hummingbird mandala and colored it cerise pink and several shades of green.

We chatted and colored for a couple of hours, enjoying the break from our other reality—the one where our partners' lives were being saved with heat, cold, light, sound, high tech machines, frequency, vibration, IV drips, food, emotional shedding, and other good stuff.

Although the rain hadn't let up, we decided it would be fun to soak in the pools. Eric joined us later, ready for a break after an eight-hour marathon of heat and liquid gold.

My Bebe and I finished the day with a game of Foo in the nurses' special care room, as his final hours of the liquid gold IV drip required the nurses to be close by.

There was a silver haired woman in the other bed, perhaps in her early seventies. She was hooked up to the IVs and moaning quietly in pain. It struck me how beautiful she was, but I noticed her sunken cheekbones, the sort of cheekbones you get when you're really sick.

Her grown daughter was sitting on the bed with her and swung her legs up to lay next to her, snuggling in tightly. The mom put her arm around her daughter and said with love and sadness, "I'm so sorry you have to go through all this." The daughter hugged her back and said, "Please don't worry about me. I'm just sorry YOU have to battle through this, Mom."

It was such a moving interaction to witness, and as I pulled ahead in our card game, I pondered the meaning of the word *battle*.

From the beginning of Eric's diagnosis, I had started calling the process a "journey" or "experience." I figured in a battle there are only winners and losers, fighters who survive the battle, and those who don't.

I wondered if perhaps the juice in the journey is more about self-reflection, self-discovery, facing one's own demons, knowing the truth for oneself, seeing through the illusion of life, and most importantly, deep forgiveness of self and others for not having played a different, better, more loving role in our lives.

Facebook Post—November 26, 2016
What our loved ones often don't realize is that it's an honor for us to be part of the journey. To be able to love, and support, and cry, and hug, and go through it all. It's sometimes messy, and often painful, but it's real, authentic and intense, and good for the heart at the same time.

— 29 —

Phillipa Misplaces Her Magic Wand

Snuggling with Eric in his bed the following morning, I enjoyed reminiscing about the days before cancer broke his back and traditional treatments almost broke him. However, as soon as he started moving, the pain and nausea started up, and we were both transported back into this rather harsh reality.

I wished I could wave my magic wand and create a different experience for my guy that day. He couldn't keep down water or supplements, and daily IVs were likely saving him from dehydration. His pain was pretty much non-stop, even with medication, and he found another lump, this time in his chest. He had been soaping himself down in the shower, and his fingers ran over the new lump. He made a mental note to tell Dr. Kind at his next session.

Eric requested a heating pad to soothe his back pain. However, Sanoviv was out and since heating pads were in high demand, there were none available in the local stores. I wondered why and then remembered it was winter. As we walked around in our shorts, t-shirts, and sweatshirts, the local staff at the facility were wearing heavy winter coats.

Dr. Kind was so concerned that the staff couldn't locate a heating pad for Eric that he asked his wife to drop off their personal one from home. This was not only personalized care but personal, and we appreciated the gesture very much.

As I wrote the day's missive that evening, my husband snored softly in the other room, thanks to the heating pad and his doctor's wife taking time out of her busy day to bring in their personal one from home.

Facebook post—November 29, 2016

Sometimes I wondered if and when all this would end, and my beloved could get back to his normal, happy, healthy self. It was too early to tell whether I would ever get him back the way he was, or even keep him the way he is, and that makes me sad.

— 30 —

Pelicans and a Liquid Gold Day

I sat in a comfy chair outside the mansion and stared out at the ocean. I was present, yet allowed the edges of my vision to go a little blurry to get into that waking meditative state I love...I'm there, but I'm not there.

I looked out at the ever-present pelicans flying by and into my awareness, mesmerized by their unique shapes and majestic energy. I looked down and noticed a pair of strategically placed pelican statues, one on each side of the path heading towards the cliff, like a pair of lion statues signifying power and prestige.

I had observed many pelican statues, pictures, and art pieces placed throughout the property, and I wondered what significance they held in the tale of Sanoviv. I figured there must be a story behind them. There was, apparently, and it was a critical one.

The story goes that when Dr. Wentz was making his decision whether to buy the property, he was standing on the cliff when a pelican flew overhead. It was one of those rare moments when the world fades away, time slows, and a living creature and a human connect. Communication passes from the animal to the person as clearly as if they are speaking directly into each other's consciousness.

Distilled down to those seconds in time, he and the single pelican shared a *moment*, and Dr. Wentz received a powerful message that this property was where his dream for the ultimate medical institute was meant to be. It was allegedly what tipped the scale for him. The pelican had spoken, and this was his sign to move forward.

I researched more about the spiritual significance of pelicans. It's said that when a pelican comes soaring into your life, it's a powerful reminder that nothing can deter you from your destiny. They are known to empower those who connect with them with determination to remove obstacles in their path. And thank goodness Dr. Wentz embodied the degree of strength, fortitude, and persistence required for such a massive undertaking.

I stared at the pelicans, grateful they had soared into his life, changing everything for him, his family, and the team of phenomenal people he brought together to create this extraordinary place. I was excited to be here, sixteen years later, completely opening up to all the options to save Eric's life.

Heading back to the room to work, I bumped into Eric's doctor in the hallway and told him that Eric hadn't been able to keep much food down in the last four days. Within thirty minutes I received a phone call from the head nutritionist calling me down to the lobby to discuss an amended nutrition plan for Eric. She wrote down a list of all of Eric's favorite foods and confirmed that the kitchen would make whatever he desired.

Eric felt like a mushroom omelet for dinner that evening, and a mushroom omelet he got. And guess what? He gobbled it all up. And it stayed down.

That day was one of the liquid gold days for Eric, meaning nine to ten hours of the day hooked up to the curcumin IV drip. I was learning more about this stuff and discovered that it's very labor intensive to produce and is consequently an expensive commodity. The charge for the curcumin drip was $500 per bag at Sanoviv, and he was up to three bags, twice per week. In the U.S., with only a few naturopathic doctors offering curcumin IVs, we were able to locate a doctor in Seattle offering it for $1250 per bag. That's a total of $7500 per week, just for this one treatment.

We knew our health insurance would not cover this, and it sounded like a lot of money. It was, but here's the kicker. When Eric's oncologist had him traveling to Seattle every day for one month for a five-minute injection and blood pull, in readiness for the blood cell harvest for the stem cell transplant, that never ended up happening, it was between $5,000 and $38,000, per injection, PER DAY. Insurance paid for that, no questions asked. It was simply covered, and at a cost of over U.S. $175,000 for that one month alone, *just for the injections.*

Even still, the insurance company didn't reject those charges after they knew the procedure had been a waste of time. There was simply no rationale behind this. Reject cheaper, natural treatments, but cover, without question, the horrendously overpriced pharmaceutical ones.

Facebook Post—November 30, 2016

We haven't met Dr. Wentz yet, the owner of this place, but I hope to be able to give him a huge hug one day to thank him for his persistence, selflessness, and willingness to bring together a team of professionals to treat and care for people as whole and unique individuals, not just a name, birthdate, and number on a wrist band.

— 31 —

Goodbye, Again, for Now

I slipped into bed with my Bebe, sweaty from my morning jog. He was sleepy but happy to hold me, knowing I would be leaving a few hours later. We talked for a bit, then lay on our backs, propped up with pillows, staring out the French doors and beyond the coconut palms, to the blue ocean. We lay quietly, saying goodbye without words.

When I heard his light snoring, I wasn't the least bit offended. I knew my beloved needed every moment of healing sleep he could get. I slipped out, careful not to wake him, to do my daily dry brushing and hot/cold shower routine. I had learned that these help improve lymphatic drainage and detox the body, among other benefits.

Brushed, showered, dressed, and packed, I roused my beloved and gave him a beautiful card our girlfriend Jill made for "brave and courageous men." She had also gifted a lovely silver necklace to Eric, so that he could wear a reminder of me around his neck, close to his heart.

It was time to say goodbye. It was hard to leave my Bebe, and I couldn't hold back my tears as I squeezed him as tightly as I dared. I whispered in his ear, "Only sixteen more sleeps before we see each other again, my love. I love you, and I will always love you."

He pulled me in tightly, put a hand on each of my cheeks, and pecked me on the lips, "I love and appreciate you, my love and yes... see you and Bella soon. And don't worry about me. I'll be fine."

At the San Diego airport, I found myself turning to him to share something or to make a joke that only he would find funny. I missed my beloved already and felt bad I had left him alone, but alas, work was calling.

I needn't have worried though, as Eric was never really alone at Sanoviv.

Facebook Post—December 2, 2016

I exchanged contact information, and said goodbye to all our new friends, our tribe, fellow souls also seeking healing options that make sense for our bodies, families, and out-of-pocket expenses. How awesome if we could heal ourselves in centers like this all over the U.S. My questions remain...why do we have to leave the country to save our lives? Why are these alternative treatments not covered under our health insurance programs? Why are natural treatments routinely shut down?

— 32 —

The Plot Thickens Surrounding Eric's Lumps

Eric woke up the next day gagging, stiff, and in pain. He found another lump in his rib cage area, making a total of four he'd discovered over the last couple weeks. They had grown and become more painful over time, so Dr. Kind ordered an ultrasound, stat. If they matched the lump they removed from his knee, they would likely be mutated cancerous lymph nodes.

Eric slept into the afternoon, and when he met with the nutritionist, she confirmed that his continued weight loss had only impacted leftover fat, not his actual body mass. Another small mercy.

Later, Eric got the results back from pathology for the lymph node from his knee. Oddly, it was a sister-cancer, and still in the lymphoma family (medium cell). They sent the results off for a deeper analysis, and that would take another five days.

He wanted to spend some time catching up on online banking but couldn't muster the energy. Sadly, although it was the best place in the world for him, the bills were mounting and understandably the accounting department at Sanoviv needed to be paid. Poor Eric wasted so much time and energy *every...single...day* reaching out to Microsoft's health insurance company, asking for responses to his questions, to no avail.

"Enough about me and my sleepless nights, my pain, my nausea and the dang bills! How was your day?" he asked when we chatted later.

"Well, Bella and I purchased a lovely Christmas tree, and we've already decorated it. It brought back memories of this time last year, when the three of us picked out a tree at the same place. Remember how much you struggled to help bring the tree inside?"

"Oh, yes, I remember that well. I remember feeling sad and frustrated that I couldn't help you and Bella much with the tree."

It took my breath away, to think about how much had happened in one year, from those first few chiropractic treatments, the big surgery, the chemo, and now over a month at Sanoviv. But Christmas was coming, and although it wasn't going to be quite the holiday we'd hoped for, I was excited to have my Bebe back home with us soon.

Facebook Post—December 4, 2016

Bella and I picked up a lovely Christmas tree today. We remembered one year ago and how much pain Eric had been in then. He's in the right place now, and we are visualizing him healthy, happy, and here with us for many more Christmases to come!

— 33 —

CBD and a Mexican PET Scan

The following morning, I heard my cell phone ping and saw a selfie Eric had texted me. He joked that he looked like a member of the cast of Breaking Bad. I laughed when I saw it, because with his hair and beard growing back in, he very much looked like he belonged on the show.

But there was something else about the photo. He looked different. The way he stared at the camera, solid, grounded and in his body, looking out, challenging both life and death, "Take me if you dare. But...not...yet. I have a lot of fight left in me!"

Eric was excited to be the first Sanoviv patient to receive CBD, (Cannabidiol), the active ingredient from cannabis, derived from hemp. It seemed promising, and multiple studies over many decades showed that CBD can help and even cure all sorts of maladies, including cancer. Of course, I wondered, *Why are we only hearing about this now?*

He had a session of minor ozone autohemotherapy later that morning, where a small amount of blood is taken from a vein and enriched in a syringe containing about 10 ml of ozone. The enriched blood is then injected under the skin, encouraging the immune system to react to the ozone-enriched blood with higher activity and production of antibodies. This treatment can effectively jumpstart the immune system, and only takes ten minutes a couple of times a week.

After lunch, Eric told me that the kitchen offered him a special steak treat, and he was sad that his body rejected it just as soon as he had finished.

He rallied, though, and in his daily session with Dr. Kind, they agreed it would be helpful to get a PET scan soon, rather than wait until the typical three-month interval, as we'd experienced with Dr. Smiley. Unlike the U.S. cost of $5,000 to $8,000 per scan, they were around $2,000 in Mexico, which I suspected was much closer to the actual cost. Dr. Kind worked on scheduling one as soon as possible.

Facebook Post—December 6, 2016

Eric has so much to live for, with his new calling, to somehow connect technology with health. He has discovered his new thing. Let's energize a reality where he is becoming so healthy, he can change the world with his superpower.

— 34 —

Busy Healing the Body

Eric had ten sleeps to go at Sanoviv and things hadn't eased up for him. The night before, he experienced intense back spasms, and he thrashed around most of the night, his knees and back on fire. He even laid his pelvis on three stacked pillows to try to get some relief.

At one point, he leaned over to retrieve a pillow from the floor and heard a "pop" in his lower back. His first thought was, "Oh shoot, what just popped?!" But thankfully it was a good pop, an area his chiropractor had been trying to get to for a while, and he slept solidly for six hours.

The nurses called to check why he had missed his 9 a.m. lab appointment, and he asked nicely if they would come to him instead. Because they loved my guy, they agreed to do "their Eric's" labs in his room. He fell right back to sleep and woke up ready to rock and to devour a bowl of fruit for breakfast.

It was one of his three-bags-of-curcumin days, with nine to ten hours of IVs. They tried a different schedule and gave him his first bag in the morning, followed by regional hyperthermia. Then lunch. He was feeling nauseous and canceled his Quiet Room and hyperbaric oxygen chamber sessions. He cracked me up though, as he kept his spa treatment, and it was a back-of-the-leg massage. The practitioner tore into the deep tissue of his leg, and it was apparently just what he needed. He came back to the IV room mid-afternoon for another curcumin bag. He took a break for dinner, rested, and he was back from 8 p.m. to 11 p.m. to finish up.

Phew! It can be an exhausting process to heal your cancer-ravaged body!

We connected that evening, and my guy was beyond excited, "Andi's coming tomorrow, Bebe! He's staying for three nights, and on the day he leaves, Bea's coming too."

"Yay! Only one more sleep and you'll spend six of your last ten days at Sanoviv with your two besties!"

I breathed a sigh of relief that Andi was going to be spending more time with Eric, as he had been struggling with his decline more than most. In Andi's case, I imagine it wasn't that he didn't want to be there for him, it was that he struggled with Eric's deterioration. He really needed his buddy, and I think he was deathly afraid his best friend wasn't going to make it.

Dr. Kind confirmed that there was nothing that needed to be treated urgently with Eric's medium-cell lymphoma, and they had time. They considered cryogenics for the four small lumps, and created a custom turmeric and ozonated coconut oil cream to rub on to the lumps daily, in the interim. In his final few days at Sanoviv, he and Dr. Kind would review the PET results and create a plan for his return to Seattle.

Facebook Post—December 7, 2016

I so appreciate the way the doctor is seeing my beloved daily, talking and communicating, and bouncing ideas off Eric and the other docs and professionals when they meet. I am beyond delighted that he's getting such a degree of personalized and personal care, and that they don't use fear tactics to scare him into taking a course of action that might not be in his best interest.

— 35 —

Eric and His Best Buddy Spend Time Together

Andi had arrived the previous morning, and noticed right away that his buddy didn't look like the "old man" he was before we had left the U.S. It seemed that pumping him full of all the good stuff had revived his bestie's damaged body.

I got a text from Andi with a selfie of the two of them, and I chuckled because it was both a terrible and adorable picture. They were squinting into the sun, and the angle was not very flattering, yet it made me so happy they were together and taking selfies.

Eric invited Andi to his body code session that afternoon. He was doing a ton of emotional clearing in those sessions and began to acknowledge that most disease starts somewhere other than the physical body and that we humans tend to internalize things that happen to and around us.

In his session, Eric asked Karen whether his body was ready to give up producing more cancer. The answer was a resounding yes. However, there was one caveat…he needed to create a stronger connection with a higher power. In all my research, believing and having faith in something or someone unseen and infinitely larger, wiser, and more all-knowing than ourselves can be an important element in the healing process.

Eric thought about it and agreed he could visualize that and make it happen.

How wonderful that my beloved had the rare opportunity to get so much intense emotional healing time and cool that his friend got to witness something that many might be skeptical about, at least initially.

Andi also joined in on Eric's morning stretch class and the cardio session at the gym, and they each enjoyed a nice long massage at the spa. He very much wanted to return with Bea and both of us in the spring for a short retreat.

When I called to check in, Andi picked up and said he was so proud of his longtime friend for his dedication to healing, particularly given all the obstacles he had faced. He said he was so glad he came and was looking forward to coming back with us for a three-day assessment the following year.

All four of us were a resounding *yes* on a return trip in the spring.

Facebook Post—December 9, 2016

Had a great chat with Andi today. He's enjoying being with his buddy, like old times. He and Bea invited us to join them for Christmas in Hawai'i, and we said we'd need some time to think about it! So much is resting on the results of the PET scan in a few days. In fact, EVERYTHING is resting on the outcome of the scan. Prayers gratefully received.

— 36 —

What We're Not Saying

Bea had come and gone, her three days passing by very quickly. She had several long conversations with Eric and she called to share that he is very much looking forward to coming home to be with us, and not dealing with all this for a while. Just to be Eric after a full year of thinking about health, treatments, and healing.

She said, "It was a wonderful experience for me to share these few days with my buddy, and I was sad to leave him.'"

It was a big day for Eric—the day of the PET scan.

We talked after his scan, but we didn't talk about the elephant in the room. What if, for example, the elephant wasn't an elephant at all, but a tiger stealthily eating up more of my guy's healthy cells, allowing the cancerous ones to proliferate? We didn't dare consider that as an option. Not on that day. We hoped for the best and focused our attention on one specific outcome...a healthy future for my Bebe.

Eric's voice was a bit shaky, and I could tell he was feeling nervous, but by that point, there was nothing more to be done. Of course, he wanted the results immediately. We all did. But we breathed through our impatience and awaited the results, as calmly as possible.

Facebook Post—December 13, 2016

In Bea's words, 'Eric was very relaxed, and I could see how well the whole body and soul practice has worked for him. Like everyone here, this is not a one-way-route. Keeping cancer under control is a good start for everyone. I noticed how different it is here, compared to talking with oncologists in Seattle. This isn't a quick treatment and it's not like it either works or it doesn't, as with traditional medicine. This is a complex process that takes time and effort, on many levels.' Eric had his PET scan today, and we are awaiting the results. Hopefully, he'll get the full report with great news soon.

～ 37 ～

Phillipa and Eric Receive Very Big News

No one else knew the enormity of the news I received that next morning.

We got the results back early. We don't know how or why, and it didn't matter. What mattered was that the news was not good. Not good at all.

Everything seemed surreal, yet I was ultra-aware of every little detail around me. The blade of grass reaching through the layer of frost as I rushed into the warm building for an early morning meeting on the Redmond Microsoft campus. The lyrics to the Celine Dion song, "My Heart Will Go On" playing in the reception area. The slow-motion sniffles, coughs, and blinks of the distracted people walking by.

I walked into the meeting and greeted everyone with a smile. One of my colleagues brought donuts with pink and white icing and multi-colored sprinkles. While they chose their pastry *du jour*, I was pondering life and death, love and loss, and life without the ones we love. I felt sick and gracefully declined the offer of a donut.

No one knew that we had received news that my husband's cancer was still fully present. Even all the advanced/alternative treatments hadn't been able to slow the speed with which the cells were mutating and growing.

No one sitting in the room knew that yesterday's PET scan revealed that my husband had several hundred little tumors. Yes! *Several hundred.*

FFFUUUUUUCCCCCKKKKKK!

Fuck cancer!

Fuck chemo!

Fuck the multiplying tumors in my husband's body!

Damn the damage chemo did to my husband's cells.

I wish we had gone to Sanoviv earlier!

Fuck! Shit!

When Eric gave me the news, my heart squeezed, and it hadn't stopped hurting since. I wanted to jump through the phone and hug my guy so tight, it'd pop those nasty cancerous lumps right out of his body. Or better yet, whisk him away to another dimension where cancer doesn't even exist.

I tried to stay present in the meeting room but felt more than a little out of sorts. I managed to smile and speak and direct the Microsoft webinar and, thankfully, no one in the room, nor any of the hundreds of people listening in, knew anything was up.

Still feeling discombobulated after it was over, I pulled out of the parking lot and started driving on the wrong side of the road! Lucky for me, there was only one vehicle coming my way, a Microsoft shuttle bus, and after hearing a loud toot on the horn from the startled driver, I quickly swerved my car to the right side of the road.

Oh shit!

Note to self—stay in my body, breathe!

Stay in my body, breathe.

When Eric received the PET scan results, he went through the full gambit, and had a tough time speaking. How do you tell your wife that even with all this intense care, cost, and energy, your body's cells are still mutating out of control? How does one even process the disappointment with news like that?

By the time I spoke to him later in the day, he was doing better. Dr. Kind had encouraged him, reminding him that he was a fighter and that he was their first patient to be able to handle three bags of curcumin, over nine hours each day, twice a week. That buoyed him up, for now.

He had looked into the doctor's eyes and asked him if he had wasted his time coming to Sanoviv, and what his chances were. Dr. Kind reminded him that he was in very bad shape when he first arrived only two months earlier. He was completely out of balance of mind, body, and spirit, and they had almost sent him home. But they had been determined to get him in balance, and together they succeeded in doing just that.

Eric had worked hard to face all his emotional demons—all the people, events, and relationships that had caused him pain, and to whom he had caused pain. He had done the work with the help of Dr. Heart and Karen. He worked on his body with the help of doctors, the nutritionist, chiropractor, dentist, reflexologist, masseuse, fitness trainer, the hyperbaric chamber staff, the IV nurses, the hyperthermia guy, drivers, the microscopic blood guy, the thermography person, the colon-hydrotherapy, and the Quiet Room women...every single person who touched his body or spirit in some way at this place of healing.

He developed a personal, spiritual connection with his version of his higher power, and committed to being in touch with them every day.

So, what now?

Eric was due to come back to Seattle on Saturday, and I continued my research for two different tracks for him. One was a naturopathic referral from Dr. Kind. He offered IV treatments, hyperbaric chamber treatments, and such. The other, unbelievably, was to find another oncologist.

Shit! Damn! Fuck!

Indeed, one of his options was to do chemo again. Yet as our friend Hilary encouraged, "No matter what, Eric is in much better shape than he was. Even if that means he's going to need more chemo, he's in a better place to receive it than he was a couple of months ago."

We also started looking into the Car T-cell trial in Seattle. We had heard about it, but didn't really understand what it was. We heard there were risks and more than a few deaths at the clinic, but it did offer promise for treating otherwise lethal cancers.

> ### Facebook Post—December 14, 2016
>
> I so wanted to be able to share positive good news with you all that Eric was either cancer-free or had a few manageable spots of cancer. But alas, that wasn't the case. The PET scan showed that he didn't just have the four little lumps, but several hundred. This was the last thing we all expected. We are not giving up though! There's a heck of a lot more fight left in both of us!

— 38 —

No Regrets, No Time Wasted at Sanoviv

We were not the only ones in shock from the PET scan results. Our Facebook family was reeling with the news. Even some of our more stoic people shed tears when they read the post. Indeed, it was a surprise for us all.

I was thankful to those who took the time to reach out with authentic, heartfelt words and sentiments, and for the recommendations, links to research, and offerings of help and support.

There was a theme that emerged from all the messages, something we were also aligned with, and that was about absolutely NOT giving up. We decided to move forward with the belief that the best and highest route would reveal itself, and the right people and connections would appear, all in divine timing.

We believed, with all our hearts, that it had been the right thing to go to Mexico. There were no regrets about that.

No matter the outcome, I fully supported Eric's experiences in Sanoviv. It would have been almost impossible to piecemeal this type of program in Seattle. If he were doing this locally, I don't know if he would have been willing to pursue the sheer depth of the emotional healing he had experienced, both with the psychology and the body code work. To have Dr. Heart's and Karen's sessions woven in and around the rest of his treatments was priceless. The daily habit of actually "going there and going within" regarding the possibility of dying, forgiveness, and letting go was something that Eric worked through intensely over the two-month period.

I chatted with my guy around lunchtime. Vitamin C and hydration IVs had been selected to shore him up for his travels back home to Seattle. The women in the Quiet Room gave him a spinal-rejuvenation session, designed to re-energize his spinal system. They used a large Y-shaped tool and a specific sound frequency, and finished up with a heavenly back massage.

He had his final body code session with sweet Karen, and they peeked at his deep sadness and where it was coming from in his body. "The sadness comes and goes," and, as he said, "not always at the most appropriate times."

It turned out his sadness was fear-centered, resulting from feeling out of control with his body. The lesson though was that he was in control after all. She picked up the beginnings of a core belief that started to form when he was five years old, embarrassed by punishment in public from his stepdad. Fast forward to the big car accident in 1989. As he was in his lengthy recovery phase, he felt helpless and out of control. For years afterward, he felt like he was crawling out of his skin, as a passenger, whenever he saw car headlights coming toward him.

Together Eric and Karen worked on a plan moving forward. His job was to find laughter in everything. This was something we loved experiencing together. We laughed. We giggled. We chortled. His mission was to seek out ways to *be* happy and *be* in a happy place.

With that in mind, we decided to take Andi and Bea up on their offer to go with them to Hawai'i for one week over Christmas. They rented a house right on the beach on the North Shore of

Oahu. We knew the house and had stayed there together once before all this. It was a fabulous location, the stuff of movies, where you can literally walk out the back door over soft white sand and dive into the ocean.

On our call that night, Eric said no matter what happened he would like to live fully and be present up until the very end...even if it meant sliding into home base with a battered, bruised, and chemo-ravaged body.

Facebook Post—December 15, 2016

No long dissertation tonight. It's been another emotional day. We said yes to our friends Andi and Bea, to join them on Oahu over Christmas. To our Big Island friends, sorry we'll miss you, but we'll look at coming over for winter or spring break next year.

— 39 —

Saying Goodbye to Sanoviv

My beloved's time at Sanoviv had come to an end. It was time. We both knew he was ready to leave. Most guests there signed up for a three-day assessment or for a one-week retreat and detox. Some stayed for up to four weeks, but very few stayed for a full two-month program.

Day fifty-five of my daily Facebook journal posts marked the finale of one chapter and the beginning of the next. It was a master number in numerology where each number, or combination of numbers, carries a certain meaning, tone, or vibration.

I looked it up, and fifty-five represents a composite energy of independence, exploration, self-determination, freedom, and adventure.

That sounded about right!

Two of our Sanoviv friends, Angelina and Kay, sent several photos of their little "IV party" the night before and of Eric getting ready to leave. Scrolling through the photos, I felt the full gambit of emotions.

The three of them by the Christmas tree in the lobby, for some reason, made me cry. They were all wearing the matching cream uniform, looking out at the camera with hope in their eyes and in their broad smiles, full of hope that their lives would have more chapters. I loved that they took that photo to send to me, and I stared at it for a long time, breathing through my tears.

I looked at the photos of their "Farewell to Eric IV party" from the night before. The first was an adorable photo of the four smiling port buddies all with IVs dripping life-affirming liquids into their respective ports. I smiled because in the second photo, Eric had fallen asleep *at his own party*, and I cried because he looked so deathly pale and thin.

There was one of him waving to the ladies from the passenger window as the van was leaving for the airport, and I was excited to be seeing my guy again soon.

Eric texted from the San Diego airport, reporting that he ate a few bites of a hot dog and that his flight had been delayed two hours. He said his butt was sore from sitting in the wheelchair for the extra hours, and he was grateful to have been upgraded to the more comfortable seating in first class.

Bella and I were at Sea-Tac International Airport to welcome and bring him home. Even though it was only two weeks since I last saw him, it was shocking to see him close-up and in person, all 145 pounds of him.

With his familiar grin, he announced proudly, "I had a beer at the airport in San Diego and a Crown Royal on the plane."

Bella and I looked at each other and smiled. That was our Eric, pushing the edge of the envelope. I replied, "It sounds like a prison break to me! Too funny, but now it's time to get you home to rest. We're leaving in a few days to go to Hawai'i!"

My guy was exhausted after his day of delays, hot dogs, beer, Crown Royale, and a sore butt, and he barely managed to get through his evening ablutions before collapsing into bed.

I held on tightly to my beloved husband that night, now barely more than a bag of bones. As his breathing slowed to a gentle rhythm, I allowed my tears to flow unchecked. I didn't know how much more time I had with him, but I knew I would be there every step of the way. I knew there was more fight in my Bebe and that he was far from accepting this was *it* for him.

I was close to sleep too, and as I felt myself falling into the void, I thought of the white sand and blue ocean, and of the house on the beach on the North Shore of Oahu in Hawai'i, aptly named "The Blue Lagoon."

Next week we would be there. Next week . . .

Facebook Post—December 17, 2016

Eric traveled alone from Mexico and has made it home safely. We chatted by the Christmas tree and fire, and Bella helped him get up the stairs and into bed. He looks very relaxed in the nice comfy big bed. Indeed, I think he's happy to be home—at least for a couple days, before jumping on another plane. This time to Hawai'i.

PART FOUR

— 1 —

Eric Comes Home to Seattle

After his two-month stay in Mexico, it was a treat to wake up next to my husband at home in our big bed.

I rested my cheek on his bony shoulder and listened to his breathing as he slept soundly. My mind wandered, and although I had been holding it together, I started crying quietly for our tough journey that year.

I cried because we didn't know what the next step looked like and how much longer he had. I cried, as I had quickly come to the realization that he was not well enough to make it to Hawai'i for Christmas. I cried for my Bebe and his lifetime of dreams not yet fulfilled.

I wondered if he'd ever get to his bucket list. Would he leave a footprint on the world in some way? Would he be here to walk his daughters down the aisle? Would he even walk again on his own without the help of a person or a device? How much of the new year would he see?

Neither of us was willing to give up, but it was tough not knowing what was next. Eric liked to have a plan, and we were between plans.

He moved in his sleep, moaning softly in pain. I watched his eyes slowly open. He smiled and pulled me towards him, whispering in my ear, "I love my Bebe, and I'm so glad to be back home with you in our bed."

"I know, my love. Me too. I missed you all those days and nights I wasn't with you."

I squeezed his fragile body tightly and felt him eventually drift back to sleep.

When he woke up, I gently broached the topic of Hawai'i. I said, "Bebe, I'm so sorry, but do you think you'll be able to handle the trip to Oahu? It's not only the flight, but the house isn't wheelchair friendly. I know you want to go, but do you think you'd have fun?"

He didn't answer for a while and surprised me when he said, "I was thinking the same thing. As much as I want to go, I don't think it'd be a good idea. I don't want you guys to have to carry me up and down the stairs and out to the sand."

I hugged him tightly but had to switch gears in preparation for the visitors about to descend upon us that day. Alison and the kids came over, and the sound of his grand-kiddos playing and racing around the house was something Eric enjoyed. Seeing six pairs of hastily strewn shoes by the front door was my favorite.

Eric passed out asleep on the couch after they left. As I scooted beside him, I thought about how none of us knows how many tomorrows we have, when it's going to be too late to travel to the faraway places on our bucket list, or have Christmas with friends in Hawai'i.

At that moment, I also wondered if Eric might outlive us all. Who really knew?

Facebook post—December 18, 2016

One of the most difficult things for Eric about his disease is the hopelessness, helplessness, and feeling out of control with what's happening to his body. Love each other, hug each other...because the truth is, none of us really knows how long we have.

— 2 —

Unusual Interactions with My Microsoft Boss and Eric's Onco-Doc

It was a dreary and cold Monday. I was grateful to be bundled up in our warm bed, my laptop balanced on my knees, journaling the words of our story.

I was needed at the Microsoft campus for a few hours that morning and slipped out of bed quietly to get ready. I brought a cup of coffee upstairs for my guy, a special treat since he'd been without it for a couple of months. After a kiss on the cheek, I told him I'd be back later to pick him up for his doctor's appointment. Bella was on winter break and promised to bring him food if he felt like eating or needed help getting around.

I told my Microsoft manager we were no longer going to Hawai'i for Christmas week, and she responded, "Okay, well, make sure you take some time off." I noted she had zero interest in *why* we weren't going and what had changed for us. In fact, she had only asked about Eric once the entire year.

At that time, I had replied, "Oh, he's doing pretty well. He's just taking some time off."

She wasn't an unkind person, she was just stretched thin and often distracted.

That afternoon we drove to the Seattle side to see Eric's previous onco-doc to stock up on pain meds. It was a strange visit with none of the previous warmth from Dr. Smiley. She had lost him to Mexico, and yet there he was. It seemed hard for her to find common ground with us. I imagine she was thinking, *Who heads to the unknown, to Mexico, to try to heal from cancer? Who gives up the safety of the medical system in the U.S. to try alternative treatments?*

That was the last we ever saw the not-so-smiley doctor. We grabbed Eric's pain meds and made a run for it into the waiting arms of their competitor network. We were on the lookout for a new oncologist and wanted to explore our options to get Eric into the only local immunotherapy/Car T-cell trial.

They were more than happy to oblige.

As soon as we got home, Eric slept fitfully on the couch for a few hours. His days started to look like this: sleep, pain meds, more sleep, eat a little, keep it down (sometimes), bring it back up (maybe), take a bath or shower (very carefully and slowly), wriggle around trying to get comfortable (whether sitting or lying down), conversation with me, maybe a visitor or two, and more sleep.

I looked at him sleeping on the couch, relieved we had canceled the trip to Hawai'i. Our friends got it. They, too, were wondering whether it would be a good experience for their best friend and buddy.

Facebook post—December 19, 2016

Please keep praying everyone, sending healing energy, blessings, love, hearts, happy and teary-eyed faces, and cute little emojis, as it all helps. Let's energize a crazy ass miracle indeed!

— 3 —

Missing the Sanoviv All-Under-One-Roof Treatments

We continued piecing together Eric's options outside the traditional medical network and made an appointment with the naturopath referred by Dr. Kind in Mexico. His office was one of the few in the U.S. offering the curcumin IV drip at a cost of $1250 per bag out of pocket. Eric would require six bags per week.

Since he was dehydrated, they gave him IV fluids on the spot. We figured we could do the hydration IVs, high-dose Vitamin C, and the ozone treatments at that location. If we signed up with them, we'd likely add in hyperthermia and the hyperbaric chamber, as they were also offered, albeit not covered by insurance. Almost none of their alternative cancer treatments were covered by insurance.

We already missed Sanoviv and the joys of having everything under one roof. In Seattle, to supplement medical treatments with natural ones, we would potentially have to schedule appointments at a half dozen locations. It would be a full-time job scheduling, driving Eric to his appointments, waiting, and driving to the next one or back home. If only there were clinics like Sanoviv in Seattle.

If only.

We got a call from Eric's mom and aunt in California asking if they could visit the following week. Eric had mixed feelings about his family arriving on Christmas Day for a few days because he was struggling with his pain and energy levels. However, since we didn't know whether he was going to recover or not, I encouraged them to come. Just in case.

Facebook post—December 20, 2016

My heart hurts for my guy, and yes, many of you are right in your assessment of us. This is quite a love story, and I'm hoping I get to post about the happy ending we are all praying for.

— 4 —

Phillipa and Eric Talk about Death and Dying

There was a moment in the middle of the night when Eric was lucid dreaming and wondered whether he still had cancer. He enjoyed hanging out in that existence, playing around with the possibilities. Sadly, as soon as he moved, he felt a bunch of nerve endings on fire and was right back into the reality of pain.

Now and again I, too, would look at him and forget what was happening in his body, as if there was nothing amiss, and we could plan out our lives.

I kissed my guy goodbye and left for the gym. Bella took over the early morning watch to keep an eye out for her daddy. We figured it wasn't a great idea to leave him alone at that point as he could easily fall, given the state of his wobbly legs.

Our dear friends Mary and Craig visited, armed with freshly baked goods and eggs from the hens on their farm. Hilary and her furry buddy Charlie popped over and, again, I appreciated that she knew to sit quietly and let Eric take the lead. Often their talks segued into strategic conversations around Hilary's life's direction, or what was next for my beloved. He treasured those conversations.

That night, after a mixed day of rest and visitors, I laid my head on that special spot. We laughed and cried and talked deeply and openly. We explored what would happen if Eric didn't make it and what his wishes might be.

"I want to be cremated," he said firmly. "And I'd like to have my ashes scattered on Lake Washington from the boat."

We talked about who he'd like on the boat. He said he'd like his daughters, Bella and Alison, Alison's teens, Andi and Bea, and their two boys.

"Make sure you go as close to the WA-520 bridge as you can," he added.

That was one of his favorite spots to view the Blue Angels air show the first weekend of every August at Seattle's annual Seafair Festival.

He paused for a moment and grinned. "If I were you, I'd keep an eye out for the direction of the wind. You wouldn't want my ashes to blow back into your faces!"

We both chuckled, imagining how that would look like a scene from a comedy. I told Eric that if there does happen to be a big gust of wind right at that moment, we'll know it was him!

Facebook post—December 21, 2016

It's all so surreal, but hope is indeed a powerful thing. I can't believe we talked about arrangements just in case he doesn't make it. Eric is struggling a bit, but he's strong, a real fighter. I'm proud that we had THE talk. Just in case. Prayers and blessings most graciously received. Thank you all.

— 5 —

Renewed Hope with the Promise of CAR T-Cell Therapy

It's interesting how much we take for granted, like taking a shower, yet that was Eric's major achievement of the morning. The afternoon accomplishment was getting him dressed, down the stairs, in and out of the wheelchair, and into the truck to meet his new oncologist. Once again, I found myself in awe of my guy, how he was able to keep his spirits up and just keep marching onward.

Later, I watched as his eyes opened wide and a grin spread across his face. It was three days before Christmas, and he had renewed hope. We were sitting in his oncologist's office, and the doctor told Eric he had a twenty percent chance of living. He wanted to get him into the CAR T-cell Trial as soon as possible. A few tests would determine his eligibility, and a call or two would confirm if it was covered by our insurance.

CAR therapy is a mix of gene and cell therapy and immunotherapy. T-cells are extracted from the blood, modified, and taught to identify and target cancerous cells. Once ready, the cells are reinfused back into the body of the patient. I was excited and visualized Eric getting on the trial and being in the lucky twenty percent to survive.

Driving home, I pondered our recent conversation about death and cremation. Although neither of us was willing to give up, Eric was now under 145 pounds and couldn't eat much. That day he hadn't been able to keep down water. He could barely make it down the stairs, even on his butt. We'd likely need to move him into the downstairs office, as the stairs were like climbing and descending Mt. Everest. He had been determined to sleep upstairs in our bedroom for as long as possible, and I sensed he felt like he'd be giving up when he gave up the stairs.

I reached over as I was driving and laid my hand on his thigh, and thought about the Pooh and Piglet quote, "I just want to be sure of you."

Facebook post—December 22, 2016

Standby and please send prayers, healing energy and blessings for Eric, that he gets on this trial, or something even better and more miraculous.

— 6 —

Phillipa and Bella Go Christmas Shopping

Two days before Christmas, Bella and I stood in the menswear section of Nordstrom's not knowing which way to turn. What do you buy for someone who's deathly ill? We walked through the dress and casual shirts, men's bags and briefcases, socks, ties, shoes, and colognes. Nothing made sense. There was an eighty percent chance he'd never need any of these items again.

I ended up getting a few gifts for my guy and decided to write him a poem. Bella had the same idea and had already started writing something for her daddy.

Although we tried not to leave Eric at home alone, he had insisted on it that day. He was holding on to the last vestiges of independence, and we got it. We texted and called regularly though, to be sure he was okay. When we returned home, we saw he had made his way into the media room with his walker and was watching *Designated Survivor* with the volume WAY up.

Aside from friends Sandy and George visiting with delicious food and open hearts, and Erin arriving with a diffuser for essential oils, Eric had a day of complete rest. It was one day at a time with his food intake and degrees of nausea.

Eric's new oncologist, "Dr. Big Boss," called and confirmed that the results of the labs from the day prior were looking good. His white and red blood cell counts were within normal range, although his kidneys could do with some help.

Facebook post—December 23, 2016
We finished up our Christmas shopping today. We're excited that all is looking good with Eric's readings. Phew, we can breathe a little easier—for now.

— 7 —

Christmas Eve Shenanigans

Mid-morning on Christmas Eve, I answered the doorbell in my nightie, a baggy sweatshirt, and with my unbrushed hair in a messy top-knot.

It was a friend of Bella's I hadn't seen in a while, and she stood there with an awkward smile and a plate of homemade Christmas cookies. I grabbed hold of the plate, pulled her into my arms for a hug, and thanked her profusely through my tears.

I had been doing a decent job of holding it together when I needed to, only letting my emotions loose in more private moments. But when someone was being kind and empathetic, that was when I most often lost it.

I ran back upstairs to my beloved. "It doesn't always happen at the most opportune times," Eric said when he looked up at my wet eyes, and I nodded.

I snuggled next to him, happy to be lying under the blankets with my Bebe.

I loved that he was reading and smiling at articles on his iPad, like the old days. I asked him what he was grateful for, and after a moment he said he was happy to still be here, to be able to spend time with family and close friends.

Since Eric's daughter celebrates the holiday on Christmas Eve, we loaded the car with presents and went off to be with her and her kiddos and friends. There were twenty-two people in total, and I appreciated that some of the young strong men in the group rushed to lift Eric up the stairs and into the house, wheelchair and all.

The food looked delicious, and I got a small plate for Eric. He managed to eat a little plain turkey, ham, mashed potatoes, and poured himself a Mimosa and a beer. I was grateful he was relaxed and eating. If he wanted a couple of drinks, so be it.

There was a half hour of chaos, high-fives and hugs, and Christmas paper flying everywhere, as six kiddos opened all their presents at once. The adults followed with a white elephant gift-giving session, and Eric got an LED light and a cool University of Washington winter hat. He told me later that if someone had tried to take away his light, he would have pulled the cancer card and not given it up.

A little later, I glanced over at my beloved. He was there, but didn't seem fully present. I sat on the side of his wheelchair and leaned in to kiss him. When someone yelled, "Photo op!" we both turned to smile for the camera. The others piled in on the photos, and in no time we were surrounded by family creating memories, and permanently capturing digital records of the fun and mayhem.

I had assumed Eric wouldn't be able to handle the noise and high energy of the party much longer. Surprisingly, he got a second wind, and we stayed until after midnight, talking, playing Scrabble, and watching videos.

It was after 1 A.M. when we finally got home and into bed, and we talked for another couple of hours. I treasured those times we were relaxed, chatting easily in bed about anything and everything, just like the days before all this.

As he slipped into sleep, I pondered the deeper meaning of celebration. I wondered if it was the beginning of many lasts. Would it be his last Christmas Eve, the last time he would open

Christmas presents with his two daughters and his five grand-kiddos? Would that be his last Mimosa? His last beer?

Facebook post—December 24, 2016

We had a fun Christmas Eve party at Alison's place. Eric was able to eat some yummy food AND have a couple drinks, and he loved his LED light gift the best! I wish everyone a fantastic Christmas, if you celebrate. I wish for you ALL—good health, meaningful friendships, sweet moments with your families, and fun and laughter for the coming journey around the sun.

— 8 —

A Different Sort of Christmas Day

When I was a girl, Christmas was the most exciting day of all. We would wake up early and run to the tree to see what gifts were waiting for us and examine the stockings, bursting-at-the-seams, hanging from the mantle. We'd jump on Mum and Dad's bed to wake them up, eager to open our stockings and bummed we would have to wait until after church to open our presents. The day would be chaotic but wonderful, and I treasured being surrounded by my loud family of nine. I particularly loved the smells of the tree, fruit cake soaked in alcohol, the turkey, potatoes, vegetables roasting, and steamed pudding cooking. So many good childhood memories are associated with Christmas.

On that Christmas day in 2016, as a grown woman of fifty-two, although I still had that underlying excitement for the day, everything was different. Bella was a teen and wanted to sleep in, I had laundry to catch up on, and I left Eric in a deep sleep to run out and pick up some last-minute groceries.

When I arrived home, Eric was in pain, rubbing his distended tummy.

"How long has it been now?" I asked.

He responded with a moan, "Over two weeks...I think, seventeen days?"

"Oh, shit! Over two weeks without pooping?!"

We agreed that even though it was Christmas Day, an enema might be just the thing. I certainly didn't want my beloved sitting in an ER on the holiday for several uncomfortable hours, so I said I would try to do it for him.

I laid a towel down on the bathroom floor and struggled to get him down on all fours. We managed, and I gently pulled his pants down and exposed his skinny butt.

"Ready, Bebe?" I calmly asked with my outer voice; all the while my inner voice was going haywire.

What the fuck?

What the hell is this fucking cancer journey?

Eric's body didn't know it was Christmas Day. We did what we had to do, and after a successful enema, it was time to get my guy showered, dressed, and ready to spend time with our Bella-girl.

Eric asked for help with the final button on one of his mod dress shirts, one I had gifted him years ago. It had been too tight around his belly then, but we kept it anyway.

I grinned and said, "You know, this weight loss program you've been on for the last year has really worked. But there might have been less painful, more graceful ways to lose weight!" Eric agreed and chuckled with me.

We heard Bella and looked up as she waltzed into the bedroom, wearing the fuzzy flannel Christmas onesie I had given her. I loved that our girl was fifteen years old yet delighted with a onesie that fit her tall body and extra-long legs. She ran over to Eric, gave him a big hug, then turned and gave me one too.

"Merry Christmas Daddy! Merry Christmas Mummy!"

We helped Eric down the stairs, into his wheelchair, and onto the couch. As we settled, Bella sat on the floor beside the tree and located a present for each of us. We preferred opening our gifts one at a time so we could savor the moments of excitement and surprise.

Eric joked that he had outsourced his gift purchasing that year. We all chortled and agreed that, indeed, it had been a different sort of a year and it was a different sort of Christmas.

Eric's family arrived from California later in the day, checked into their hotel, and came straight over to see their boy/nephew. If they were surprised that he was a shadow of his former self, they didn't show it. They took him and his dire situation in stride and hugged and held him. Then we all talked and talked.

Eventually Eric needed to lie down and migrated upstairs. We followed and sat around our special man, chatting and watching as he moved in and out of sleep.

Between us, we managed to prepare a delicious holiday dinner with most of the usual fixings. My Bebe handled a few mouthfuls, but the grape juice didn't fare so well.

Later, as Eric's relatives stood to leave, we agreed that, health issues notwithstanding, it was still a lovely Christmas day.

> *Facebook post—December 25, 2016*
>
> Merry Christmas everyone! Ours was a little different this year. Yes, it was about family and laughter and stories and food and a fire and gifts and photos. But it also involved laundry, grocery shopping, an enema, and not keeping down grape juice. We take the good with the not so good, and these are the things we deal with, even when it's a special holiday.

— 9 —

Eric's Family Visits from California

It was the day after Christmas and I found myself wishing, yet again, I had a magic wand.

I would have waved it over my Bebe to ease his pain and the ravaging effects of the disease and gently transmute the lumps pushing out of his skin.

I would have had his body take in all the good food we were providing, adding muscle mass to his fading frame rather than rejecting almost every morsel.

I would have dried his tears as he was sitting on the edge of the bed, slumped over in frustration that his body was giving up on him.

Up until then, he had assumed that his pain was temporary. He had a clear direction, something to believe in, a path to follow. It was hard for him to stay positive on that day. He felt like a cork bobbing helplessly in an ocean of unknowns. We hadn't heard back from the folks at the CAR T-cell trial and figured they were likely enjoying the holiday too.

Eric's family came over, and this time I observed that his mom, in particular, had difficulty knowing what to talk to him about. The topics we usually discuss no longer carried the same significance, and at times it got a bit awkward. Eric was gracious and allowed them to do the talking, yet there were times I wanted to intercede and say, "Stop! Let Eric speak. Ask him questions about his life, and what some of his best memories are," but I didn't. I think people don't always realize that it needs to be about our person in these moments, and it's okay if there are stretches of silence.

As his physical body ached and screamed, Eric was consciously looking for positive things to inspire himself. Later that night, after his family left, I asked him what advice he would give people, knowing what he knew about life in his fifty-five years. Being a deep thinker, my Bebe started pondering and came up with a list of insights.

Facebook post—December 26, 2016

Tonight, Eric came up with a list of top 10 things to have a happier life: be more conscious, work to be the best you can be, be in gratitude for what you have, don't take for granted the amount of time you have left, be less "squabbly," avoid squandering your lives away, treat each day as precious, move forward more gracefully in your own lives, be less worried about what other people think, and don't get so involved in other people's stuff. Well, there we have it. Eric's advice for a happy life!

— 10 —

A Professional Photographer Comes to Visit

The next morning we had a professional photography session scheduled. Our friend Karla had told her photographer friend, Michelle, about our story and my Facebook posts, and she could see that Eric wasn't doing well. Michelle works with a non-profit organization, Soulumination, that offers professional photos for families with a terminally ill child under fifteen or a deathly ill parent with a child under fifteen.

Michelle had read about our journey and wanted to take photos for us. We had a full house for the shoot with Alison, the grand-kiddos, Uncle Bob, Aunt Carol, and Eric's Mom, Bobbie. Michelle did an awesome job and got some incredible family shots. She knew I loved to lie on Eric's chest and offered to take that exact shot. So she climbed up onto the bed and stood over us to get the best angle. Without question, that was my favorite picture of the day.

That evening, we had a phone session scheduled with our friend Jane and her healing, dancing hands. Throughout the year, Jane had done some healing on Eric, and each time he had had a burst of good health. That night he lay on the couch to receive the healing energy from a distance, and he appeared to be sleeping peacefully, all snuggled on the cushions and under the blanket.

At one point he started moaning in pain and asked if I could run upstairs and grab an oxy painkiller. Before that kicked in, he started crying out in pain. I panicked and texted Jane. She said the fairly intense long distance healing work would continue for a while, and that she would check in again with us later.

Facebook post—December 27, 2016
I am grateful for a day filled with family, love, friendship, intense discussions and healing sessions, new awakenings and insights, a family photo shoot, and above all, kindness. In turn, I send out thousands upon thousands of blessings to each and every one of you!

— 11 —

Eric's Healing Session with Jane and a Goodbye with His Mom

When we connected with Jane again, she reminded us of the first time she went on a wild dolphin swim and watched Eric and me in the water. Apparently, when we thought no one was watching, we swam towards each other, kissed, and did the dolphin dance. I loved that she remembered that moment. On the healing Skype session that morning, she saw that the dolphins and whales were sending their healing frequencies to Eric too.

I listened to part two of the healing session and watched the screen as Jane's hands danced in joyful expression with the possibility of a full and complete healing for my guy. She could see Eric as whole and healthy and dancing with me on a beach in the future. She also saw us writing a book together, and I held those images tightly wrapped in my heart.

During both healing sessions, Jane saw a beautiful cloak of white feathers, singed but transformed, like a Phoenix rising out of the flames. She could see that Eric was involved in the coolest cutting-edge technology, even beyond our imagining. Yet the jury was still out, and he was at choice. She and her team worked on unlocking a part of Eric's brain that most of us never utilize, teaching his body a new way of being and inviting his cells to bathe in that delight.

Eric had three sets of visitors after his session with Jane. The first was a friend he had known since they were in the navy together, over thirty years earlier, Damon. He joked that he lived vicariously through Eric's shenanigans. He confirmed that Eric liked to push the edge of the envelope, even back then...*especially* back then.

Andi and Bea came next and brought some goodies from Hawai'i at his request. It was wonderful to see them and to catch up, although it was bittersweet for Eric knowing that he hadn't been well enough to enjoy Christmas in Hawai'i with them.

Eric's mom, aunt, and uncle arrived soon after with some delicious food they had ordered, and a slice of cake for Uncle Bob's birthday. We sang Happy Birthday to Bob, and Eric and I thanked them profusely for coming up and spending time with us. I wouldn't say that it was an easy visit for Eric, who stayed awake for hours trying to remain present. But he did enjoy their time together.

It was a particularly tough goodbye for his mom, as she didn't know whether she would ever see her one and only boy again. At the front door, she pulled me into a tight hug, and I could feel her breath catch as she said, "You should never have to see your child go before you. That should never be part of God's plan."

"I know Bobbie, I know," I whispered back through my own tears. "I'm still holding out for a miracle. Let's pray that your boy can get on the trial and that it works its magic."

— 12 —

Eric's Belated Christmas Gift for Phillipa

I had the essential oil diffuser on all night, pulsing with healing frankincense and turmeric-filled steam, illuminating the room with ever-changing colors. Each time I awakened, there was a surreal glow coming from the reflection in the window, and I saw that Eric was either lying still deep in thought or massaging the parts of his body causing him the most discomfort. We talked a little, savoring every moment together.

Early in the morning, as Eric was finally sleeping deeply, waves of sadness engulfed me. I had trouble breathing, imagining a future without my Bebe and I fell into a deep sensation of loneliness. I imagined waking up in an empty bed, no one to hear me call out "Beeeebeeeee," no favorite spot on his chest to lie on, no blue eyes to lose myself in, or to crinkle and sparkle as he chuckled at my jokes, no one to share my GOCs with every day, and no one to talk to about life.

It was too much. We both figured we'd be together for decades to come. I, for one, hadn't consented to an early departure. I had visualized we'd be together until we were old and gray and we eventually passed from this world, ideally in each other's arms.

Still, I gathered myself and got on with my day. There was mom duty to do, and I took Bella to the orthodontist to have her post-braces check-up. As I was driving, she clicked play on a song she knew her daddy and I loved: "Chasing Cars," by Snow Patrol. *"If I lay here...If I just lay here...Would you lay with me and just forget the world?"*

I tried to stop them, but my tears flowed again. I wondered why it's considered a thing to be stoic, to hold back our emotions in front of our people. My girl noticed my wet face, and squeezed my thigh as I was driving.

We followed her appointment with a trip to the mall in Bellevue. It felt good to take a break, to be just mummy and daughter, rather than a wife to a husband and a daughter to a daddy who was struggling to stay alive.

We enjoyed our time together, and I relaxed knowing Eric was connecting with his buddy Damon at home. I had no doubt they were talking non-stop for hours.

When we arrived back at the house, I picked up an Amazon package left by our front door that was addressed to Eric. I ran up the stairs and handed it to him. A big grin spread across his face, and he asked me to open it. He watched as I tore open cardboard packaging, more animated than I'd seen him in a while. Beyond the cardboard and bubble wrap was a periwinkle blue box with a beautiful soft black ribbon. I tugged on the bow, eager to see what treasure was hidden inside. I pulled the lid off and there was a hummingbird necklace, in sparkling fourteen karat yellow and white gold. He said it was a belated Christmas present for me.

"Oh my gosh! I love it! How do you do it? How do you always pick out the most amazing gifts? It's got to be one of your superpowers. Thank you!" and I kissed him fully on the lips.

I exclaimed again, "Thank you, my Bebe!" as Eric was sitting against the bed headboard with his biggest of smiles.

Facebook post—December 29, 2016

My guy never ceases to amaze me. Who has the wherewithal to get through their pain and nausea, and secretly order an absolutely perfect gift for their wife who just happens to adore hummingbirds? Eric, my Bebe. That's who.

— 13 —

It's Back to Hospital for Eric

Eric's medical adventure took an unexpected turn the following day. I had been concerned that he was throwing up with or without food or water, and I wanted to see if I could get him hydrated. I called the Oncology department and asked to schedule an appointment to get IV fluids. Dr. Big Boss, although not officially working that day, broke away from his family to come and see Eric. This was very much appreciated by us and not something we had come to expect with the American doctors.

Thankfully, most of my beloved's critical blood counts were within range, with the exception of his creatinine, the waste molecule generated from muscle metabolism and transported through the bloodstream to the kidneys. The kidney's role is to filter out most of the creatinine and dispose of it in the urine. Normal levels of creatinine are 0.6 to 1.2 for an adult male. To be accepted into the CAR T- cell trial, his creatinine needed to be 1.5 or under. On that day, Eric's was 2.6.

The oncologist decided to hospitalize Eric to get his kidneys fully functioning again. He told us that the team would come at him with all guns blazing, and they loaded him up on IV fluids, anti-nausea medicine, nutrition, and more. He wanted to ensure Eric was back on track, first and foremost for his health and wellbeing, in addition to getting him well enough to get on to the CAR T-cell trial.

The good news was that the insurance company confirmed they would cover the cost of the CAR T-cell trial, at just under a half million dollars!

What. The. Heck?!

They said yes, in less than twenty-four hours, to a half million-dollar trial, and yet we still haven't heard what's happening about the rest of our bills from Mexico?

The medical team had their work cut out to get his kidneys functioning well enough to get on the trial. There was also one week of additional testing and cell harvesting before we would know for sure that Eric was eligible.

I left my Bebe at the hospital alone that evening, and that night I did something I almost never do. I made myself a Mimosa and drank alone while watching a show on TV. We were going through a seriously intense time, and it felt decadent, but I figured, "Why the heck not?"

Waking up at 3 a.m. with the TV still on and the empty champagne glass in my hand appealed to my sense of humor. I managed to drag my heavy body to the bedroom, collapsing in a heap on our big empty bed, clothes and all.

— 14 —

Bella and Eric Speak from the Heart

We had no big plans for New Year's. My Bebe was in the hospital fighting for his life, and I was giving everything I had to support him.

I had only two wishes for 2017. First, I wished for my beloved to live through the year and beyond, healthy and happy. Second, I wanted him to be accepted into the trial so those T-cells could work their magic, hunting down and killing the nasty cancerous cells throughout Eric's body. I figured if the trial had worked for others, why not him?

Eric's two girls and I were in the hospital room visiting with him. Bella had been open about having difficulty working through her emotions this last year. To help her process, she wrote a beautiful and authentic piece for her daddy about an evening that occurred almost one year earlier. It was the night we had chosen to tell Bella that Eric had (as we thought at the time) stage four bladder cancer and that he may not make it.

So, on that first evening of the new year, Bella took a deep breath and read her piece to Eric as he lay in his hospital bed.

In Bella's own words:

"We each had our own way to process what was going on around us. One night, I was called into my parents' bedroom. I walked through the door, saw the looks on their faces, and I knew the news was not great. I felt the tension in the room and sat beside my father, his dark blue eyes weary. I felt my stomach drop, and my heart was heavy. I looked up and stared at my mom lying behind him, her eyes a vivid green, the color of trees in the spring.

My mother started to speak, and I could hear, through her blurry words, that she was trying to hold her tears back. I couldn't listen, and honestly, I didn't care. I didn't care why they couldn't fix him, or what was wrong. I didn't care about the tests, or the doctors, or even the cancer. I cared that this was the end. I cared that in front of me lay my hurting mother, and my breaking father.

My dad had struggled to get his words out, and said, 'I am proud of the people in my life. I am proud of myself, and the life I have lived. I love you both very much. I love my eldest daughter, I love my grandchildren, and I love my family and friends. I am so grateful to have lived this life with you all and had so many amazing opportunities. But it's likely my time, and it's your job to stick together and stay strong.'

I had never heard my father speak with such raw emotion, and I admit that it was heartbreaking. I had to accept it, and I don't think I've been closer to anyone than in those few moments."

After Bella read, there was silence, and heartfelt emotions ran deep in the hospital room.

Eric took a breath, and I clicked record on my phone as he responded,

"Being surrounded by such a loving family, along with close friends, gives me the strength and courage to live each day the best I can, with grace and dignity. When Bella read her piece just now, with both my daughters and my lovely wife present, there wasn't a dry eye in the room.

One of my biggest concerns has been that Bella was keeping so much inside, yet I could see the pain in her eyes. She has a gift in poetry and writing that is beyond her years, and I'm proud she uses this gift not only to help herself process but to inspire others.

This type of loving kindness and deep inspirational thought gives me the power to fight this disease and walk this journey with courage, and have a strong desire to be around for each of my daughters' milestones and enjoy the smaller things in life like seeing my grandkids playing and having fun.

I love having similar heartfelt discussions with my eldest daughter, and as you can probably guess from her daily posts, with my wife. We have a lot more open and deep discussions than you see on Facebook. I feel truly blessed to have such a wonderful family. Thank you, Bella. I am so looking forward to your next inspirational insight."

Facebook post—January 1, 2017

Oh boy! How blessed am I to have Eric as my husband and life partner, and Bella as my daughter, both able to articulate and share the toughest of stuff! Hugs to you all, and Happy New Year!

⎯ 15 ⎯

More Liquid Therapy for Eric

It was January 2, and although it was hard to get our heads around it, they told us that Eric would likely need more chemo.

He had declined rapidly in the previous two weeks with something called spontaneous tumor lysis. It's where a bunch of tumor cells die off at the same time, releasing their contents into the bloodstream, changing the blood electrolytes and metabolites, and not in a good way. These metabolic abnormalities, in Eric's case, had led to intense nausea and vomiting, and the first stage of kidney damage.

I felt like I wasn't totally up to speed with what was happening, and was appreciative that Dr. Big Boss had offered me his cell phone number. I called, and he kindly spent thirty minutes on the phone explaining his strategy and walked me through the current plan. Unbelievably, I agreed that chemo seemed to be the only traditional medical route to take, with the goal of getting Eric well enough to meet the criteria to be accepted into the trial. At that moment, with his kidney readings, he was still ineligible.

The nurses hooked him up to the skull and crossbones, and after they left the room, I watched the liquid poison start dripping into his veins. I kissed him on the top of his smooth head, and said, "Bebe, I'm so sorry, but I have to go to work. I love and appreciate you, and I'll be back later."

I drove over the 520 Bridge and marveled at the snow-peaked mountains and ranges looming above and beyond the city: Mt. Baker to the north, Mt. Rainier to the south, the Cascades to the east, and the Olympics to the west.

I felt an angel tap on my shoulder, a reminder that those majestic beauties, reaching up toward the stratosphere, are always there, always present, albeit often hidden behind the veil of clouds in the gray overcast Seattle weather.

At that moment, I felt intense gratitude. I wondered if maybe that's what bliss is, those magical moments of gratitude. Even in the worst of times, they're there if we take a moment to breathe them in and stay present.

Time slowed, and I thought about the conversation with my beloved about scattering his ashes if he didn't make it. This was it, this was the place, right here, under the 520 Bridge.

OMG! OMG! OMG!

Is this really happening?

Did we actually have THAT conversation?

Did we really talk about where we would scatter his ashes?

Facebook post—January 2, 2017

After a busy day, I made dinner at home and soaked in the bath with some delicious-smelling Ylang Ylang bath salts. I looked up the benefits of Ylang Ylang afterward and apparently, it is, amongst other things, an aphrodisiac. Oops! That totally appealed to my sense of humor. Thankfully though, the bath salts also serve to calm the nerves and generally relax the body. Phew!

— 16 —

Eric Hallucinates and Gets a Little Loopy

It was dark in the hospital room, but sensing Eric was awake, I swung my legs over the side of the hard cot and climbed onto the bed to snuggle with him. The doctors confirmed he had tumor lysis, the thing that happens when the kidneys struggle to filter out the toxins. His kidneys were also damaged from the chemo and his creatinine levels were still too high.

Yesterday he had been incoherent, and last night he hallucinated.

"There're fleas everywhere! They're in my bed! Help!" he had shouted out in the middle of the night, kicking off the linens. The hospital staff kindly changed his sheets and blankets, and he went right back to sleep. Of course, there were no fleas in the hospital bed.

I watched him spend thirty minutes trying to type a text to Damon, who figured out the main gist of the text, even though most of it didn't make sense, especially the part where Eric signed off, "Love, Dad."

If it was scary for me to see these developments, I couldn't imagine what it must be like for him.

What's happening to my guy?

Is it too many meds?

Or is this the beginning of the end for my Bebe?

No, no, no, noooooo!

Many of our people started dropping by the wayside. They asked what they could do, but what could they really do, aside from sit with him and take whatever the day brought? It was difficult for them to see him like this, and even Andi was still having difficulty. Their absence spoke volumes, but our core people kept calling and showing up. They were there, no matter what.

The food tray arrived, and he picked up his spoon to feed himself, and once again fell asleep before it reached his lips.

Where has he gone?

Will I ever get him back? Is he scared?

If I'm fucking terrified. What's it like for him?

I sat quietly, watching him sleep. If only I could twitch my nose and take him back to the days when he wasn't loopy and sending incoherent texts to his friends…back to the days when it was just us, our love and gratitude, our little family, our plans for the future, and excitement for all the big adventures yet to come.

> *Facebook post—January 4, 2017*
> The last twenty-four hours have been a little scary. Eric has
> been feeling sick to his stomach, is on more meds than I
> can count, and he's been incoherent and hallucinating.
> Your prayers are needed more than ever.

— 17 —

Eric Moves into the Downstairs Office and Phillipa Leads a Double Life

I received the call to pick Eric up from the hospital the next morning. When I walked into the room, he was sitting in his wheelchair with a grin on his face.

"Take me home, Bebe."

However happy he was to be getting picked up, I was praying I could get enough fluids into his body at home to keep up the slow but sure improvement of his kidney function.

It took a while, yet I got him home, and before long he was happily ensconced on the temporary twin bed in the downstairs office. The idea was to keep him comfortable and get in as many fluids as possible, so he could get on that darned elusive trial.

He ate pancakes for breakfast, wasn't so successful with the yogurt for lunch, and for dinner he was able to handle some canned chicken noodle soup. He didn't want to try the organic chicken soup I had made from scratch that afternoon. He wanted the genetically modified, MSG-laden big-brand soup.

On the work front, the good thing about the fact that almost no one at Microsoft asked what was going on for me was that no one knew what was happening. It allowed me to have some normalcy in my life, as everything else revolved around Eric, as it needed to.

Facebook post—January 5, 2017

On one hand, I am the wife of a very sick husband, and I'm writing and posting like crazy to help process the unbelievably fucked up cancer journey. On the other, I am a Microsoft consultant, where only a couple close colleagues know what's going on with my beloved. I'm leading a double life, and I think I'm okay with that. It's better that way. For now.

— 18 —
The Creatinine Game and the Professional Photos Arrive

After a couple rough days, without much success keeping down food, water, or even canned soup, Eric was back in the hospital for round two of chemo at the hospital in Seattle for 2017.

He felt nauseous, drowsy, and wasn't sure which end was up. I sat beside him as he quietly slept, holding his hand and trying to stay positive.

He enjoyed having Bea and Alison there and did his in-and-out-of-sleep trick while they were present. When they left, he and I sat on the bed together, with me hugging him around his shoulders and back. I asked him whether he had hope.

He said, "I don't have dis-hope. I don't know what my next step is, but I want to keep an open mind."

I loved that Eric had coined a new word, "dis-hope," because I totally understood what he meant. It was all about Eric, and I loved him so much.

The good news was that his creatinine level was 1.41, down from the 2.0s. That was encouraging and the main point of focus. But he also needed to be eating, drinking, and more mobile to get on the trial. It was a bit like managing bobbing balls in the water. Just when we were able to hold down one of the balls and get it under control, another one or two bobbed to the surface.

I brought in a package from home to share with him. It was the photo frames and albums from the non-profit that had taken our family photos. I had been super impressed with the organization, in part because hiring a professional photographer is typically the last thing on your mind when you're supporting someone who's fighting for their life. Although Eric was a little surprised to see how ill he looked, we both loved how the photos turned out.

Facebook post—January 7, 2017

Thank you for all your heartfelt encouragement. You all, in turn, are inspiring me to stay strong, stay connected, keep writing, and be a loving and supportive wife for my guy on this crazy fucked-up cancer journey.

— 19 —

It's Groundhog Day for Eric

My heart broke as I arrived in the ward and saw his skinny "chicken legs" wobbling along, getting weaker by the day.

The doctors had wanted Eric to get some exercise walking around the ward with his walker, and this was the first time he'd had the energy for it in a few days.

My guy felt like he was in Groundhog Day, with the "same old, same old." Eat oatmeal, jello, pudding, rice, get a drug every hour for something, sit on the side of the bed to pee, get his vitals taken…rinse and repeat.

Thankfully, Dr. Big Boss was pleased with Eric's kidney function, as his reading continued to drop into the normal range. But then he started worrying about Eric's white and red blood cell counts. Those bouncing balls in the water . . .

The treatment plan was adjusted yet again to encompass meds to assist the blood cell counts. The idea was for him to come home again soon, and the hospital staff worked with me to ensure that I felt somewhat ready to be able to handle life at home.

It became even more difficult for people to sit quietly and just *be* in the room, particularly as Eric was in a drug-induced state of sleep. Ironically, that day, when everyone was out of the room except me, he woke up and was happy to chat.

Sitting next to my husband, loopy with meds, I felt both intense love and sadness. I had thought we would be together forever. And at that moment, I just didn't know how long forever would be for him.

I sat on the couch to write my daily post and thought about what was going on with my beloved. I tried to be light and stoic to get through these days, but there was nothing light about my beloved's decline.

To round out my post, I added a photo from our wedding day in New Zealand in July 2010. My Eric, as he often would, liked to reach out and lay his hand on the small of my back. In the photo, we're walking along a country road, heading back from photos by the lake on the property. I had hitched up my wedding dress so that it didn't drag on the road, and Eric had his hand on the small of my back to support me as we walked up the hill.

In that moment I couldn't have imagined that, not even seven years later, I would be sitting on a hospital bed with him, holding and supporting him in the small of *his* back as he tried to pee into a plastic container, breathe through the pain and nausea, and reconcile with his mental decline.

Facebook post—January 8, 2017

I am grateful for each and every person in our extended Facebook family who reads my posts and shares in our journey. I am grateful for the prayers and blessings and healing energy and thoughts each and every day from our people. I am grateful to be alive, and I am grateful to have Eric in my life.

— 20 —

Bad News from the Insurance Company and Imaya Comes to Visit

The next day we heard from our insurance company that they had denied the remainder of our claims from Mexico. The most frustrating element for Eric was that before we left for Mexico, his main point of contact had told him that most of the claims would be covered. The denial meant we had over $80,000 left to pay on credit cards. Eric was devastated and felt responsible for our finances.

Rather than dwelling on this, I held Eric's hand and asked him to tell me the highlights of his day. He loved his visit with Imaya, a colleague previously based in India and on one of the teams that Eric managed in his last few years at Microsoft. Although my beloved had found it hard to stay focused and awake, he appreciated that Imaya had flown in from Florida just to spend a couple of hours with him.

Eric also had a sense of achievement with two walks around the hallway on his walker. This was more movement than he'd had in quite some time, and it was monumental for my guy.

I reclined on the bed with him and watched as his eyelids fluttered, and he fell asleep. Soon after, I closed my eyes and slept next to my precious person, at least until I moved to the hospital cot when the nurses made their rounds a few hours later.

Facebook post—January 9, 2017

Imaya's letter to Eric: 'It is impossible for me to simply use the words 'thank you' and move on. Our relationship bloomed out of nowhere and was totally unexpected. Eric, you made that happen. You were not just a manager for me, you were more of a mentor, friend, guardian, and huge supportive pillar during the entire time we worked together. Your heart is lovely, huge, and warm. That is something unique, and very few people possess that, and even fewer are willing to exhibit that quality. You literally channeled my career and offered great support and guidance during a very critical point as I was deciding on moving to the U.S. A BIG THANK YOU for that. I'm confident this trial is going to do the magic and put your life back on track again. I promise I'll come back again next year to see you happy and smiling and in GREAT health.'

— 21 —

Phillipa Sets Up a GoFundMe Account

January 11th was a day for gratitude. Eric was still with us one year after his cancer diagnosis, and he was in good spirits, getting around on his walker, and smiling.

The night before, I'd started a GoFundMe account. The year prior, I wouldn't have thought it necessary, and I don't think we would have been willing to reach out and ask for help from the people in our network. However, when you go through what we'd been through the last twelve months, humility and strength show up in the most unanticipated ways.

Dr. Big Boss called and said, "I'm hoping Eric will be well enough to go home in the next few days and start on the trial next week. If not, he may need another few rounds of chemo."

Oh, yay?

The doctors made their rounds that morning, and as soon as they left, my beloved ate a bowl of cereal. It was only down for a few minutes, and he grabbed a bag. I asked the nurse to bring one of the doctors back to find out why he was still feeling so nauseous. The doctor didn't know but came up with some theories. They had endless theories. One was that it was a side effect of the most recent round of chemo from a week ago. The other was that it was the lymphoma. He shared that the ultrasound indicated there was lymphoma present in the kidney itself.

Well, shit!

Why didn't you say anything?

He has cancer in his kidneys?

As Eric slept, I reached out to a mobile nursing agency for help and IV fluids for my beloved for his time at home.

We got more bad news from the Microsoft insurance people that even basics like radiation, biopsy surgery, and IVs from

Mexico would not be covered because although they were standard treatments, they were ordered from an "experimental facility." This was indeed tough news for Eric.

Later, I sat staring at my laptop screen, struggling with my daily post. It stayed blank for a while, as I was at a loss for words. Of course, I wanted Eric to be okay—to live, to heal, to walk, and to love in a pain-free way again. Sometimes I could see it, feel it, and know it. Other times, I wondered whether he had the will to keep fighting, particularly feeling so sick to his core.

I couldn't imagine how tough it was to be positive and believe "I can do this...I am doing this."

Facebook post—January 11, 2017

We have been humbled to see the donations flowing in from our friends, friends that are family, and even people that we have never met. In the first twenty-four hours, fifty-four kind folks donated and/or shared the GoFundMe account with their networks. It is extraordinary, and we are very grateful for every donation or share, no matter how large or small.

— 22 —

Low Platelets, Nausea, Chemo and Purple Stockings

Eric was home again and I hadn't meant to wear purple stockings that morning. I had been running late and had dressed in a semi-dark closet, so as not to wake Eric up. It wasn't until I was driving to work that I looked down and surprised myself with my purple stockings. I smiled and felt like that might be something Piglet might do, if Piglet were to wear stockings.

Later, Eric had a rough evening, and my heart plummeted. He took oxy for the pain and settled down. I snuggled next to him on the new hospital bed I had ordered to watch *House of Cards* and eventually broke away to sleep upstairs.

My phone rang in the middle of the night, and it was Eric asking me to come downstairs to help him out, as he was going through a tough episode. I stroked and rubbed my beloved's back, sang the lullaby, "Go To Sleep My Baby," and he eventually fell back asleep.

At 6 a.m., it was time to get him up and into the shower. He needed to get ready for our friend, who had graciously volunteered to take him to the hospital for his appointments. Sandy bundled Eric and his walker into her truck and off they went to Seattle for his labs, IV fluids, and a visit with the nurse practitioner. It turned out that Eric's platelets were low, and he required a bag to get the level back up again. My guy was in good hands, and I was grateful that Sandy was flexible enough to stay with him for what ended up being a full day.

It looked like Eric would need more chemo before the CAR T-cell trial started on the latest target date of February 6th. The hope was that the team could figure out a chemo cocktail that wouldn't make him feel nauseous. This was a tough journey at the best of times but worsened significantly when nausea set in.

> *Facebook post—January 13, 2017*
>
> It was a crazy day today – low platelets, nausea, chemo, purple stockings and all. That Eric might get on the trial in early February is great news. As always, any and all healing energy, prayers, visualization, and any other healing offerings, modalities, and intentions you have up your sleeve are absolutely appreciated! Thank you all so much.

— 23 —

A Seahawks Game and Eric Confirms He Is Not Ready to Go Yet

Although his body was much weaker, it was great to have Eric home. However, he struggled to stand up to use his walker or get in and out of the wheelchair. That worried us the most.

That afternoon, we were excited to dress in our Seahawks football colors and went off to Andi and Bea's to watch the game. We ate snacks, laughed, and posed for some fun photos during the ads. We hadn't watched football at all that season, other priorities and all. It didn't matter that the Seahawks were out of the running for the Super Bowl. It was lovely to spend time at our friends' place, talking, eating, and catching up. Sort of like the old days, but not quite.

My guy, a daredevil behind the wheel most of his life, was no longer able to drive. As we were leaving our friends' home, I reached over to help get his legs in a good position and to buckle him into the passenger seat. His breathing was labored, and I sensed he was on the verge of having an emotional moment. However, he held back on the drive home, not ready to go there yet.

When we arrived home, I initiated one of our tough conversations for a few reasons. First, I noticed Eric's mobility had declined rapidly, even during the last twenty-four hours. He had struggled to get from the bed to his walker, from the walker into his wheelchair, and from the wheelchair into the car. He had also needed full support from Andi and me to move him around at their home.

Additionally, we discussed how close he was to requiring twenty-four-hour care. Although we had home nursing options, that would mean he was no longer eligible for the CAR T-cell trial. The participants in the trial had to be somewhat mobile and functional. In other words, they can't manage patients in the trial if they are hospitalized or require extra care to get around.

I picked up his hands in mine, and said, "I love and appreciate that we can talk about everything, Bebe, even death and dying. I know many people can't, and they must have unfinished business, so much left unsaid."

Perhaps there's an element of denial for many, or they're too afraid to discuss a taboo subject like death. As a result, if and when it does happen, arrangements have often not been discussed: funerals, wills, logistics, real estate, portfolio management, bank accounts, passwords, and such.

"If it's your time Bebe, are you ready?" I asked quietly.

His answer was an emphatic, "I am NOT ready to go yet!"

"Okay, great! I'm fully on board. Let's look at your options," I said.

First, Eric could get into remission, either with another round of chemotherapy or the CAR T-cell trial, and assuming he started to feel good all-round, he could potentially start working again at Microsoft.

Second, if he could get into remission but was not well enough (physically, mentally, or emotionally) to go back to work in his previous role, there were other roles he could potentially do in a business capacity at the company.

Finally, if Eric couldn't get into remission, either with additional chemo, the trial, or any other traditional or radical treatment, and started needing twenty-four-hour care, given the aggressive nature of his cancer, this would ultimately lead to going into hospice.

I shared with him that I had reached out to a local hospice organization, and they would only get involved when there was no other option…no more chemotherapy, no more radiation, no more surgery, and no more medication or sustenance of any sort. Their sole focus is on palliative care and comfort until the end.

"I'm going for option one, Bebe! I want to get better and go back to work," he said with as much passion as he could muster. We agreed that there was no question for us. We were energizing the first option. At the same time, I was glad we discussed the other two, so there would be no surprises if or when either one of the other options occurred. Or at least that was my theory.

Facebook post – January 14, 2017

I didn't feel like writing a post tonight, so I wrote a poem:

Please Don't Go!
Written for Eric, by Phillipa

Please don't go!
Selfishly, I am not ready to lose you . . .
I am not ready to explore who I am
without you by my side.
Please don't go!
You've fought so hard this past year . . .
Dealt with more than most can bear,
Please don't go!

We have come so far, and gone so deep . . .
Yet, we have only begun to explore
the universes of each other.
Please don't go!
There is more work for you to do,
more of YOU to Become . . .
The world needs the rare and unique BEing you are,
To help connect the dots with health,
big data and technology.
Please don't go!
You've learned so much throughout the journey . . .
About yourself, me as your life partner,
our friends, our families.
Please don't go!
Your daughters need the Life Coach in you . . .
Your grand-kids need the Wise Man within . . .
coaching, guiding, and role modeling for them.
Please don't go!
What about all the things left unsaid?
What about all the places you yearn to visit?
I'm asking nicely,
But I mean it . . .
Please don't go!

~ 24 ~

Phillipa and Eric Explore Eric's Legacy

I noticed there were fifty-six infusion rooms at the cancer care facility. Cancer is prevalent in Seattle, and this is where many on the journey come to get outpatient services, like IV fluids and chemotherapy. On that day, it was all about fluids for my husband. Later in the week, he'd be back for more of the nasty stuff.

Ugh, sigh.

Seriously, more chemo?

Isn't there anything else they can offer?

Almost unbelievably, I agreed with the doctors. At that stage, my beloved's body required radical treatment to kick him into remission. Ideally, that would be chemo initially and then, hopefully, the CAR T-cell trial the following month.

It's a double-edged sword with the doctors prescribing chemo to potentially kick their patients into remission. At the same time, it's widely known to be carcinogenic or worse, oftentimes morphing the cancer into something different and more resistant, as happened to Eric with both the two main chemo protocols: R-CHOP and RICE. Another sigh, but the goal was to get Eric into remission and make a new plan from there.

As we drove home from his appointments, I asked Eric about his legacy and what that looked like. Of course, I knew of the difference he had made in the lives of others throughout his life…in the Navy, at Microsoft, and in the various business and management coaching roles he had over the decades. I was curious what a more recent legacy might look like.

"What about the amazing impact you've had by allowing me to tell your story?" I asked. "You've seen people's comments. They're moved by your journey and some have been inspired to make healthier changes in their lives."

"Yes, and maybe there's a way we could create a charity or organization that would leave a greater impact?" he pondered.

"Lovely," I said, and followed up with, "How about we focus on getting you into remission first, and then we'll see what sort of a legacy you can create?"

He nodded as we drove up our driveway, parked in the garage, and went through the new normal routine: me, bringing the wheelchair around from the back of the car, Eric slowly bringing his legs around, grabbing onto the door for stability, slipping into the wheelchair with a grunt, and finally me pushing him up the ramp and into his temporary lower floor bedroom.

"Want to watch a movie with me?" he asked. I grabbed some water for us and snuggled next to my guy. We hadn't quite decided what to watch when I spied he was already asleep. So that evening, I watched a movie as my Bebe slept soundly beside me.

Facebook post—January 15, 2017

Things don't always go as planned, and sometimes love looks like me watching a movie as my lover boy lies next to me, snoring softly.

— 25 —

Two Hot Blond Chicks Touching Eric All Over and Some Bad News at the ER

"Two hot blonde chicks touching Eric all over," was the text I received the following morning during a meeting with real estate clients. I grinned, grateful that two friends were with my beloved at home. I had put a call out asking for help to get him to his first appointment for IV fluids. My plan was to meet him in Seattle and escort him to his next appointment to see an orthopedic surgeon and his oncologist, Dr. Big Boss.

Sandy had responded right away, saying yes to transporting my guy to the hospital. Thankfully, Hilary was already at the house visiting Eric, as it took both of them, performing all sorts of gyrations, to get him into Sandy's big Yukon truck.

By the time I took over hours later, my Bebe was exhausted. When we met with Dr. Big Boss, we told him that Eric had been losing more mobility each day, with a particularly drastic decline over the last few days. Even more ominous, he noticed that Eric had no reaction when he did the hammer-to-the-knee reflex test. Nada.

"Can you try to stand up?" he asked. "Without your walker?"

I found myself holding my breath.

Indeed, Eric couldn't stand, and the doctor said, with his fingers cupping his chin, "Hmm, you're going to need to get an MRI to see if there is any spinal involvement. But if we order one here, it'll take some time. I suggest you head over to the Emergency Room right away."

We swung into action, and I drove him to the ER. I flagged down someone to help lift Eric out of the car, as he could no longer swing his legs nor hold his own weight. The ER was full to overflowing and unfortunately, he was not a top priority given that his was a diagnostic need.

After a few hours, Eric was taken to a bed in the hallway, out of the ER intake area. He was slightly more comfortable lying down, and two different doctors and a nurse kept an eye on him, examining him out in the open. He didn't mind. We were grateful that the medical professionals were taking care of his needs, and we knew he would eventually get his MRI. As always, Eric didn't whine and complain. He just got on with it.

Finally, at 2 A.M., my beloved was whisked away for the long-awaited MRI. It was supposed to be in two parts, the spine first and then the right hip. However, after the spinal session, he was in too much pain to continue.

Please please please!

I pray to God, Goddess, All That Is, all angels and archangels and benevolent beings . . .

Please send a miracle for my beloved!

Pleeeeeeasse!

We had an inkling we weren't going to like the results and we were right. Eric was finally taken into an ER room at 3 A.M., and the doctor came in to share the news that there was evidence of multiple tumors in his lower spine, the lower lumbar, and sacrum sections.

Oh no! Oh no! Oh no!

Shit! Fuck!

No Car T-cell trial now!

No fucking trial at all!

Oh no! Oh no! Oh no!

They took him straight up to the top floor, the floor dedicated to cancer, and admitted him. I laid on the bed with him. We held each other.

There were no words.

For now.

Facebook post—January 17, 2017

Sadly, there are more tumors in my beloved's spine and surrounding areas. Praying and hoping this is not the end and that his time is running out. Please everyone, please pray for a miracle for my guy.

— 26 —

Ropes and Pulleys and All Hope for the CAR T-Cell Trial is Gone

M orphine and Oxycodone had the desired effect, but, whereas Eric was feeling no pain, I continued to feel it all.

The MRI results confirmed he was now completely ineligible for the CAR T-cell trial, and in fact, any trial. He was going to need ten radiation sessions to reduce the level of pain and increase mobility. There were a couple of drugs they could try, but Dr. Big Boss warned me that both were not only expensive, requiring a substantial co-pay each month, but they were not necessarily designed to treat lymphoma. Like a lot of drug discoveries, in using this medication for other maladies the doctors inadvertently had some success with lymphoma patients.

The news was not great, the prognosis worse, yet we still held out for a miracle.

In a lucid moment, I asked my Bebe how he felt about the new developments. He decided he'd rather spend time daydreaming of a vacation to keep his mind off the news. I jumped on board and asked him where he'd like to go.

Of course, he said the Seychelles. He had always wanted to go, and he visualized going with Andi, Bea, and me. I was right there with him and knew that our buddies would go with us in a heartbeat, if only he could get to a point of reasonable mobility, could eat, drink, and have fun. We figured there was no harm in dreaming.

When Bella and I walked together into his hospital room that evening, Eric was in la la land, and feeling pretty happy. Morphine and Oxycodone can do that to a person. The nurses had an alarm on in case he tried to get out of bed, as he needed to be lifted with a sling contraption, with ropes and pulleys and all.

Oh God.

Ropes and pulleys?
What is happening?
This can NOT be good!

I reminded myself of the parable, "It's not good, it's not bad. It just is."

We operated on a one-day-at-a-time basis. It was about being present in the moment, catching up with bills to be paid, things that needed to be handled, and getting everything in order. Spending time with each other and the girls and close friends was right up there too.

When I got home, I allowed all sorts of emotions to come up and pass through. I was sad, angry, in shock, but most significant of all, I still had hope. For my daily post, I felt driven to write a list of urgent reminders to everyone to go and live their lives.

Facebook post—January 19, 2017

Everyone, listen in . . .

If you want to go to the Seychelles, please go! Just do it!
If you have a dream, live it!
If you don't have a dream—get one! (I think
everyone ought to have a dream.)
If you are drawn to help out kids in an orphanage
in Thailand, or Ecuador or Rwanda—go for it!
If you want to start a business—what are you waiting for?
If you want to get healthier and fitter—
just do it, with no excuses!
If you are unhappy in your relationship—make a change!
If you don't like your job—get a new one!

They say life is too short, and they are right.
Do what you want to do,
Feel what you want to feel,
Be what you want to be,
See what you want to see,
Open up doors that scare you!
But, most of all...just go live your life!

— 27 —

Rainbow Healing Colors for Eric

My journal put me at Day 90. Ninety days since I started writing daily about Eric's journey to Mexico to heal from his foray into the underworld of traditional cancer treatments.

He had started having anxiety attacks during the night. These events of sudden onset terror were frightening for him. Being a deep thinker, in his calm moments he figured out what was triggering his attacks. He tracked it back to a nurse telling him he needed to get regular movement and change his position regularly or he would develop bed sores, and those can be tricky to heal.

That may have been true, but I think it went deeper than that. Perhaps something like, "What will happen if my body doesn't heal at all?"

As I was lying in the hospital cot, I looked over at Eric sitting up in bed with his hospital gown hanging off his frame. His body had continued to waste away, and, although I had never experienced full-on panic or anxiety attacks, I did feel a catch in my chest when I acknowledged how sick he was looking or when I imagined what it would be like to lose him. If I allowed myself to dip into the fear, even for a moment, I tried to stay conscious enough to bring myself back out quickly by thinking good thoughts.

I loved imagining, for example, Eric wake-surfing behind the boat. I visualized him holding on to the rope and doing the infinity movement with his lower body and legs. He would get into the zone and become one with his body, the board, the wave, and the universe. It was easy for me to picture, as I had taken hours of video of him behind the boat over the years—in the mist of early mornings, the heat of summer days, and as he turned into a silhouette against the setting sun.

I reached out to Clara, a long-time spiritual teacher I had reconnected with recently. She recommended we visualize a few strategically placed golden balls in Eric's body. Their job was to go throughout his body like little "pac-men," gobbling up every cell of cancer. The final step was to thank them for doing their job and send them packing back home.

We also called on the healing angels and asked them to multiply the effects of the radiation a thousand times. We asked them to shower Eric with the rainbow healing colors he needed for perfect health and wellbeing. As Clara reminded me, Eric could potentially neutralize every bit of cancer in his body, if he could imagine that as a possible outcome.

Where is that miracle we have been holding out for?

Is it just around the corner, or did it slip by unseen?

Come back miracle! Please.

Hover over my beloved's body and shower him with healing rainbow-colored light.

We haven't finished all the chapters of our love story.

Now is the time, please, if you're out there, miracle…come back!

I needed a break and scheduled a massage at a place called "The Tummy Temple" in Seattle. I experienced a divine slice of heaven in their capable hands. I had a hard time not feeling guilty and reminded myself that the caretaker needs to be cared for too sometimes.

> *Facebook post—January 21, 2017*
> We are staying hopeful, daydreaming about going to the Seychelles and visualizing a miracle. As my spiritual teacher said, 'It's not over yet, and we are not giving up.'

— 28 —

Eric Gets His Affairs in Order and Offers Bella Financial Advice

The following day, I saw an email Eric sent Bella. In it, he was giving her financial advice for her future, and it made me cry.

You need to transfer $ from your savings to your checking account. You have already used 2 of 6 of your allotted overdraft protection allocations this month. Remember the tricks to getting around this type of situation are to:

Transfer larger amounts of $ from savings to checking (like $100 or more, for example)

Monitor your checking amount via your phone app prior to spending, so you know what is exactly in your checking account

Use $50 as your bottom-line threshold instead of $0

Follow these simple principles, or minimum rules, when it comes to operating your checking account, and you will never bounce a check or go into overdraft. Master these rules when you are young so you will have high credit scores in your future. This will be very important to you later on in life.

Love Daddy xxx

I cried because Eric was giving advice to our fifteen-year-old daughter, with the assumption he wouldn't be around to ensure she learns good financial principles.

Prayers. Prayers. Prayers.

Our girl needs her daddy.

She's too young to lose her daddy, so . . .

Please, I pray to God for a miracle for her daddy.

Eric had a busy day. He had physical and occupational therapy. He talked on the phone with Andi, and Damon came by the house to pick up computer stuff and a small table to take to the hospital, as Eric had requested.

When I spoke to my guy later, he was giving instructions to Damon about the computer setup and was keen to get off the phone so he could get caught up on paperwork and such.

I wondered if that meant he was getting his affairs in order?

Facebook post—January 24, 2017

I had some tears on my keyboard with the possibility that my beloved was getting his affairs in order and giving financial advice to our fifteen-year-old Bella. There's something to be said for denial from time to time. Just sayin'.

— 29 —

Eric Sets Up His Computer and a Desk on the Transplant Floor

I walked into his hospital room and stopped in my tracks. There, against the far wall, Eric had the full-size computer table from home and his desktop computer and monitor all set up, complete with power strip, and ready for business.

"Oh my god, Bebe! I like your new office! It looks pretty cool!"

My Bebe's grin was priceless. He also cracked up the hospital staff. When they walked into his room, they too did a double take. I'm guessing most patients on the penthouse transplant floor are typically too sick to work on their computers.

It was also the day for more radiation treatment and a spinal tap. They injected chemo into my beloved's spine, and the spinal fluid they removed was sent to pathology. It was now a waiting game to get the results and to adjust the plan…again.

Eric was excited to have an appetite and had fried chicken and a bottle of Coca-Cola for dinner! It wasn't food approved by me, but he was putting on weight, and that was the main goal.

We had a good cry that night. Through his tears he told me his biggest fear.

"Bebe, I've been worrying about something. I'm afraid that you'll forget me."

I jumped on the bed with him and held him tight. I spoke quietly but vehemently, "No matter what, you will NEVER EVER be forgotten!"

I stayed on the bed for a while, even when I realized his breathing had slowed into sleep. I thought about his biggest fear to assure myself too. Whether he had a miraculous recovery and lived a long time, or faded away soon, I knew I *would never, could never* forget him—my unique and unforgettable life partner.

He was so intense, yet able to be light and have fun. He was a deep thinker and could articulate beautifully what he was thinking and feeling. He was the first person I had ever met who created the space for me to express my truth. There's such freedom of spirit to be in a relationship where we encourage each other to feel what's true for us, and to be safe enough to express that.

I whispered into his ear before leaving the bed, "Nope, my love, there is just no way you could ever be forgotten."

Facebook post—January 25, 2017

Eric told me today he was afraid he'd be forgotten. I reminded him we've been sharing his journey with our Facebook world, and he has many supporters following the journey every day and cheering him on from the sidelines. I reminded him, who knows, maybe I'll write a book about his journey. Either way, he will never be forgotten!!

— 30 —

Phillipa and Eric Come Back from the Abyss

We were back from the abyss! It was pretty scary. Feeling helpless, hopeless, and fearful was not a great place to be. Eric had felt like he was fading away and that the worst was yet to come, and I had dipped into feeling what that was like for him. Typically, if one of us took a dive, the other remained strong and helped our beloved see things from a different perspective. The day prior, I was experiencing so much compassion for what he was going through, though, that I dove in deep too.

To switch things up, I massaged Eric's body and poured love into every stroke, despite the little bumps and tumors all over. I focused on love, not fear, when my fingers unearthed new lumps under his armpit and on his chest. It was an act of love, and something I hadn't been able to do in recent months because he had been in too much pain or hadn't felt like being touched. Lucky for me, his skin had been drying out in the hospital room air, and he asked me to massage some moisturizer into his body.

While I was loving on my Bebe, I thought again about what he meant to me, this man, my beloved husband. We had learned the power of conscious relationship in marriage together. I had always wanted something like that, without even fully knowing what it meant. I just knew I wanted something more. And we did it, we got there. We arrived there by doing our daily GOCs. We did it by being open and honest and allowing the deepest level of communication, always.

Over the previous year, we had been able to give each other strength and courage when the other was running short of one or both. We cried, we laughed, we sat in silence, we played cards, and we watched movies. We talked and talked about anything and everything. We enjoyed dreaming together about things we hadn't yet done and still wanted to do.

Back to the reality at hand, it was a day of radiation, food, and rest. No friends called or came to visit, and he was okay with that. Thankfully his kidney creatinine level was trending down again. The docs said a little of his spinal chemo was filtering through into his bloodstream, but it wasn't too bad.

The big decision for the doctors was what systemic chemo treatment to give him, and whether the medical professionals would allow it on the rehab floor. I think we already knew the answer to that.

Dr. Big Boss confirmed that the one drug in pill form they were considering had a co-pay of $4,000 per month.

$4,000 per month?

More out of pocket expenses.

Oh yay! Just what we need!

Even so, if that was the one with the fewest side effects for the kidneys, then that had to be the frontrunner.

— 31 —

Eric's Fragile State and Bougainvillea Murals

We looked around the tiny room and marveled at the bright colors of the mural painted across the walls. It was a vision of sunshine, warm sand, turquoise waters, and cerise-colored Bougainvillea. We could almost imagine the hammock swaying gently in the breeze. We wondered whose idea it was to paint it and how they got permission in an otherwise white-walled, sterile hospital environment.

I had seen lovely paintings hanging on the walls and hallways throughout the hospital, but this mural was located where patients could enjoy it as they were waiting for their next radiation treatment. Eric told me they had also painted tulips on the ceiling above where you lie to receive the radiation.

It ended up being an emotional and anxious day for my beloved. When his tears first started, I rubbed his back, stroked his shoulder, and laid my head on his. I climbed onto the hospital bed, and we cried together. Kudos to the nurse and doctor who came in, didn't say a word, turned around, and left.

My beloved reiterated to me that he was not ready to die but realized there might not be much more anyone could do at that point.

"I feel like I'm just rotting away," he said.

We hugged, and I whispered words of encouragement, "I love and appreciate you Bebe and I am so proud of your determination and strength to keep going. I need you and your baby girl needs you, and we are here for you."

It felt raw and real and sad, but it was somehow freeing to be open and authentic too.

I had planned to go back home that evening, but with Eric in such a fragile state, I decided to sleep over again. I wanted to be there for him, whether he was asleep or not.

Facebook post—January 27, 2017

I'll finish up with a wonderful A. A. Milne quote from the infamous Pooh and Piglet duo. Piglet: 'How do you spell love?' Pooh: 'You don't spell it, you feel it.'

～ 32 ～

Eric's Spiritual and Emotional Journey Intensifies

We had my spiritual teacher on speaker phone early that morning. Clara could see that my beloved was at a crossroads. The timing of his healing, or not, was between Eric and God, but the how or when could be heavily impacted by Eric's hope and belief.

"Even though your body feels and looks weak, Eric, your spirit and life force are still REALLY strong," she reiterated. "You are at choice. The doctors and medical professionals are doing everything they know to do, but they're not inside your heart, and they're certainly not a part of your relationship with God."

Clara reminded Eric, "If your mind starts to daydream about negativity," she said, "Stop it before it can go any further. Make your movie about the life you choose, not what you don't want to manifest. The best way to create the reality you want is through your thoughts, words, emotions, behaviors, and actions—starting with a dream, a prayer, or a request to God or the Universe.

"Eric, there are also a lot of stored emotions in your body starting to surface. Like most people, your tendency is to push down what's painful, the things you don't want to deal with. It's important to allow all the emotions you've hidden away over your lifetime to surface. This is not so you can get stuck and consumed with them, but they're surfacing so you can let them go."

I asked how Eric could deal with his emotions as those big feelings were surfacing. Clara said that a great tool is to visualize a burning violet flame and direct it to burn negative thoughts and emotions, effectively transmuting them.

Eric asked point blank, "Why is cancer happening to me now?"

She said that although it might seem like a horrible situation, it could be turned into a gift . If this hadn't come up when it did, he may not have had the opportunity to discover that these emotions needed to be cleared out, and he wouldn't necessarily have had a reason to wake up. His cancer journey presented him with that choice to do the tough work.

"This is not a punishment. You are not a victim in any way, and Eric, you can get through this!" she said.

Whether he was going to choose to or not, she didn't have that answer. She told us that she had seen a lot of people who were given two days to two weeks to live and are still around now, years later.

"It can happen! It happens all the time," she said. "The time for action is now, and I recommend that you are open to receive the healing energy available for you."

I was proud Eric was willing to work with Clara and consider more than one outcome. I was amazed he was receptive to go even deeper, to start releasing another layer of stored emotions, and that he was open to fully healing on a spiritual and emotional level, regardless of the outcome. Most of all, I was happy he was not willing to give up on his dreams. Not yet.

Facebook post—January 28, 2017

For the last 100 nights, Andi and Bea have been setting off 'wishing lanterns' across the lake every night in honor of Eric. They called and said, 'Tonight, we let go two wishing lanterns, and, while we made our wishes, a shooting star joined the two lights and added another wish to this night. Sweet dreams, Sir Eric!! We love you so, so much!!!' Oh boy! Tears on my keyboard! Go Eric—you can do it! As our wonderful spiritual teacher reminded us today, 'ANYTHING is possible!'

— 33 —

Eric Has Another Healing Session

The next morning, we heard a gentle knock on the sliding door, and Jane peeked in. We hugged and kissed our hellos, and she got busy.

She started working on my beloved's body, her healing hands flying and fluttering all over. She danced around the room and stood quietly beside his body. She was, at one moment, etherically massaging him, and the next, leaping to a different spot by his head, his feet, or by his side. She had music playing, and it reminded me of Eric's favorite song, the movie theme from *The Gladiator*—at times soft and unobtrusive, and at others powerful and strong. I could see the healing session was impacting him. He smiled, had tears in his eyes, and went into a deep sleep.

Once the session was complete, Jane pointed to the hallway so we could chat without disturbing my beloved. She said the healing session went well, and she could see that although Eric could make a full recovery, the jury was still out. It could go one way or the other. She shared that when she had first *looked* at him several months earlier, she saw what appeared to be a network of brittle coral where his bones should be. This time she saw a stronger grid throughout his body.

Towards the end of the session, when I was sitting at Eric's feet, Jane had witnessed a powerful vortex coming through her hands and from my heart. She had heard, "Miracle man," and responded, "Bring it on. He can be the miracle man!"

Jane had energetically removed what didn't belong and said she could see light going into Eric's body on a schedule. To complete the healing, she set the intention that every person entering his hospital room comes in with harmony and light to bless him on his journey.

Facebook post—January 29, 2017

I am so blessed to have had two powerhouse healers working on my beloved over the last 24 hours. I appreciate Clara and Jane! I am blown away by their level of commitment, skill, humility, and power. It's like magic, what they can see and do. And they both see a path forward for Eric. This is so encouraging. And I hope to God it's not too late.

— 34 —

Dr. Big Boss Announces His New Plan to Get Eric into Remission

Jane slept over at our home in Kirkland. Like me, she's a morning person, and we dressed for an early morning hike into the neighboring forest. We chatted excitedly, as you do when you've been friends for many lifetimes and you're excited to have recognized each other again in a different body and at a different time.

The forest was breathtaking, with its vivid green leaves and swollen streams. We skipped over muddy puddles and balanced on homemade wooden bridges. We stopped and breathed in the feeling of life itself and listened intently to the sound of the coursing water as it rushed over pebbles and stones on its way to the lake.

"Thank you, dearest Jane, for coming to spend some time with us, albeit short! How wonderful you are, and how blessed we both feel," I said as I hugged her goodbye. And off she went, back to California, as I drove into a different reality to see my Bebe in the hospital.

Dr. Big Boss came to visit and started off with the more palatable part of the conversation. He said he was happy with Eric's progress and was looking to the future. If he was doing well in three months, he may yet get on the trial. I could tell Eric liked that, judging by the size of his smile. He needed something to look forward to.

The current plan was to keep the pain at bay, get him into remission, and give him more mobility in his legs and hips. Eric was pleased that after the fifteen radiation treatments, he was able to get himself from the bed to the wheelchair and back again.

"Sure beats getting lifted by that sling contraption," he added with a grin, "Although it was kind of fun."

Then Dr. Big Boss gave us the shock of the day when he told us that they would likely be putting a port in Eric's head. "The purpose of the port is to drip chemo directly into the brain, which we hope will also feed into the spine." I looked at Eric, but instead of sharing my horrified reaction, he was listening intently to the doc.

"There's also the matter of systemic chemo, to work on the cancer in the rest of the body. We are considering using the immunotherapy drug called Rituximab."

Eric looked at me with a slight grin, and I knew why. Two words, "mouse nuts." At the beginning of this whole chemo journey, we learned that the antibody was from a one third non-human source, and in this case, mice.

Facebook post—January 30, 2017

I'm going to finish up today's post with another quote from the infamous Pooh and Piglet. 'Promise me you'll always remember: You're braver than you believe, stronger than you seem, and smarter than you think.'

— 35 —

Eric Gets Some Good News, But With a Twist

Today Eric had some good news but with a twist. He heard from Dr. Big Boss that after studying his MRI brain results, Eric didn't have cancer in the brain. The twist is that the doctors had assumed that he did.

Hello, people!

Don't tell the patients they have cancer in the brain if you don't know.

Best to wait until the results are in.

Even with the good news, his nausea continued to build in intensity, and he requested that he have no visitors during the day. Instead of going to the hospital in the morning, I was able to spend time with my dear friend Gail, in town from Hawai'i and staying at our place.

When we arrived at the hospital in the late afternoon, Eric was very sleepy and slightly incoherent. He had just completed his radiation sessions and had moved wards so they could administer another couple of rounds of the dreaded liquid therapy.

He passed out asleep regularly, and Gail and I would just turn to each other and talk. I loved that Gail would often come to visit for a week and end up staying two weeks or two months. She's that sort of a friend.

As we were driving home, Gail mentioned that even though Eric was a bit loopy on his medication, he was still pretty funny.

Later at home, sitting on the comfy couch in front of the fire, she asked gently, "How are you really doing my friend?"

I stared at the fire in silence for a moment, unable to form a coherent answer right away but felt a tear slip out and slide over my cheek. She scooted over and hugged me tight as I bawled.

I cried over the unfairness of it all: the horrendous journey and my guy's failing body. I cried over the possibility that after all the hard work of the medical professionals in two countries, with two diametrically opposed medical systems, he still might not make it. I cried for me and for his two girls, grand-kiddos, and friends. I cried because I could and I needed to at that moment.

— 36 —

Will Eric Ever Catch a Break?

I could see it, and Eric could feel it. The medical professionals confirmed the radiation had helped enormously with his mobility. Indeed, Eric liked being able to move about more and enjoyed his short walks around the ward with his walker. That was the good news.

The bad news was that Eric's kidneys were now seriously struggling.

Ugh! Good grief!

Will my Bebe ever catch a break?

It turned out there were three problem areas in his kidneys. His creatinine level was high again, the BUN was not at a healthy level, and there was confirmed significant cancer involvement in his kidneys.

What the heck? Ugh, what next?

The doctors believed the cancer was producing protein deposits in the kidneys, the main reason for the damage and dysfunction. Eric met with the kidney doctor, as he would be overseeing the progress of his kidneys and was hoping to have some good news in the coming weeks.

I spoke to Dr. Big Boss, and he confirmed that the timing for everything was now critical. The radiation team preferred a gap of least seven days before the next main systemic round of chemo. Then, a week later, the surgeon would insert a port into his brain for the Rituximab to cycle around his brain and spine.

In the interim, they were going to drip in a steroid called Dexamethasone to try to calm down the inflammation of the kidneys and clear out some of the proteins prior to the next chemo session. It's been known to counteract certain side effects of their antitumor treatments, and ironically, the reason it works so well is still unclear.

OMG! The medical professionals don't have a clue as to why and how it works!

Good Grief.

Facebook post—February 4, 2017

I'm remaining positive and hopeful.

— 37 —

Eric Sleeps Away His Days and Swallows Pills in Caramel-Flavored Pudding

I sat beside Eric's bed and watched him sleep, wondering if this was all there was for my beloved. Sleeping away his days, swallowing pills in caramel-flavored pudding, slipping in and out of awareness while hooked up to machines to ensure he was still breathing and his heart still beating.

Eric woke up and asked for a strawberry milkshake but promptly forgot to order it, then woke up again wondering where it was. I called and ordered his shake, and when it finally arrived, he had two sips before falling asleep again, milkshake in hand.

With his brain cleared of cancer, Eric's increased signs of confusion continued to baffle his doctors. They couldn't determine the cause. The team of a half dozen doctors descended upon the room and one of them took the lead. He read basic questions, dutifully taking notes of Eric's responses.

"Can you tell me what year you were born?" Eric looked confused and sheepishly turned his head to look at me. He knew he should have known the year of his birth, but he couldn't pull the data from his brain. He turned back to the doctors and shrugged his shoulders.

"Can you tell me your name?" He smiled; he could remember that one.

"Eric," he said.

"Can you tell me the date?"

He smiled again and said proudly. "February 22." His daughter Alison's birthday.

It was February 6th. They all looked at each other. After another few questions, I held up my hand in the universal stop sign and said, "I think we get the picture. Any chance we can move on?"

Once the team left the room in a swish of white coats, I was alone with my guy. His eyes said it all.

"What's happening to me, Bebe?" he asked.

"Don't worry," I answered. "They have you on so many medications, you barely know which way is up. You're going to be just fine, my love."

As he slid back to sleep, I wondered.

OMG!

What IS happening to my Bebe?

Is this it? Is this all there is?

Where did he go? Will he ever come back?

I laid down by the window and curled into a ball, feeling quite alone. I looked back over at my sleeping, loopy husband and picked up my journal. I wrote about some of the things I would miss about my big love should the worst come to pass. It was painful to think about, but things were not looking good for my Bebe, and I figured it was healthier to sit with the what-ifs, even just for a moment, in the event he didn't have much longer.

Facebook post—February 6, 2017

I know I've mentioned this quote before, but it's worth repeating, 'Some people care too much. I think it's called love,' Pooh says to Piglet. All prayers and blessings desperately and gratefully received.

— 38 —
The Word Love and a White Winterland Landscape

I had come home late the night before and awakened to a winter wonderland. I sat on the edge of our bed and took a picture of the gorgeous white landscape visible through the bedroom window. A metal art piece with the word LOVE sat on the windowsill, in the forefront of my photo. I wanted to share a little scene from home with my beloved and texted the photo to him.

I had lost count of how many days and weeks he'd been in the hospital, but it was around three weeks at that point. It felt weird wandering around the home for such long periods of time without Eric in it. He was such a large presence, always felt and noticed by me. I stepped into the walk-in closet in the master bedroom and looked at his clothes, most of which were going to be too big for him moving forward. I stood at the top of the stairs, knowing it was going to be a long while before he could tackle stairs again. It was surreal, and a part of me expected the front door to open and hear him bounding up the stairs, two at a time, coming to me for kisses and hugs.

Everything was different now. When I wanted to see my guy, I had to plan ahead—pack a bag, jump in the car, drive over the bridge, park in the underground parking lot, walk through the long hospital corridors and wards, and head up eight floors in the elevator. I would enter the hospital room, and he'd be lying in the bed looking so small and fragile. I loved him just as much, but it was a shock each time I saw him. It took a while for my brain to calibrate what was happening with my beloved husband, sometimes even on a daily basis.

Thankfully, the team of doctors was not giving up on him. They were doing the steroid medication that day, and Eric had had a spinal tap the day prior. His kidney reading was through the roof though at 3.2, and the doctors were hoping that both the steroids and the chemo would normalize this. But they didn't really know for sure.

I wanted my guy home with Bella and me for a while, but knowing that he would need 24/7 care, I let it go, and enjoyed the moments and hours we spent together at the hospital. At times he was his old self, sometimes loopy and not present, and at other times he was cranky and short. I imagined I might be irritable too if I had been in a hospital for weeks at a stretch, no end in sight.

I just kept on loving my guy, hoping and praying he would make it through the next few weeks of tough treatments.

Facebook post—February 7, 2017

Sometimes I can see it, feel it, and know it—that he is going to kick this dis-ease to the curb. Other times, I just don't know. Of course, as my spiritual teacher reminds me, it's not up to me. It's between Eric and God. So, I take deep breaths, and let it all go...the holding on to a certain outcome. Eric's spirit is strong and grounded, so let's see what the plan is for him.

— 39 —

Eric Contracts MRSA and Phillipa Dreams of the Seychelles

I peeked through the glass sliding door, and when I went to open it, I felt a gentle tap on my arm. It was one of the nurses gently explaining that Eric had contracted MRSA, (Methicillin-resistant Staphylococcus aureus), and that in order to enter the room, I had to be gowned, gloved, and masked up. So, I did all that and gingerly entered. He was awake and watched me come to him, with my pale yellow gown and powder blue mask and gloves. He reached up to hug me, and I held his thin frail body in my arms.

"How are you really, Bebe?" I asked him.

He shrugged his shoulders and repeated, "It's the same old, same old, Groundhog Day."

"I know, I know, my love. It seems if it's not one thing, it's another. But, I love you, and I appreciate you!"

He hadn't had the energy or been present enough to do our daily practice of GOCs for a while, and he grinned. We sat quietly, just holding hands, being sure of each other—gloves, protective gear, and all.

He eventually fell asleep again, and I jumped online to learn more about the MRSA infection. I had heard of it and knew it was both common and contagious in a hospital environment. I read that it's an infection caused by a type of staph bacteria that is resistant to standard treatments for ordinary infections.

Yep, here we go again with those fucking bobbing balls!

Will he ever catch a friggin' break?

The nurse woke Eric up to prepare him for his battery of tests. It was a big day with a brain CT and stomach ultrasound. I sat with my guy between the tests and followed him back to get the care he needed at the Intensive Care Unit, once he was done.

That night, as I slept near Eric in the hospital, I had a wonderful dream. In the dream, my Bebe and I were on a plane traveling to the Seychelles. He was fit, vital, and a picture of health. He was wearing exquisite white linen pants and a matching shirt, open to a few buttons down and hanging loose over his pants. His face was tanned golden, and he had a full head of hair, shimmering with varying shades of silver. He was looking at me and glowing with a sort of bright light from within.

The dream jumped ahead, and we were on the beach. It was a gorgeous day and we were walking on an expanse of fine white sand, and the ocean to our left was a vivid turquoise. There were people all around, but they were blurry, like they didn't fully belong in our dreamy world. Rather than walking, we were holding hands and skipping high, eight feet in the air. We would come back down to feel the soft warm sand on our feet and then rebound in slow motion up in the air again. We were laughing and happy and totally focused on each other, staring into the other's soul. We understood that this is where we should be, always.

I woke up abruptly to the alarms blaring on Eric's monitors. The nurses rushed in and adjusted his lines and called for the doctor. I was bleary eyed and still waking up from that exquisite dream with my beloved and me skipping high above the beach in the Seychelles. I wanted to go back to that reality, and I could imagine that my Bebe would like that too…at one with God and the universe, healthy again and living his best life, in the place that remained on the top of his bucket list.

The harsh reality was that he was very sick, and I heard the doctor talking in hushed tones to the nurses, giving them updated instructions for his medications. They talked about dialysis and scheduled it for the following day.

Everyone had just left the room, when I saw something happen with Eric and completely freaked out. I noticed a flickering in his lids, and a sort of momentary rolling back of his eyes into his head. I called out to the nurses and asked them to get the doctor back—stat!

He came right back in and checked on Eric again, but didn't witness anything out of the ordinary. I was hoping I had imagined it and told them I'd reach out if I saw it happen again.

After all the excitement, Eric looked unperturbed and closed his eyes to sleep. I eventually went to sleep again too, sitting in the chair next to the bed, with my head and arms draped over his body. I felt sad that we weren't in the Seychelles, leaping above the beautiful white sandy beaches, at one with the universe, but I figured we first better deal with the reality at hand, in the all-that-is-right-here-and-now reality.

Facebook post—February 8, 2017

His daughters came to visit, and our friends Gail and Bea. We all laughed and cried and shared memories together. Bella created another amazing poem for her daddy and read it out loud. It was so beautifully written and heartfelt... no dry eyes in the room. Just an intimate time for our little family and friends who are family. Love!

— 40 —

Dialysis and a Brainwave Test for Eric

The good news was that Eric was in capable hands in the ICU and that he made it through the night. The not so good news was multifaceted. His blood sugar level had dropped to a new low, there was some confirmed lymphoma involvement in the liver, he had an inflamed lining of the brain, his level of presence waxed and waned, and his lactate levels were dangerously high and climbing.

They said this was all more than likely related to the lymphoma disease in his kidneys and throughout his body.

I'm sorry, but no shit?

Their new plan was to do kidney dialysis every one to two days, to filter out some of the lactic acid, yet also keep up the lumbar puncture chemo *and* systemic chemo over the next couple of days.

I had heard of kidney dialysis but had never seen it firsthand. I watched intently as they rolled in a big machine and hooked up the tube to a needle in Eric's arm. They explained that the blood would travel along the tube, into the large machine that filtered it, and then it would pass back into his arm through another tube.

The docs were hoping that the dialysis would bring down the BUN reading. However, even after almost five hours of dialysis, Eric's was still way up there. A healthy reading is under 2.0 and Eric's was at 18.

Holy shit! 18?!

That CANNOT be good!

In addition to the dialysis, he had a ninety-minute EEG, to measure his brain waves as lights flashed into his eyes, both awake and at rest. There appeared to be no evidence of tumors or seizures but rather a "slowing" of the brainwaves, which was apparently to be expected given the state of his labs.

I barely left his side. Overall, it wasn't looking good for my guy, and we had some good crying sessions together. One of us would inadvertently start with a catch in the throat or some tears, and the other wouldn't always be able to hold back. We held on tightly to each other, as if that might stave off what seemed to be a likely outcome.

We spent some time playing the "remember when" game.

"Remember when you winked at me on Match, and I replied back with a really long email?" he whispered looking at me with his sad blue eyes, in his chemo-chiseled face.

"Yes, I loved that you did that! If you hadn't responded with such intense gusto, we may never have recognized that we were the ones for each other!" I replied. "Do you remember when you were so nervous the day you proposed to me, with one knee in the sand at the Four Seasons in Kona?" I asked.

His eyes twinkled, and he smiled. I waited for his next "remember when" but his lids fluttered and sleep came quickly.

Oh boy, that was enough to start me up again, and I cried softly to myself, curled up in the chair by the window. After several minutes, I dried my tears and looked outside.

I took in the beauty of the view over the lake and cityscape from this room in the hospital and thought about what was happening to my beloved. Aside from not knowing whether there was a miracle out there somewhere, the toughest thing for me was that his mental capacity was so severely impacted. I learned to go with the flow as he waned in and out of presence.

I spoke to a kind social worker about this, and she said this is often one of the hardest elements for the family, to see their loved one not be fully functional and lucid.

I moved back beside my Bebe, in the event he woke up. As I was falling asleep that night, I imagined him walking out of intensive care with a fully functioning body, incredible health, and going on to live a long and adventure-filled life. I could see him with his huge smile, exclaiming, "Phew, that was a close call, but look at me now!"

"Yay, Bebe! I did it!" he would say. Let's go celebrate life!"

Facebook post—February 9, 2017

Thank you all soooooo much for your continued prayers. It's quite wonderful for us to know how many loved ones are out there cheering for him, our beloved guy-husband-friend-brother-cousin-nephew-coach-father-mentor. I am still picturing Eric in full health and literally walking out of here miraculously…so, I shall end with that image tonight!

— 41 —

He Has a Name, and His Name Is Eric

"I really hated it, Bebe. I'm so glad it's over, it was so uncomfortable."

I pondered his comment and found it a little surprising that after everything he'd been through in the last thirteen months, he hated dialysis the most.

He'd made it through nine months of systemic chemotherapy, local spinal chemo taps and injections, blood transfusions, thirty days of injections and blood pulls, twenty radiation sessions, several surgeries, multiple biopsies, and he'd been poked, prodded, tested, scanned, and x-rayed every which way. Incredibly, for him, dialysis was the worst of it all.

We had just finished talking about this when the white-coat entourage walked into the room. They did not look like doctors with good news and stood uncomfortably at the end of his bed with their coat uniforms on and the barrier to their hearts and emotions firmly in place.

The most senior of the group, Dr. Ice Queen, took a step forward and said emphatically, "Sir."

I wanted to stop time and her next words.

I felt like reaching out to take her hand and gently place it in my beloved's.

I wanted to connect the two of them, this icy intelligent lady with the bad news and the love of my life.

I was tempted to say, "His name is Eric. Please don't call him Sir. He has a name, and his name is Eric."

But I froze, swallowed my words, and the moment was gone.

"Sir, the dialysis last night didn't really move the dial as much as we had hoped," she said quickly and took a breath. "Your kidneys are still struggling to clear the chemicals in your blood. You're going to need twelve to thirteen hours a day of dialysis for the foreseeable future. Without it, your prognosis is not good."

Oh shit!

Oh no. That is not good!

No, no, no, nooooo!

He hated dialysis more than anything else!

Oh no. This is not good at all!

Time slowed, and I turned towards my Bebe with a sick feeling and figured I knew what was coming.

Although he had been fading in and out of awareness in the last couple of weeks, in that moment he was completely aware, and present in his body. His head swiveled in slow motion to look me in the eyes, and I just knew.

All of time and space slowed.

That was it. It was one of those choice points, where we could choose to take the left fork in the road or the right. Take the red pill or the blue. He snapped his head back to Dr. Ice Queen and said, "Okay, that's it. I'm done. I don't want to do that. I don't want to do this anymore."

Oh my God! Oh my God! Oh my God!

No, this cannot be!

This is it?!

My Bebe is choosing to die?

Please, oh God no!

He looked at me again with his big sad blue eyes, his sunken cheekbones, and breathlessly said the words I shall never forget.

"I'm so sorry Bebe, but I have to die now."

Then he started pulling out the wires and IV tubes from his arm, trying to disconnect from his sustenance and from life.

We all jumped in that instant to stop him from hurting himself, and we managed to halt the immediate damage, at least until the team could figure out the next steps.

Oh shit, I can't believe it!

This is it?

But, but, but...how did we get to this point?

Where's that fucking miracle that was supposed to waltz in through the glass sliding door?

I sat there in disbelief, squeezing his hand tightly, as if that could stave off the inevitable. My mind was racing, but somewhere in my consciousness, I knew that when a patient is no longer receiving sustenance or medication, and is terminal, they likely get moved somewhere else, away from intensive care, right?

I didn't know if they had a hospice unit in the hospital, somewhere where the patients go to die, or if they had to transport them out from the hospital to a hospice off-site. I panicked with the thought of moving this fragile man, my big love, for his final days.

Thankfully, I didn't have to sit too long with my mind spinning and emotions churning, as the kindest, sweetest nurse came back into the room. She went right to Eric, laid a gloved hand on his leg, reached out for my hand, and with a quiet voice, full of compassion, she said, "It's okay. Eric, you can stay right here. We'll keep your catheter in, but we'll stop the fluid sustenance. We'd also like to keep the IV in for your palliative care."

She efficiently administered the new palliative medication prescription, adjusted a few things, and disappeared quietly through the sliding door.

"I'm so sorry, Bebe. I'm sorry. I'm sorry," he repeated over and over with his soft gravelly voice. I let my head fall forward onto his shoulder and allowed the tears to flow.

He repeated again, "I'm so sorry Bebe, I'm so sorry…"

We hugged for dear life, and I replied through my tears, "It's okay, Bebe, you gave this battle everything you had. I'm so proud of you. You tried so hard to live. It's okay, Bebe. It's okay."

Truth be told, this is FAR FROM FUCKING OKAY!

My Bebe has chosen to die!

But he can't keep going like this!

He can't keep wading through this nightmare another day!

And I couldn't blame him. Not at all.

He laid back down and stared up at the ceiling. He closed his eyes. As soon as he was asleep, I figured I had better call my beloved's closest people to let them know the hard news. I peeked into the family room right across the hall, saw that it was empty, and sank down on a chair.

It was surreal.

I called his eldest daughter first so that she could gather her kiddos and bring them to the hospital to say goodbye. Somehow, I managed to hold it together.

"I'm so sorry, but it's time. I'm so sorry, it's not going to be long now. You might want to pick up the kiddos from school and bring them in."

I answered a few of her immediate questions and told her I'd see her soon.

The second call was to Bella's school. I didn't know what to say when a woman answered in a cheery super-helpful voice.

"Good morning, this is Finn Hill Middle School, how may I help you?"

I blurted out, "Bella needs to leave early. Her daddy is dying, and she needs to come to the hospital to say goodbye!"

There was silence on the other end, but the voice recovered quickly and asked who would be coming to pick her up. I told her Bea would be there soon.

I called Bea, and, thankfully, she was available to jump in the car and scoop Bella up from school and drive her to the hospital. I figured Bella would be in good hands with her, given the shocking news she was about to receive. I called my girl on her cell once they were on their way to reassure her.

"Oh, my Bella. I'm so sorry that this is it for your daddy. But we're going to be okay. I promise, you and I will be okay, and we'll figure out a way to move forward. It's going to be okay."

She was quiet and numb, and I got it. It was big news to handle for a fifteen-year-old. Very big news indeed.

I called Eric's mom and said quietly, "I'm so sorry Bobbie, but your boy is not going to make it. He decided he just can't keep going, and they don't think he'll have long."

"Oh no," she said, fumbling her words, "I've been praying so hard for a miracle. Oh, dear God."

I gave her a long-distance hug and told her I'd call back again later so she could say goodbye to her son directly.

I called Aunt Carol and gave her the news next. I told her more of the story so that she could share it with her big sister. She was very sweet and focused on how I was doing, and then I did lose it. Through my teary hiccups, I said, "I know, I know, I know, it's just so hard to believe. Until this morning, I really thought he was somehow going to make it. I truly believed a miracle would show up somewhere along the way. It's just so surreal, and I'm still processing."

Back in the room, I heard a noise at the sliding door and some whispering outside. I peeked around the curtain and saw two elderly ladies. One of them had stuck a temporary hook on the outside of the glass door and was in the process of hanging a beautiful multi-colored lead glass butterfly. I figured in an instant the meaning of the butterfly and lost it afresh. It was a not-so-secret code signifying that the person in the room wasn't going to make it…that just like the spiritual meaning of the beautiful creature, a significant transformation was about to take place.

Once the butterfly was hung, they gowned up and came into the room with their big hearts and big love. One reached into her bag and pulled out the most extraordinary blanket. It was a handmade patchwork quilt, and the dominant color was bright yellow, the color of happiness and sunshine. She got busy laying it out on the bed and said, "This is for you. And it's yours to keep."

I looked up at the other dear lady and raised my eyebrows slightly in question. She said gently, "The nurses told us that Eric loved the color yellow the best."

She reached out for me and even though she was about half my size, I walked into her arms, and she held me tight. She didn't seem to mind that my tears were falling onto her hair. She reached up, pulled me down, and said quietly into my ear, "I'm so sorry you are going through this my dear, and we hope that the yellow blanket will bring moments of joy in his last days."

Before leaving, the other sweet lady handed me a brown grocery bag and smiled. I hugged her too, and they left the room to continue on with their day of volunteering.

Eric was watching me closely and asked me what was in the bag. I reached in, pulled out a book, a collection of short pieces on dealing with grief, *Safe Passage—Words to Help the Grieving*, by Molly Fumia.

It was too soon for me, and I pushed it back into the bag quickly. There were also a bunch of bananas and a few oversized, plastic film-wrapped chocolate chip cookies, Eric's favorite. I figured they were to provide some comforting sustenance for the special people present for his last days, as he was done with food and eating for...well...forever.

I felt their presence before I heard or saw them and looked up. They had all arrived at the same time. Eric's eldest daughter, four of the five grandkids, and Bella walked into the room en masse. Bea and Gail hung back for now.

It was heartbreaking and awkward, but each grandchild said goodbye, one by one.

The first gave him a quick kiss and muttered, "Goodbye Grandad. I'll miss you" and reached in for a hug.

One of his granddaughters said, "Here's a picture I drew for you. Goodbye Grandad," and handed Eric a stick figure picture of her with her two sisters and two brothers, her momma, Bella, and Eric.

One just stood there in shock, tears pouring out, not knowing what to say.

My heart broke again. How do you say goodbye to your grandaddy when you haven't a clue what death and dying is all about?

The final grandchild hugged Eric, said, "I love you, Grandpa," and they left the room one by one.

Their mama hugged her daddy goodbye and spoke in quiet, private conversation with him for several minutes. Bella followed, crying and hugging her daddy. She read aloud another poem she wrote, and we all lost it afresh.

Both his daughters said their final goodbye, gave their last hug, and looked into his deep blue eyes one last time. Eric had been emphatic he didn't want either of his daughters present when it came time for him to pass. So, when they left the room, they knew they would never hear his voice again, have another daddy hug, groan at another bad daddy joke, or look to him for sage advice. They walked away from their daddy...forever.

Eric seemed relieved once they all left. It was a lot to deal with for my poor Bebe. It's tough to say your forever goodbyes to your grandkids and your daughters while you're feeling so deathly ill. He closed his eyes, opened them again to look at me, and reached for my hand.

"I'm sorry, Bebe. I'm so sorry." And he promptly passed out asleep.

I felt like I was going to start hyperventilating and walked out into the hallway. I saw Dr. Big Boss and his PA walking my way, asked if I could have a word and guided them into the family room across the hallway. They sat, and I stayed standing. I spoke my mind, leaving nothing out as they stared at me, their mouths open wide.

"I know that you guys are amazing people and incredibly smart doctors. I never thought differently, and that's not the issue. It's just that the system is stacked against your patients, our beloveds. I know; I've seen the statistics. So many of your patients don't make it, and it's not just your organization, it's all of the big hospitals and corporations across the country. I know that you think you're doing your best, but you're not!"

I kept pacing back and forth and paused to lift my arm to point to the room across the hallway where Eric lay dying.

"MY HUSBAND is lying in that room and he's DYING! He didn't have to die! There are cures out there in the world for cancer. There are so many supplemental and alternative treatments available. I just can't understand why you don't stand up to the big bosses and insist on being able to explore more ways to actually CURE and HEAL your patients!"

They sat there like stunned mullets, not used to being read the riot act from their patient's family members. I didn't care and kept going.

"You must know that there are things you could be doing better. WHY DON'T YOU FIGHT to make it happen?

"For starters, feed your patients healthy food while they're in your care. Find ways to boost their immune system, which is something you just don't do…you don't even seem to have the terminology in your vocabulary!

"Do your own research and see what's out there. There's more than just chemo and radiation and surgery. THERE'S SO MUCH MORE!

"Go visit clinics like Sanoviv in Mexico and see what they're doing. They've been saving people using functional medicine since 2000!

"There are so many clinics and hospitals around the world that are way ahead of you and your doctor-colleagues across the country. There are so many books written on this stuff and literally thousands of case studies AND peer-reviewed articles! So much material is online these days. You're all completely missing the point!"

I slowed down, lowered the volume of my voice, and implored, "Why? Why don't you make changes? Why don't you fight? It's not all about pharmaceuticals and trials and money and maximizing profits—there's food, there's oxygen, there are plant-based therapies, and light and sound and frequency, emotional release, psychological, and energy work.

"For God's sake, they even have machines with thousands of programs that can diagnose and treat people in Mexico! Sanoviv has a ton of data proving their successes, and hundreds, probably thousands of case studies to share. But your medical authorities don't want to know! They label these doctors as quacks, performing quackery, and they not only reject the tons of data and research they've been offered, but they're still, even after sixteen years, trying to SHUT THEM DOWN!"

I sat down heavily and looked them in their eyes.

"Look, all I'm asking is that you do better. If you can figure out a way to do better, many more of our beloveds won't have to suffer so horrendously and die such horrible and painful deaths.

"I know you are good and kind people. Thank you for everything you did. We are super grateful, but now that you know there's more out there to learn, you can't un-hear this. Please, I beg you. Do better."

I went straight into the ladies' room, locked my stall, sat down, and wept.

That was quite a session with the docs, but I meant it. Every word. I truly believed that the whole industry could do better.

I dried my tears and slowly made my way back to the room. I tiptoed past Eric and sat on the window ledge, my knees pulled up. I opened my journal to pen a letter to my sleeping beloved, snoring quietly in the bed. The words poured onto the paper directly from my hurting heart, and a fresh steady flow of tears slid down my face as I realized the words were for me, not for him. . .

"Dear Bebe,

I miss you already! You're there, but you're not there. You're fading fast now, and I am devastated. Totally devastated.

Oh God, I miss our daily gratitudes! I missed them the most as they began to fade. I don't know when it started, but I've missed their depth, and now they've gone altogether. I have loved that our GOCs have been such a big part of our story. I loved how you would hold me as I cried tears of gratitude… for you seeing me, looking into me, and loving me…ALL the parts of me. Now your brain can't hold the thoughts and turn them into words for you to share. Oh, my heart . . .

As you fade away, I know I'll miss those gorgeous blue eyes… eyes that carried me away for years. I feel like I've been peering into their blue depths for many lifetimes.

I have been missing your smile, and soon it'll be gone altogether. Your beautiful broad wide smile, even when it slips to the side and becomes a grin. God, I shall miss your 'Eric grin.' I so loved when you wrote me cards and emails for all those years, and how you added the <grin> at the end.

Oh, my love, I've already been missing your arrivals at home, and you calling out,

'Bebeee,' your way of saying, 'Yay, I'm home with my big love. I am so incredibly happy to be seeing you.'

I've been missing your kisses and hugs and your touch. The seat beside me on the couch and the space beside me in the bed have been empty. For a while now, it seems I've been practicing walking through life without you by my side. You tried so hard to keep up, you so wanted to stay, and I know your place will remain beside me, very soon, in your spirit form.

My darling Bebe, it's been over a year since we knew you were sick. It's been both horrific and beautiful, sad and joyous, shocking and not.

To see you transition from great health to looking like death, just thirteen short months later.

To go from being so vital and alive, to experiencing constant pain and suffering.

To go from having so many hopes and dreams, to fighting to live another day.

To go from looking forward to visiting and experiencing your bucket list places in the world, to just thinking about how to get from home to the doctor's office, and eventually from your hospital bed to the bathroom.

My darling Bebe, I can't believe it!

I can't fucking believe it's happening!

I'm losing you,

Oh, shit, it won't be long now."

Facebook post—February 10, 2017

The dialysis machine has been turned off, sustenance and fluids have stopped. Now, it's all about pain medication and palliative care. Eric tried so hard in the past year to have a different outcome, and I was with him every step of the way, encouraging and showing up for him. We were so close. But he wants it to be over fast now, without too much suffering. Please everyone, your prayers are welcomed, but instead of prayers for life and wellbeing.... Please pray now for peace and a gracious next few days and beyond . . .

Angel Wings
Written by Phillipa Leseberg

I've earned my angel wings in the last year,
Or so my ailing husband tells me.
But does he know that without him,
They would never have sprouted and
grown to such epic proportions?
Serendipity brought us together,
My etheric team and his, the
universe, working in concert.
Whispers through all time and space
That we were meant to be.
Although in this lifetime,
It was only for a short chapter in our books of destiny.
Not quite eight in human years,
But an eternity by any other measure.
We made it through ups and downs and roundabouts,
We beat the odds and went deeper
into our heart of hearts.

There I found you,
There I find you,
There you shall stay.
What does life look like without you?
I'm not ready to consider that.
Oh, how sad I am that the time has
come to unearth this truth!
The time has come to let you go.
But before you go . . .
Please know that through you I gained my voice,
Please know that through you I found my written word,
Please know that through you I shored up my strength,
Please know that through you I am inspiring others.
When I reach into my core, I AM strong!
Stronger than ever before!
Now is the time to say goodbye,
To share with the world what an
honor it has been to know you,
What an honor it is to BE present with
you as you prepare to transition.
Thank you Bebe,
Thank you my love,
Goodbye, my Bebe,
Goodbye, my love!
Love always,
Your wife and life partner,
Your Forever Bebe

— 42 —

Our Final Goodbyes

He looked freaky with red teeth and bloody lips. I couldn't remember why his mouth was bleeding profusely, although I'm sure I asked the nurse at one point.

Standing to the side of the bed, I leaned into Eric, dipped the sponge-on-a-stick into water, and put it into his mouth to provide a little moisture. The sponge was soaking up the blood, and he was oblivious that it was pouring from his mouth.

Bea arrived a few hours after everyone had left, to sit with us through the night, and she and I took shifts. Eric had been moaning and writhing in pain intermittently during the late afternoon and into the evening. It was physically exhausting and utterly heartbreaking. Although it was shocking to think about, we figured it was because his body was shutting down, one organ, one system, at a time.

His breathing became more labored, his voice quiet and raspy, and he apologized again, "I'm so sorry, Bebe. I'm sorry. I'm sorry."

At one point, he reached up gingerly, put his shaking hands on either side of my face, and pulled me in to kiss me on the lips. In a slightly cowardly move, I shifted my head a little to the left, and his kiss was redirected to my right cheek. To be honest, I was afraid of getting MRSA and didn't want that to be the final gift from my dying husband. He struggled with his breath but managed to say, "I've loved being married to you, Bebe…you were the best…thing that ever happened to me…you were my best."

I wasn't sure if he was referring to best wife, best person, best partner, or best lover? But it didn't matter. I understood the sweet and heart-wrenching sentiment.

"Oh Bebe," I cried in return. "You were the best thing that ever happened to me. You were my best too!" And I meant it. He was my best husband, life partner, lover, life coach, mentor, best friend. All of it.

Bea and I took turns stroking his face, his bald head, and his arms. We filled up a trashcan of bloody sponges and red-stained tissues. His moaning kept up and he cried out in pain, delirious at times. I asked the nurse if she could step up the morphine, and she said she was giving him the maximum dosage.

In the wee hours of the morning, Bea got up and walked around to my side of the bed. She put her arms around me, hugged me tight, told me it was her shift, and that it was time for me to get more rest. We had taken turns all night, and it had been horrendous to see my beloved groaning in pain as his bodily systems slowly stopped working.

No one ever tells you what it's like in those final hours and days, and I learned why, the hard way. It's a very painful process for the one departing, and agonizing for those in support, being present for the final decline.

I witnessed Bea saying goodbye. She took both his hands and held them close to her heart. She leaned in and kissed his forehead, "Goodbye, my friend. I love you so much. Andi and I will miss you every day. Thank you for being a great friend to Andi and to me and to the boys. You tried so hard this last year, and you can be very proud of yourself. Phillipa will be fine. We'll be here for her too. Go in peace my friend. We love you."

Later in the morning, Bea decided to go home to rest. She said she'd be back later in the day for another shift.

I reached for my journal and started writing,

"Then, all too quickly came the final, the "last time" of so many things we took for granted.
The final time you sat up in your bed . . .
The final time you walked on your own . . .
The final time you could operate the wheelchair . . .

The final time you knew, with certainty, what year it was and what month it was and how to read the time.
Your final goodbye to your grandkids.
Your final goodbye to your eldest daughter.
Your final goodbye to your 15-year-old daughter Bella.
Your final goodbye to your close friend Bea.
I know that before too long, it's going to be
Your final hug with me.
Your final kiss.
Your final conscious moment before your final sleep."

At one point, when Eric was going in and out of consciousness, in pain and choking on blood from his mouth, he shouted out, "The ghosts need to let me go! The ghosts need to let me go!"

He repeated it several times, so it was quite clear what he was saying. I didn't have a good answer, so I called Clara for advice. Serendipitously, she picked up right away on that morning, and after we spoke briefly, I put the phone up to Eric's ear.

She reminded him that the reason he was seeing the ghosts was that the morphine had "opened him up" to other dimensional realities, particularly where many had passed and are still hanging around. She reiterated that the ghosts cannot harm him, and to remember his own bright light.

Clara could see he was feeling a ton of emotional intensity around the "dings" he had experienced throughout his life. She could see he was feeling into, "Oh, this person did that to me… that person did that," and she assured him it would be beneficial to allow those intense thoughts and feelings to spin out of his heart center right away, as he didn't need to take those with him. She helped him work on that and saw the heavy emotions lift from him.

Once he was sleeping again, I shared with Clara that he was still in intense pain. She agreed he should not be feeling anything at this point and to insist that the nurses give him more of whatever they were giving him. I thanked her profusely and hung up.

I called the nurse in, and in hushed tones, begged her to step up the meds.

"I know you're probably not supposed to, but it's the only humane thing to do. It's what we should do for him now."

I'm not sure if she did, and I didn't need to know. Either way, he fell into a deep sleep, and since the hospital bed was in an upright position, his body slowly fell forward. I didn't want to disturb his sleep, so I left him like that for a bit.

What I hadn't realized in that moment was that Eric would never again be conscious. He would never be able to sit up from that slumped forward position.

No, no, no, no! That's it?

Oh my God! Oh my God! Oh my God!

I'm not ready!

Was that really the last time he's going to be conscious?

Seriously, no more conscious moments for my Bebe?

No more opportunities for goodbyes with his eyes open?

Noooooo!

I want more time to say goodbye!

No, no, no, no! Seriously? That's it?

Oh my God! Oh my God! Oh my God!

No more kisses!

No more hugs!

No more chuckles!

No more GOCs!

No more blue sparkly eyes!

No more anything…just a long stretch of unconsciousness.

No, no, no, no! Seriously?

That's it?

Oh my God! Oh my God! Oh my friggin' God!

I laid down in the little cot beside his bed, to be close but also to rest. Everything was incredibly hard to take in, so I didn't. I closed my eyes and slept for a half hour or so.

I woke up as Hilary came flying into the room. I hadn't known if she would make it, since she had to travel from her new Boston home base. She looked at Eric, unconscious in the bed and then at me in the little cot. Without hesitating, she slid into the bed beside me, spooning me from behind. She held me as we both cried hard, although mine was the sort of crying with snot and big ugly red splotches.

"How are you doing my friend?" she asked gently.

After a minute, I said, "I think I'm okay. I don't know. I can't believe that he probably won't wake up again and that he's unconscious. That's what I'm finding hard. I won't be able to have another conversation and be able to look into his eyes. He won't be in pain anymore, and that's a blessing, but I won't have my Bebe… ever again."

After another cry, I asked her how she had made it in time. She said that it was meant to be, because she'd had to contend with snowstorms, flight delays, cancellations, inserting an IV into an unconscious passenger on the plane and all. She sensed Eric didn't have long and came straight from the airport to see her buddy.

We got up to stand vigil on either side of the bed. We stroked his arms and stood, present in the moment.

I said to him quietly, "It's okay to go, my Bebe. It's okay to let go. They're ready for you on the other side. I love you, Bebe. I love you so much. It's okay, Bebe. It's okay to let go now."

I reached out for some of the sentiments that people in Eric's life had sent to him. I had printed them out and read some out loud. I paused and just stood there, stroking my unconscious Bebe.

Hilary urged quietly, "I'd love to hear some GOCs if you'd like to."

I wasn't sure I could, but I took a deep shaky breath and through tears, started quietly with, "I love and appreciate that you have been the big love of my life" and, "I love and appreciate that you fought so hard to stay here with us and get well, and I'm so proud of you." I repeated through blurry, wet eyes, "But, it's okay to let go, Bebe. I love you, my Bebe."

I paused and was just feeling into what I wanted to say next, and Hilary looked up at me. She whispered quietly, "Oh, I think he just stopped breathing."

Oh…Oh no.

There were no machines blearing, sounding the alarm to mark the moment of his passing. He had been unplugged eighteen hours earlier, as soon as he had decided he couldn't do it any longer, couldn't fight the cancerous curse for another moment. It was only eighteen hours since he had tried to pull the wires and tubes out and made the decision to die.

I glanced at the clock and it was 4:17 pm. I leaned forward, gently kissed his cheek, and put my forehead on his.

In that surreal moment, I thought about how hard it must have been for a strong Leo like him to let go, to say goodbye to his wife and daughters and grandkids, knowing that he was no longer able to provide for his family or be there for their big milestone moments.

I walked over to the window, plunked myself down and looked out at the sun, now low in the sky. I was completely out of sorts, but felt a sort of relief that the fight was over and my beloved was now pain-free.

Hilary came and sat with me on the window ledge. We hugged and held on to each other, two people with hurting hearts, all geared up in protective clothing. A nurse came in and busied herself clearing and cleaning up his space and straightened the sheets and the yellow patchwork blanket over his body.

She offered to take a few photos of us as we sat there, and in the weirdness of that *sur-reality*, we looked at the camera. And I'm not sure why, but we both smiled.

I texted Bella and Alison and gave them the news. I invited them to come back in to say a different sort of goodbye. I called Eric's mom, who had been anxiously awaiting word.

"I'm so sorry, but your boy just passed at 4:17 pm. He's no longer in pain, and, at least, we can be grateful for that small mercy."

There was silence on the other end, then, "Oh, dear God. I was waiting for the news, but it happened so fast. Oh, dear God. Yes… yes, it's a blessing he's no longer in pain."

I told her I'd call her later, and in a moment of déjà vu, called Aunt Carol and Uncle Bob next. We spoke a little longer, and I gave Aunt Carol more detail on Eric's last hours to share later with her big sister.

As soon as Alison and Bella came in, Hilary gave me a big squeeze, and I said, "Thank you! Thank you! Thank you so much for showing up. That was huge! I am beyond grateful. Talk later?"

She responded, "It was my honor to be here. I love you, my friend." And she slipped quietly out the door.

Bella leaned down to kiss the cheek of the adopted daddy she loved so much…the only daddy she ever remembered living with. She kissed him on the head and sank down heavily in the chair next to the bed. She touched his arm and just sat there. Alison privately did what she needed for closure, and the girls sat in silence.

The three of us said our final goodbyes, and in another moment of *sur-reality*, we left to go home, walking arm in arm down the hallway…leaving the body of our beloved husband and father on the bed wrapped all comfy in his yellow blanket, with his sunken eyes closed, and his slack jaw hanging loose.

I don't remember driving home, but I do recall opening the front door to our home, Gail coming out of the kitchen and walking towards me. She already knew somehow, and I said the three words she will always remember, "My Bebe's gone." We rushed into each other's arms, and I held on tight and finally sobbed.

Facebook post—February 11, 2017

Today, the 11th of February at 4:17pm, my beloved husband, Bebe, life partner, best friend, lover, life coach, and biggest cheerleader left his body. He is now free from bodily pain...at last.

Auspicious timing with the Snow Moon Eclipse & Green Comet, and of course, in our own little universe, day 111 of my journaling. As Eric's girls and I walked away from his hospital room, having said our goodbyes, we joked that he's riding the comet all the way home. For those of you who know Eric personally, you can totally imagine that, right?

When Eric took his last breath, our good friend Hilary and I were standing on either side of his bed, stroking his arms and head.

I had told him how much I loved him and that he was one of the best things that ever happened to me. I told him that it was okay for him to go any time and that everything was in alignment for him. Hilary noticed some movement in his eyes, his breathing gently catch...and then stop. It was a beautiful gentle lifting away of his spirit.

What an honor to be a part of that process. At first, I couldn't believe it and am still only just beginning to process it all.

I thank you from the depths of my soul for being on our journey. This is not the outcome any of us wanted. Even up until 4:17pm, I was still hoping that by some miracle of miracles, something would magically shift and change. Of course, something did shift and change...Eric's time with me, our families and friends, and on the planet, at least in his physical form, was up.

Love and blessings and "warrior wings" to you Eric...you earned them!

Your loving wife, Phillipa xxooxxoo

Epilogue

I've never had to look hard for signs of his presence, as my beloved has been making himself known from the other side since he left the physical world, exactly seven years ago, as of this writing.

Perhaps the most extraordinary happening took place eighteen months after Eric's passing, in the South Pacific Kingdom of Tonga—a tiny nation archipelago that encompasses hundreds of islands, to the northeast of my country of birth, New Zealand.

Jane and I, along with our retreat clients, had been on a magical island for almost three weeks. We swam in the turquoise and green Pacific waters with the humpback whales by day and danced on the sand as the sun sank beneath the horizon each night.

On this particular day, I was standing on the sand with my eyes closed, my body swaying in time with the music. I was aware of the sounds of the ocean as it gently lapped onto the beach. The sand was soft, and I noticed the way the grains squeezed up and around each foot every time I moved, supporting me and massaging my feet at the same time. My arms were swinging and my shoulders were moving in the opposing direction. There was music playing in the background, and the energy changed as each new song on Jane's playlist stopped and another began.

A faster song played and all ten of us, as if we were of pod mind, started moving from our spots around the circle, dancing with abandon. The sun was lowering, and when I opened my eyes, I could see the light had dimmed into a warm orange.

Without warning, the song completely stopped and another started. It was something unexpected, and it shifted things. I recognized it right away: it was my Bebe's favorite song—the soundtrack to the *Gladiator* movie, "Now We Are Free," composed by Hans Zimmer and Lisa Gerrard.

I looked over at Jane, and nodded a quick thank you to her for adding this song into her collection. I figured she must have remembered it was the one Eric loved the most. I closed my eyes again and swayed, my movements pulling in or extending out as the orchestral piece swelled or contracted.

Partway through the song, I sensed Eric's presence and I stopped moving. I felt his angel wings around me, hugging me from behind, his breath on my neck. We started swaying, he and I...me on the sandy beach, and he, all love, light, and angel feathers. I wanted the song to go on; I wanted to stay there, moving in his arms forever. I swear I heard him whisper in my ear, "I am with you. I am a part of you, and I shall always be. You'll be okay. I love you, my forever Bebe."

I felt his presence slip away, and a single tear slid down. By the time I reached up to touch my face, it was covered with tears, my heart big with love for this man...my Bebe in angel form.

After the group session was over, I sank down onto the sand, my legs criss-crossed in front. The others started to meander towards the traditional gathering *fale* for dinner, and Jane approached and sat with me on the sand. I could tell she had something significant to share.

We were the only ones who knew that during one of the intense healing sessions, when my beloved was fighting for his life, Jane had received a crystal clear vision of Eric and me dancing on a beach, happy and in love. She also saw that we would write a book together.

Unbelievably, she did not have the *Gladiator* theme on her playlist. She said that Eric had decided to make himself known to us, and found a way to insert his powerful message of love from the great wide unknown into our group dancing session on the beach that day.

My Bebe, my big love—if you were here today, in person, exactly seven years since you transitioned, I would tell you how much I miss you every day. I see you in the yellow trucks that drive by, in every yellow flower, and each time a hummingbird hovers close. I sense you every time I hear, "Chasing Cars" by Snow Patrol, our song that we played at your celebration of life, or one of our wedding songs. I feel you when there's a whisper of a breeze on the back of my neck.

I love that you joined in with Bella and me when we traveled in Hawai'i and Africa, and with me in Tahiti, Tonga, New Zealand, Iceland, Peru, the Galapagos, and Guatemala. We always wanted to travel the world together, and I'm delighted to have you along for the ride...you, in your etheric form.

I would tell you that you were right, all those years ago at the spiritual retreat on the beach on Treasure Island, in Tonga. You said I would be okay, and I want you to know I am...I am more than okay. And you would be so proud of your daughter Bella, in Hawai'i, finishing college and exceeding even her own expectations.

I know you've been wondering why it's taken me so long, but I am finally ready to open my heart to another big love. He'll be a different sort of love, and please know you will always hold a very special space in my heart.

And Jane was right. We danced on the beach, and we wrote a book together, me here and you there...visiting from the big, wide beyond.

You thought you would be forgotten, and when I assured you, "Never!" I meant it. I truly did.

I love you now and always,
Love, your Bebe,
xxx

Facebook post—February 11, 2024

How is it seven years since we said goodbye to each other in physical form? Bebe, I am so happy we are staying forever connected. I knew you would never be forgotten. You live on in our hearts, in our minds, and through my stories. Love is saluting the space in my heart where you, Eric, my Bebe, will always reside.

Acknowledgements/Special Thanks

Thank you, Eric, my Bebe. Through you, my extraordinary husband and life partner, I learned to stand in my truth and in my power, and to engage in and enjoy the freedom of conscious relationship. Without permission to tell your story, journal, and post on social media, this book would not have been possible. You were a private man, yet realized early on the power of the written word and in sharing your story.

Second, my daughter, for teaching me the strength of staying present and conscious, and the importance of quality time as your language of love. You are an extraordinary young woman and your resilience and emotional intelligence continue to blow me away. Thank you for sharing your time with me and my laptop, as I wrote this book, and for pushing me to be a better parent, friend, and human.

To my remarkable friend, writer's workshop facilitator/ director, and editor of this book, Beth Bornstein Dunnington. I am beyond grateful for your time, guidance, friendship, killer editing skills, patience, love, and care with my words and my husband's stories. Your extraordinary writers' circles allowed my skills to develop from being a beginner writer, to someone with the confidence to put my words out into the world.

To the extraordinary team at Storybuilders, thank you for being there to graciously polish the words of my finished manuscript, design, and format the book and get it ready to be published.

To all the wonderful, kind medical professionals we met in the big Seattle hospitals, thank you. May you one day discover and incorporate new healing elements, and feel the joys of helping those on their cancer journeys to truly and thoroughly heal. There is a better way.

To Sanoviv, thank you! You're doing it right! You have in your minds and hearts an intention to heal the whole person through functional medicine. After all, what else is there?

To those that showed up big time to love on Eric and me, and to help us out in every way they could:

Hilary, for being a regular visitor...always being there for your friend, mentor, and port buddy, right up until his last breath. Eric thoroughly enjoyed his time with you and loved to talk and strategize about business and life.

Karla, for introducing us to Sanoviv, for showing up, and for your willingness to share your cancer story, gifting me the confidence to share too.

Andi and Bea, Eric's best friends for twenty years, for being there throughout his journey. Eric loved you two deeply and would be so proud of your new life developments.

To all those we met at Sanoviv. Your stories, insights, kindness, and love allowed us to bond with like-minded people and acknowledge that we weren't going crazy in our shock and horror at what's handed out as standard care these days.

To those who called, texted, showed up with food on our front doorstep, sent cards and postcards in the mail, spent time rearranging the garage and building a wheelchair ramp, transporting Eric, you all helped us more than you know. There are too many of you to acknowledge, and you know who you are. Thank you and bless you.

To our Facebook family...as I was losing my blood family throughout our journey (a story for another day), you were there— liking, love-hearting, sad-facing, commenting and encouraging us every...single...day. I swear you helped me get through many days when I wondered if I could keep up the level of intensity required to be the support person I wanted and needed to be for my Bebe.

About the Author

P hillipa Leseberg is a Kiwi-American adventurer, dolphin & whale swimmer, advocate for juicing and organic food, and debut author. As her husband battled cancer, she began to journal daily, a practice that was both cathartic and purposeful. The words she penned during those moments of vulnerability became the foundation of her first book, *His Name is Eric*. Phillipa shares her deeply personal story, inspiring readers to seek, question, and advocate for their own health. Based in Seattle, she lives a life filled with travel and adventure, frequently visiting her daughter and beloved pup in Hawai'i.